THE six essays which appear in this book were first published separately in the series of University of Minnesota Pamphlets on American Writers and, together with the other pamphlets in the series, are intended as introductions to authors who have helped to shape American culture over the years of our colonial and national existence. The editors of the pamphlet series are Richard Foster, Allen Tate, Leonard Unger, and Robert Penn Warren. Many pamphlets, in addition to the six represented here, are available, and many more are scheduled for publication by the University of Minnesota Press.

Richard Foster is a professor of English at the University of Minnesota and a member of the board of editors of the University of Minnesota Pamphlets on American Writers (see back of jacket).

❧ SIX AMERICAN NOVELISTS OF THE NINETEENTH CENTURY *An Introduction*

EDITED BY RICHARD FOSTER

UNIVERSITY OF MINNESOTA PRESS, MINNEAPOLIS

Contents

SIX AMERICAN NOVELISTS OF THE NINETEENTH CENTURY

Introduction

⚘ GAUGED by the test of history, the writers surveyed in this volume certainly have major importance. Gauged by the test of art, some are great writers, and some less than great. But such a distinction in criteria is difficult to maintain, for in practice the norms of historical and artistic importance tend to interpenetrate. To find that William Gilmore Simms and Ambrose Bierce are less important writers historically than Cooper and Twain involves an aesthetic as well as a historical judgment: they were less inventive, so their work had less generative impact upon the direction and momentum of the life of literature. And to find that Hawthorne and James are greater artists than Charles Brockden Brown or Sarah Orne Jewett could be the core of a historical as well as a critical discourse. Given a little time, usually a generation or two at most, literary history — the topography of the literary past as known — will tend to confirm whatever perdurable canons of literary excellence there are. Perhaps this means that individual artistic genius can, after all, affect history, or at least "literary" history, simply by being what it is.

But sometimes a whole literary era or movement will have a kind of genius of its own, giving a dimension of stature and interest even to the secondary figures participating in it that, had they lacked their historical context, they would not have possessed in their own right. This is true, I think, of the lesser figures considered in this volume, the creative vitality of whose time and place in literary

3

history lends to their talents an extra glory. The genius of nineteenth-century American literature among other national literatures — its special identity and value in a world perspective — is a function, it seems to me, of its marked originality. For as a literature of innovative vision, it is unique in its time.

This is not to claim that these writers owed no debts to Europe and the past. Among those before us, only Twain was essentially free of European influence. The literary heritage of Howells and James was very substantially European — French and French-influenced realists and naturalists. Cooper's debts to English novelists Scott and Marryat were unconcealed. Hawthorne, whose native sources — the colonial annalists — tended to be more "Elizabethan" in thought and feeling than indigenously American, was a frequent borrower, like Irving, from European popular fiction. Melville's fiction is a richly variegated texture of echoes and adaptations from European classics — Rabelais, Cervantes, Shakespeare, the King James Bible, Goethe, Carlyle, and many, many more. Other American writers of this period showed similar influences from the Old World. Poe's borrowed gothicism, thickly encrusted as it was with arcane learning and pseudo-learning, confirmed the cosmopolite stance of his literary essays. Even Stephen Crane, who was by no means well read, absorbed a timely dose of European naturalistic doctrine, supplemented later by personal associations with such lights of the European literary scene as Conrad, James, Hardy, and Ford Madox Ford.

But this record of indebtedness to Europe, which most of America's best writers were at no pains to obscure, only serves to dramatize their essential originality, an originality which Europe itself, despite its early response of condescension to the signs of American cultural nationalism, did not fail to notice. Such a phenomenon as Blake's making progenitive myth of the American historical experiment suggests that our life and literature alike implied, to the underside of European consciousness, at least, a near-miraculous rebirth of effective human creativity. Carlyle's recognition of Emerson, Baudelaire's of Poe, Swinburne's of Whitman, were early expressions of surprised discovery that European calls for renewal, inspired by a conviction that Europe was approaching ultimate exhaustion, were being answered from unforeseen quarters and in unexpected accents. Our writers were voicing a fresh and vital, if indeterminate, vision — social, spiritual, aesthetic — that seemed to be springing from the very soil of the new nation. Because of its natural derivation from the materials of real life, prose fiction is likely to be the most revealing literary source of a people's shared vision. And the novelty of the American vision, revealed by comparison of its norms with those of European fiction, is striking indeed.

In the typical European novel of the nineteenth century, the resistant otherness of the world confronting its protagonist — the ego-imprisoning cage or treasure-guarding shell of "reality" which must be breached if the Self is to be fulfilled — is identical with society. But in the typical American novel of the same period, society is only one element, perhaps even a minor element, in a much more complexly constituted reality, which may comprise not only society and its laws, but also the moral law, and perhaps even God, too. The American protagonist, thus, from mild Leather-Stocking to fierce Ahab, from innocent and open Isabel Archer to proud and injured Hester Prynne, will be likely to seek his fulfillment in some absolute realization of integrity, justice, or truth; his European counterpart — Dickens' Pip or Flaubert's Emma Bovary — will seek his, on the other hand, in some purified form of socially sanctioned freedom, status, or "success." Because the European protagonist is typically at war only with society, and because society has long ago made its working peace with the cosmos, a great many more personal, private, even "fanciful," if entirely natural, human desires lie outside the novel's legitimate field of conflict; the normal modes of this fiction, therefore, are ironic or comic. But in America, perhaps because the very nature of its history implied the nullification of this anciently agreed compromise between dream and reality, the heroic imperative was again in force as a human option. American protagonists thus tended to be — to use Melville's word — "isolatoes" in a way that even the most deracinated European protagonists were not; and as a consequence America's fiction, even when

5

its natural texture was comic, was deeply responsive to the tragic mode of feeling and perceiving.

Integral with these themes is the typically borderland or threshold nature of setting in nineteenth-century American fiction, the borders marking the separation not merely between differing strata of a single world but also between separate and distinct — often metaphysically distinct — worlds: Hawthorne's created settlement and uncreated forest, Melville's known shore and unknown sea, Cooper and Twain's formed East and unformed West, Howells' rooted traditional town and rootless modern city, James's innocent America and decadent Europe, and Poe's and Crane's variously delimited psychic realms of apparent and real. In such settings the main action will usually be a hazardous but necessary crossing of these borders from a known to an unknown world. Whether it is an action willed (like Isabel Archer's) or imposed by circumstance (like Huck Finn's), and whether it is informed by conviction (like Basil March's) or the result of mere compulsion (like Henry Fleming's), it quickly generates symbolic dimensions, becoming a voyage of moral discovery or a spiritual quest. The goal of the symbolic venture may be uncertain at the outset, as in *Huckleberry Finn* or *A Hazard of New Fortunes*. And if ascertained, it may be only tentatively achieved, as in *The Scarlet Letter* or *The Prairie*; or it may be achieved at ironic, even tragic cost to the achiever, as in *Portrait of a Lady* or *Moby Dick*. But in any case, as these novels affirm, it is not the venture's end but the act of venturing itself that matters most, suggesting that it is in the nature of man to seek new forms of value and significant life, both personal and communal, beyond the known world defined by tradition and history.

And just here a third major element of these writers' originality comes into view: their vivid sense of the changed nature of time in the New World — past and future having collapsed into a kind of eternal present. Perhaps no American writer realized this theme more inventively and suggestively than did Melville in *Israel Potter*, where he rendered, by means of a nearly surreal or expressionist adaptation of picaresque, the enormous acceleration of history under the new American dispensation. Melville's thematic preoc-

6

cupation in this novel, and less intensively in two or three other novels and a handful of tales, was also a hovering concern in the work of most of his contemporaries. Hawthorne's fiction, and before him Irving's, is literally haunted by the ghosts of a vanished world. The world of their grandfathers was ancient history; and before that there was only the unmeasured, uncreated wilderness — silence, prehistory. During the mere lifetime of Cooper's Leather-Stocking, who begins as Adam of the forest primeval, America recapitulates centuries of European development, and he disappears at last as a faded relic on the threshold of the post-imperial world of eighteenth-century commercialism. The American landscapes of Howells and James, and of such varied regionalist compeers of theirs as Jewett, Cable, and Garland, are strewn with artifacts, living and unliving, of their ancient or primordial pasts. But always the actual measure of elapsed historical time presupposed by the story or novel is about equal to the span of a man's life — like Leather-Stocking's, or like William Dean Howells', which began in an agrarian age of yeoman village culture and ended in industrial megalopolis. Confirmed and augmented by poets as different as Whittier and Whitman, and by philosophers as different as Emerson and Adams, these nineteenth-century novelists created the mythic understanding of what was then, and perhaps still is, the most extraordinary fact of American history — the unchecked power of the new laws of change that had been inculcated by the nation's dizzying rate of growth.

Only one other national literature of the nineteenth century was so marked by intensity, idiosyncrasy, and the spirit of discovery as America's — that of Russia. Both nations were, in a sense, provinces of Europe, one having been spun off, like a satellite, from the main body of the continent, the other deeply stamped with the oriental customs and temperament of its vast eastern reaches. Though full of themselves as a people apart, the Russians nevertheless produced writers whose minds, strongly magnetized by the cultural authority of Western Europe and its past, yearned westward in the fashion of unwilling expatriates. And so, however "Russian" their work was, it was also measurably "European." America, however, had willed to break away, and even the most inherently conservative and "European" of its writers — Cooper and Longfellow, for example — reflected something like a national will to thrust forward, taking for use on the journey whatever was viable from Europe and the past, toward the discovery or creation of a new and independent cultural identity. As has already been noted here, this proud impulse elicited a certain amount of reflexive European scorn, especially from visitors from abroad who came to witness American rawness firsthand. But in spite of that surface rawness and the prejudice of some of its foreign observers, America did win, and rather quickly at that, a good deal of respectful attention from the very culture from which it had declared its independence. That American literature has become accepted as a major world literature in the twentieth century perhaps obscures the remarkable fact that many of our earlier writers had achieved the status of world figures even in the nineteenth. To cite only the most dramatic examples, the nineteenth-century vogue of Cooper and Twain abroad, and in a quite different way, Poe, was no less than enormous. Bryant and Emerson, Longfellow and James, and only a little less so Hawthorne, were not merely American writers of curious interest to Europe, but important citizens, within their own lifetimes, of the international community of letters. Through its writers, it appears, America's original impulse of withdrawal was generating an unlooked-for motion of return.

If their typical postures in relation to "Europe" were different, American and Russian writers of the nineteenth century nevertheless had in common something far more significant: the uniquely dramatic subject matter, bequeathed them by history, of a nation's self-discovery and self-creation. Though endowed with centuries of Europe's traditional culture, the peoples of both countries, living beyond Europe's formal dominion, inhabited inchoate realms of possibility which seemed to be symbolized by the vastness, variety, and mystery of their natural territories. To cite Robert Frost's famous line, "The land was [theirs] before [they] were the land's." For both peoples, the social and spiritual orders of a dying past were yielding, in the living present, to the raw energies of an unknown future, and the land itself was an ambiguous symbol of their destinies. This was epic material; and fiction, especially the novel, was the aptest means of imaginatively encompassing it. And though both nations produced major writers in other forms, perhaps their fiction writers — fortunately for the requisites of the life that was demanding expression — possessed, in the aggregate, the densest accumulation of creative genius.

ROBERT E. SPILLER

James Fenimore Cooper

If ANYTHING from the pen of the writer of these romances is at all to outlive himself, it is, unquestionably, the series of *The Leather-Stocking Tales*," wrote James Fenimore Cooper in 1850 when he first brought the five stories together to make a single tale of the life of his wilderness scout.

He was right in his belief that something far more than he had planned — a folk epic of the settlement of America — had emerged of itself from his efforts and that these novels would outlive him. He also guessed unhappily that, with a few exceptions like *The Spy* and *The Pilot*, the rest of his novels, collected into the handsome set of the Mohawk Edition, and his critical and historical prose would be largely forgotten. Memorialized by children in their games of Indians, hunters, and trappers, and acknowledged by adults as the creator of the American wilderness myth — more real than reality — this writer of stiff and wordy romantic prose was for many years little read. Then, in the general awakening of curiosity about our national culture that took place in the 1920's and 1930's, Cooper came into his own. He was, it would appear, the first American man of letters to take the whole of American experience as the private preserve of his ranging imagination and his critical mind.

There is no doubt that, as a man of thought and feeling, Cooper, more than any other writer of his generation, understood the time and place in which he lived and gave them voice and meaning. It is he who stands at the portal of American literature, rather than

Freneau or Brown, Irving or Bryant, and who is recognized at home and abroad as the first and one of the greatest of American writers of fiction.

How then should the serious reader or scholar go about the task of breaking down the barrier that stands between him and this serious writer, the first truly professional American man of letters? How can he become acquainted with this towering figure of his own literary past?

The modern critic would probably answer: "Lay aside your prejudices, read all the text, analyze carefully the meaning and the structure of at least a part of it, and make up your own mind." This is good advice, but the literary historian would approach the problem from a different angle with different results. He would suggest that the reader should try to reconstruct as best he can the point of view of the writer and the circumstances of the writing and, with an understanding of the meaning of the work in its own context, he should read and evaluate it both as art and as historical document. From the days of his first biographer, T. R. Lounsbury, down to the near present the best Cooper criticism has been historical, but there have also been critics like D. H. Lawrence, Marius Bewley, and Donald A. Ringe who have attempted a more nearly intrinsic and impressionistic criticism, with mixed results. Of them Ringe — perhaps because he first establishes and then maintains a basically historical perspective — provides the best balanced if not the most exciting evaluation. There is still much research to be done on Cooper, particularly in the problem of his literary sources, and much careful analytical criticism is needed, especially for the relatively forgotten novels and some of the critical prose, but the essential fact that Cooper is an organic artist for whom the subject is more important than the form, rather than a consciously technical artist like Henry James, will always make the substance and process of his work far more interesting and important than its structure and texture.

Up to the age of thirty, Cooper was a reader, not a writer, of fiction. Suddenly then, he developed the conviction that as an American he had something to say which desperately needed saying and which could only be said effectively through the art of the novel. He spent the rest of his life — thirty years — in a passionate and persistent effort to get that something said. Egged on by success and stung by failure, he never fully gave up his relentless crusade, even though he suffered periods of deep discouragement, and he produced an average of a novel a year up to the eve of his death, plus a dozen or more works of history and criticism. Translated and appreciated abroad, he was criticized and condemned at home, while his fame increased all over the world and his ideas and his art created a chapter in the intellectual and imaginative history of the American people. Insatiably returning to the attack after each partial failure, he never wearied of experiment or lost his faith in the validity of his efforts. Rough hewn as it was, his total work stands today as a massive monument to his vision and his courage. Perhaps no one of his novels can successfully weather the close examination that a masterpiece demands, but his total work is unquestionably the achievement of a vivid and powerful imagination.

With Cooper's first half-dozen novels American literature came into its own. By 1829, they had been republished in England and were translated into French and German. Several had also found translators in Italy, Sweden, Denmark, and probably other European countries. A critic in the London *Athenaeum* in that year linked Cooper with Irving and Channing as the only American writers who were generally known abroad. At home, *The Spy* was appearing in its seventh edition, *The Pioneers* in its sixth.

At first Cooper did not believe in himself as a literary man, and he was not so considered by others. Samuel Knapp, the first historian of our literature, does not mention him, and he stated his own primary purpose in a letter of 1831: "[My country's] mental independence is my object, and if I can go down to the grave with the reflection that I have done a little towards it, I shall have the consolation of knowing that I have not been useless in my generation."

Moral rather than aesthetic purpose motivated his work as it did his character. Always a man in whom impulse stimulated mind, he absorbed the thought currents of his day and of his inheritance with eager enthusiasm, and he spoke for his cause with the energetic dogmatism of American youth. Whether or not we attribute this moral enthusiasm to his Quaker ancestry as Henry Canby suggested, or to other conventional causes, we can find at least one source for it in the blind optimism and vital energy which are natural products of frontier conditions and unfolding civilization. He lived at a time when American culture had sent down its first firm roots into the new soil, but what fruits it might bear were still uncertain. It was Cooper's task to profit by the autonomy which political independence had brought and to enlarge the spirit of that independence to include the sense of security which only self-knowledge can produce. Never a man of the frontier himself in spirit or in fact, he was a product of the frontier conditions which became the material of his novels. Literature for him was merely the expression of opinions and imagination in accord with actual conditions. "It is high time," he wrote in 1837, "not only for the respectability, but for the *safety* of the American people, that they should promulgate a set of principles that are more in harmony with their facts." This was the basic motive for his writing. The forms which that writing took were largely accidental. Fortuitous circumstances determined his choice of themes for *Precaution, The Spy, The Pioneers,* and *The Pilot,* the novels which in turn determined the material for most of his later work: American society, American history, the American backwoods, and the sea. He fell into the forms of the domestic novel of manners and the romantic tale of adventure because they were easy and familiar to him, not because he cared deeply about their requirements and uses. The literary principles which he gradually evolved from his experience were not narrowly aesthetic, nor were his social and religious principles the results of imposed or formulated doctrine.

A codified analysis of his position would therefore be fruitless. Rather we must follow him through the stages of his development as a moving, growing, vital, and expressive force in the evolution of American culture through a period of stumbling self-discovery.

Born in 1789, Cooper published nothing until 1820. In the early years, his character and his dominant ideas were molded by his inheritance, by the influence of his father, William Cooper, his home, and his father's friends, and by the post-pioneer conditions in central New York State, as well as by the more highly cultivated society of New York City and the settlements along the lower Hudson and the Sound.

All that Cooper himself has to say about this first and unliterary period was written in later years and is strongly colored by his developed personality and doctrines. Much light is thrown upon it, however, by his father's record and rules of his own experience, *A Guide in the Wilderness*, and by the prefaces and memoirs of his daughter Susan, as well as by what we know of the circumstances of his childhood and youth from other sources.

It is well to keep always in mind the fact that he was not himself a pioneer even though he wrote so extensively of the pioneers and of life on the frontier. His childhood was formal, in a closely knit home and community life, and his own moves were always toward the East and its culture rather than toward the western fringe of civilization. His father, although a pioneer of the homesteading generation, was a Federalist in politics and had many of the attributes of the aristocrat in his social thinking. The Cooper family life was shaped on the patriarchal model. His mother devoted herself to her home and her children who, in their turn, grew up with a strong feeling for family loyalty and integrity and attachment to place.

Compared to the Dutch patroons and the English patentees of northern New York, however, William Cooper's theories of property rights, suffrage, equality, and other "American principles" were liberal and democratic. "The mirror of partisan perfection as a Federal squire," Dixon Ryan Fox has called him, and he appeared to his son as a democratic gentleman, privileged because of his business sagacity and control of his fellows. Cooperstown was named after him, developed by his theories, and shaped around his personality. The "Mansion House," later replaced by Otsego Hall, a large structure at the foot of Lake Otsego, was Cooper's boyhood home, the embodiment of his father's integrity and power. All about this industrious squirearchy were the neobaronial tracts of the Dutch patroons who rented their land to tenant farmers, and beyond them was the unsettled and wooded wilderness; while sixty miles to the east was the town of Albany, capital of an agrarian aristocracy. The picture is vividly painted in *The Pioneers*. "There existed," explained Henry Cabot Lodge, "in New York an upper class, stronger and better defined than in any northern province . . . and closely allied to the ruling class in Virginia." The Cooper home was in accord with this tradition.

When Cooper and his brothers were sent to Yale and Princeton for the education which their father lacked, they went, therefore, with an assurance that they would be permitted, both by him and by the society of which they were a part, to use their intellectual powers to build on the material foundations of family stability which their father had laid. To Cooper, there was nothing inconsistent with democracy in this assumption that wealth permits privilege, as his later attitude toward his own children demonstrates. Furthermore, when he married into one of the Tory families of New York, he adopted and carried on its traditions. He may, therefore, be considered in these early years as an aristocrat in the social sense, as a man who accepted an unequal society and his own place of priority in it.

His experiences at Yale and in the Navy, where he served from 1808 to 1811, were, of course, important to Cooper's development, but they did little to alter his basic attitudes. His marriage, on the other hand, was a profoundly significant influence. Susan Augusta De Lancey was the granddaughter of James De Lancey, chief justice and governor of New York, and leader of the Loyalists in that state during the Revolution. The De Lanceys lost their power with their land when the Loyalist cause was defeated, but Mrs. Cooper inherited a share of the Heathcote family holdings at Mamaroneck on the Sound through descent from James De Lancey's wife, Anne Heathcote. Cooper was married at Heathcote Hall and built his new home, Angevine Farm, a few miles inland. This background is reflected in the social novels, particularly those of the later years, which present us with perhaps the best picture we have of life as Susan De Lancey must have known it, modified by the ideals of William Cooper and seen through the prism of Jeffersonian democracy.

When Cooper began to write novels, he was already established in his own privileged place in a stable society. As yet he took no deep interest in social or political causes. He looked about him with an observant rather than a philosophical eye, and he believed in his country and in the principles of its Constitution because he had nothing to complain of in his own lot. Always a lover of books, he loved life more, and he drew his conclusions mainly from the facts about him and from the opinions of such friends and relatives as Judge William Jay, Governor De Witt Clinton, and Bishop William Heathcote De Lancey. He worshipped at an Episcopal church, joined the local agricultural society and the state militia, built a house on a hill overlooking his land and the distant sea, and brought up his family in all the proprieties and accomplishments of the day. Like the Squire of Bracebridge Hall, he steeped himself in local tradition and history, and he had a lively interest in the characters of the people around him.

In the novels written during the decade 1820–30 — ten in all — his attitude is primarily that of the observer rather than that of the critic. In his first, *Precaution* (1820), the moralizer is dominant. It is significant, in the light of his later work, that Sir Edward Moseley "was descended from one of the most respectable of the creations of his order by James, and had inherited, with many of the virtues of his ancestor, an estate which placed him among the greatest landed proprietors of the county," and that his wife was "a woman of many valuable and no obnoxious qualities, civil and attentive by habit to all around her, and perfectly disinterested in her attachments to her own family." We are to meet these types again and again in the novels. The life at Moseley Hall and in the Rectory was presumably English, even though Cooper had never, up to this time, left his native shore. The details were gleaned from his reading, but the social pattern was far from alien to the comparatively crude approximations of aristocracy which he had experienced on the fringe of the wilderness.

He had written the novel, according to a family story told by his daughter, in answer to the challenge of his wife when he had complained of an English novel he had been reading aloud to her: "Why don't you write a better one yourself?" and there is some question how seriously he took the task he had set himself. It was rather the challenge of his own failure that spurred him on. The choice of material was wrong; he should write about what he knew. Both the writing and the printing were careless; he should do well anything that he thought worth doing at all. Accepting full blame for the failure, he would try again, and the world of imagination opened before him.

The ten early novels were experimental in more ways than one although Cooper seems to have sensed from the start the main objectives and the principal ways of reaching them that were to guide him throughout his career. Each of these novels represents a new start and each has in the background one or more models to provide semblance of literary form. From his reading he was familiar with the historical romance of Scott and the domestic novel of manners of Jane Austen and others. Later he turned to Balzac, Dana, Smollett, and other novelists, as well as to biography and travel narratives, for hints on how to organize his material, but what he had to say was always vigorously his own and he contributed more than he borrowed in every case. When he took the neutral ground around New York City for the scene of his Revolutionary War novel, *The Spy*, he probably had Scott's border country in mind, and it was the poor seamanship of *The Pirate* that, according to his own account, inspired *The Pilot*. His use of a single cycle of the seasons in the life of a country house in *The Pioneers* resembles Irving's in *Bracebridge Hall* and he did genuine research on his historical sources for the New England backgrounds of *Lionel Lincoln* and *The Wept of Wish-ton-Wish*, and on his vision of the open West for *The Prairie*.

Donald Ringe has suggested that it was probably the aesthetic requirements of the associationist psychology of Cooper's day rather than a narrow nationalism that led him and other early American poets, novelists, and painters to turn to familiar materials and themes in order to arouse a suitable train of associations in the reader's mind and thus convey to him a fundamental truth. If so, the turn from English to American material and from the themes of love and marriage to those of rebellion and war in *The Spy* was instinctive rather than planned, for Cooper was never a deliberate and careful artist. It would seem that his first experiment in the art of fiction, by its very failure, taught him that he had something to say about the world he knew and that the English domestic novel of manners was not the form in which it could effectively be said. A tightly constructed society is essential to success in this mode and the primary fact of the American experience was the creation of an open and fluent society in which habits, manners, and ultimately morality were threatened with disintegration. The task of the American writer was therefore more than merely the finding of the most suitable literary form; it was that of probing the effects of democratic theory on inherited and transplanted values. Cooper was not himself aware for a long time of the full implications of his own challenge and it took many experiments to make the issue clear to him and to others; but, long before Hawthorne or Melville, or even Poe, he became deeply conscious of the spiritual and cultural ambiguities of life in the New World. His use of native materials drawn from the primitive wilderness of America's recent past and the sea of her present absorbing interest provided the substance, and the developing themes of these first novels set the issues and the patterns, for the best American literature of the following years. It was necessary to twist and wrench English literary modes to make them fit American materials, but it was also necessary to face the fact that the moral structure of English society was in process of becoming, first flexible, and then disintegrated in the natural and open environment of the new continent. Often as literature in the past had revealed the tragic issue in human destiny, man seems not to have learned his lesson: he was again pitting his will against fate as though it had never been done before.

This revelation was of course only dimly glimpsed in *The Spy*

(1821). The turns to American history for his materials and to the historical romance of Scott for his model were drastic enough experiments, and they brought success. With this novel, American fiction was fairly launched. Whatever its inadequacies as art, it released the pent-up energies of its author into a form of expression which set his problem clearly and gave him the range and the instruments to deal with it effectively. He chose the neutral ground around the British-held New York City for his setting and for his central character a man who, by masking his identity, freed himself from the normal laws and manners of formal society. The role of Harvey Birch, together with his humble origin, frees him from the rigid social structure which remains as background in the two armies and offsets his violations of their limitations and requirements; and the looser technique of the historical romance provides an opportunity for fast action and vivid description, both of which were to prove important gifts of the author. The ambiguities of life in America had found, in a combination of the romance and the novel of manners, a sufficiently flexible mode for their fictional expression and, in Cooper, an inventive and courageous writer who was ready to commit himself to the task. The long road ahead was open.

In *The Pioneers* (1823), Cooper faced his problem even more directly and wrote the semi-autobiographical story that every serious novelist must get out of his system before he knows what he has to say or how to say it. Turning to the scenes of his boyhood for his setting and to his father for his central character, he raised again the question of how democracy can create in a wilderness a society stable enough to preserve the values essential to civilized and moral living. Here was a small though primitive community that was attempting to carve out of the frontier an integrated way of life. With a setting sufficiently contained to lend itself to the technique of the novel of manners, the theme demanded the scope and freedom of the historical romance. A laudatory review of Catharine Maria Sedgwick's *A New-England Tale*, tentatively identified as Cooper's by James Beard, in *The Literary and Scientific Repository*, suggests his principal source, and the pattern of the seasons and the milieu of a country squirearchy suggest Irving's *Brace-*

bridge Hall, which he also reviewed in the same journal. But the spirit of the novel is anything but domestic. With the introduction of such characters as Billy Kirby the woodsman and the versatile if somewhat meteoric Dickon Jones, the native quality of the village life takes over; and with the introduction of Cooper's master character Leather-Stocking, he discovers for the first time the romantic possibilities of the wilderness forest, lake, and stream, even though Natty Bumppo is here realistically presented as a dogged old man of seventy, toughened in both skin and convictions by his long years in the open. His idealization was a slow process which culminated only in *The Deerslayer* two decades later.

We come to *The Pioneers* then with the realization that Cooper intended it as a work of art and that he knew instinctively what he was doing even though more interested in the subject than in the form of his experiment. Its power and its purpose strike home, however, only after the patient acceptance of long and unrealistic dialogues which the author confesses are his means of presenting ideas and actions, of a plot which is full of coincidences and stupidities, and of characters who are either idealized or burlesqued beyond credibility. But when such weaknesses are recognized and forgotten, a vivid picture of the American past comes to life in the imagination. Characters step from the pages by their responses to nature in both her savage and her contemplative moods, and scenes of grandeur and terror unfold in unhampered romantic description. Setting — character — theme: the steady hand of an inexperienced but controlled and directed literary imagination is evident at every point.

The thematic structure of the novel comes to a focus in the conflict between Judge Temple and Leather-Stocking on the issue of killing a deer out of season. Their friendship breaks down because the Judge's belief in the social control of individual "rights" has no common ground with Natty's reliance on the laws of the forest and of God as moral absolutes. These two idealized prototypes of real characters, both of whom Cooper fully understands and admires, admire each other but are critically irreconcilable. The Judge symbolizes the value system of civilized society; Natty that of the single solitary natural man. When Natty loses the battle and turns his eyes to the western prairie, the Judge is left with the realization that there are still more profound and complex ambiguities that even the settlement of this issue cannot solve. Novelist rather than dogmatist, Cooper leaves the problem unresolved to follow Natty later into the setting sun and the open prairie.

Meanwhile, however, romance took over and a younger and further idealized Leather-Stocking leads his four civilized friends through an Indian-infested forest in *The Last of the Mohicans* (1826). For sheer vitality, suspense, action, natural description, and story interest, this is perhaps the most successful, and certainly the most popular, of Cooper's romances. All the conflicts of individual and social values of the other novels are here again but they are so buried in the requirements of the story that they do not intrude, even though, on second thought, one realizes that in his Indian Chingachgook and in his wilderness scout Cooper has now defined his two types of primitive conduct, the noble and stoic savage and the Christian man of nature, and has given them an epic dimension as part of the American myth upon which Mark Twain and others could draw. Natty came to grips with civilization in his clash with Judge Temple; here he turns the other way and confronts the primitive absolute.

In the third chapter of *The Last of the Mohicans*, these two meet on the banks of a small but rapid stream. Each presents to the other the chief point in his philosophy of life, and they find in each other a deep and primitive sympathy, although the issue of their debate — whether or not the white man has a right to the new lands — is not resolved. Racial traditions contain all the philosophy of the Indian. He believes only what Nature and his fathers have told him: "The land we had taken like warriors, we kept like men." But to the trapper, "everything depends on what scale you look at things." Because he rejects the sophistication of his people, can shoot to the mark, and can respect honesty and courage in his fellows of whatever color, he feels himself on a par with the red man. The right of the intruders to the land depends on their superiority as men, their justice, and their humanity. The scale which Bumppo supplies to enlarge that of the Indian comes from the Bible as interpreted in Protestant tradition. Under Christian influence, the red warrior forsakes his inhuman ways, his brutality, and his ignorance, to rely upon justice and charity. Cooper's primitivism is thus in no sense pagan; it is a complete acceptance of Protestant ethical tradition qualified by a rejection rather than by a reform of the social sophistications and corruptions which had resulted in three centuries of evolution in that tradition. Cooper's argument has, therefore, little relationship to that of the "noble savage"; his values are Christian rather than pagan. When in a romantic vein, he assigns ideal primitive traits to the savages; when in a critical vein, he calls for their cultivation in civilized society. But he still believed that the problem of differing value systems could and should be dealt with on the level of human reason and justice; it was not until much later that disillusionment made him transfer it to the wisdom of God.

The third novel in the Leather-Stocking series, *The Prairie* (1827), picks up Natty's life where Cooper left it at the end of *The Pioneers*. Unable to reconcile his moral integrity as an individual with the restraints of the civil law, the trapper has now followed through on his decision to move further west. Cooper himself had never seen the prairie and he was now writing from Europe, but the perspective of distance, buttressed by research and imagination, merely sharpened the themes of his story of the quest for moral integrity, this time offset by another of Cooper's symbolic types, the shrewd and unscrupulous squatter Ishmael Bush. Again the question is asked: Is moral integrity, based on a firm faith in Divine wisdom, sufficient to protect human values from the selfish despoiler of nature that is in every man, without the support of civil law and a structured society? The trapper's death supplies a negative answer as well as a moment of high tragedy.

During this early period, Cooper also wrote two historical novels of New England, *Lionel Lincoln* (1825) and *The Wept of Wish-ton-Wish* (1829), which, in spite of careful research and important themes, lacked their author's sympathy and therefore never took fire as did the forest romances. But in the first three sea romances, as in the Leather-Stocking series, he discovered an American myth and from it developed a wholly new kind of fiction which he taught to a generation of followers. Even though *The Pilot* (1824), *The Red Rover* (1828), and *The Water-Witch* (1830) are as experimentally and romantically interesting as the tales of land adventure, to discuss them here in the same detail would be repetitious. Ringe prefers *The Pilot* as a more daring break with convention and a better vehicle for Cooper's ideas; Thomas Philbrick, whose work on this aspect of Cooper's art is thorough, has chosen *The Red Rover* for fuller analysis as a better told story and a more satisfactory representative of the genre. Both agree that Cooper's heavy hand with allegory makes *The Water-Witch* the least acceptable of the group, even though it also reflects an important element in the growth of Cooper's restless imagination.

The inspiration for these three tales of the sea runs closely parallel to that of the three romances of the woods. Launched on his project by a more or less accidental challenge, Cooper discovered, once he was deep in the work of imaginative re-creation, that he had more to say than conventional modes of fiction writing would allow. The theme of maritime nationalism was in some respects even more compelling than that of western expansion, for by 1823, the infant Republic had survived its first major test of strength and was an acknowledged rival of the expanding British sea power. Furthermore, the theme of personal integrity and freedom from civil restraints was more effectively expressed in Cooper's freelance ships and captains than in his Indians and woodsmen, even though Long Tom Coffin is a less convincing seagoing Leather-Stocking and the pirate and smuggler of the later tales assert their rights and live their own lives in their own ways and to their own cost. If the plots of these stories lean even more than do those of the wilderness tales on the mechanics of conventional romance, their settings and characters have more freedom for the development of dominant themes, and it is herein that Cooper's originality finds its opportunity. As Marcel Clavel long ago pointed out and as Philbrick has more recently emphasized, Cooper's break with Smollett and Scott and his anticipation of Melville and Conrad was accomplished singlehanded, with only a slight assist from Byron. So fully was he seized by the power and freedom of the sea that, in his descriptive passages, the setting comes fully to life, taking over from the dwarfed humans and becoming itself the hero of the narrative. This was Cooper's invention and it gives his sea tales a unique place in the history of fiction; but the absence of a Leather-Stocking to hold them together makes them, even so, of less importance than the wilderness tales in the total evaluation of his work.

The last four of the tales of this first and experimental decade were written after Cooper had taken up residence abroad, but they show little or no influence of the impact that European life was having on his feelings and his thoughts. With the *Notions of the Americans: Picked up by a Travelling Bachelor* in 1828 he had initiated a decade in which he turned his main attention from American to European and comparative political and social problems and from fiction to critical and historical prose. The instigating motive for this book was patriotism, as in the case of his earlier efforts to delineate the American scene and character. It is Cooper's first direct statement of his social philosophy, and, instead of expounding his position theoretically as he did later in *The American Democrat*, he attempts, not without critical reservations, to prove that America is a living embodiment of his beliefs.

The immediate provocation of the *Notions* was the increasing flood of books on America by English travelers. "It is with feelings of deep regret that I observe the literary animosity daily growing up between England and America," wrote the mild-tempered Washington Irving in 1819, and by 1828 some forty pretentious works of travel in America by English authors had already appeared. American replies were taking two forms, direct rebuttal and mock travel. To the latter class Cooper's *Notions* belongs, with Royall Tyler's *Yankey in London*, Charles J. Ingersoll's *Inchiquin, the Jesuit's Letters*, and J. K. Paulding's *Sketch of Old England by a New-England Man* and *John Bull in America; or The New Munchausen*.

Notions is the most temperate, the best informed, and the best written of the group. Cooper looked upon this book as the most important of his writings up to that time and devoted the summer of 1827 to its composition. He had wished to memorialize in some way the triumphal visit of Lafayette to America in 1824 but the appearance of the general in the resulting fictionalization of his travels was only incidental to the itinerary of the "Travelling Bachelor." In February 1828, Cooper took the unfinished manuscript with him from Paris to London and personally supervised its printing, returning immediately upon its completion late in May.

"The American who gets the good word of England," he wrote later, "is sure of having that of his own country, and he who is abused by England will be certain of being abused at home." The American character and American manners had reached a low ebb in the English mind, and the American mind in its turn was habitually deferential to English opinion. Cooper addressed his *Notions* to both peoples, hoping that a fair and sympathetic picture of America might influence the English and indirectly raise the level of self-respect in America itself. It was an ambitious undertaking, certain of failure in immediate effect, although undoubtedly of ultimate influence. The semifictional formula represented the book as having been written by an English gentleman who was guided in his travels and in his observations by a New York counterpart. His readers on both sides of the water misunderstood his intentions and were irritated rather than soothed by the parts which they understood. He offended both the English sense of superiority and the American spirit of independence. The book had a small sale in comparison with his novels.

Cooper was careful of his facts and studied reliable sources in preparation for writing the book. He was one of the best informed men of his time on social conditions in his own New York State, and he tended to generalize for the nation from the particular locale which he knew. Although this prejudice somewhat detracts from his reliability, a more serious bias was his deliberate intention to present things in their most favorable light. The book may be accepted, however, not only for the value of its opinions, but for its understanding of actual social conditions.

The presumed author is an enlightened European, a man of sound learning and aristocratic taste, but broad in his sympathies, a character familiar in various guises throughout Cooper's novels and easily to be identified with his own ideal conception of himself. He is here a member of a club of such gentlemen of various nations, bachelors all, who devote their time to travel in various parts of the world to learn what they can of man in his social being as expressed in the ideals and manners of civilized peoples.

Cooper adopted in this work for the first time the epistolary form so common in eighteenth-century English novels and to be used by him again only in the travel books. He did so, he says in his Preface, because "a close and detailed statistical work on the United States of America, could not keep its place as authority for five years." Rather he prefers to emphasize "the principles of the government and the general state of society," which are not so readily subject to change.

During the months — one might almost say years — of preparation for the *Notions* he had been gradually clarifying his ideas about America. The discrepancies between her principles, as he defined them, and her practices had not yet become apparent to him, but his experience with European society would provide him with an admirable background for judgment. As his mind developed, he came to identify conventional ethics and even etiquette with political theory and he wove them all into a social and moral philosophy which he preached in novel after novel and tract after tract without pause. The integration of his morality and his historical sense took place during his European years when he observed the antithetical political ideals in open conflict. The code which he had at first applied successfully only to individuals he gradually learned to apply to society as a whole.

The *Notions* appeared before he had been in Europe long enough to come into close or varied contact with the life about him. So far he had been concerned almost wholly with the two purposes which had taken him from home: the education of his daughters and young son and the business arrangements for translating and publishing which he hoped would secure his financial independence as a writer. But France and England were in these years testing political liberalism as a means of avoiding the extremes of revolution and the old order. France had tried reaction in the restoration of the Bourbons Louis XVIII and Charles X, and England was on the eve of the overthrow of her Tory government. When Cooper arrived both countries were still at the right; during his residence both swung to a hypothetical middle ground with the July Revolution of 1830 in France and the passage of the Reform Bill of 1832 in England. Cooper took part in the discussion which preceded these changes, and sharpened his political wits. In the main, he was in sympathy with the turn of events, but he was intensely critical of compromise.

The longer he remained in Europe the firmer his friendship with Lafayette became and the more definitely the latter molded his opinions. Lafayette was, for a brief moment in July of 1830, the deciding political voice in the affairs of France. It was he who made the gesture of awarding the throne to Louis Phillipe, of the collateral Orleans dynasty, instead of to the legitimate and reactionary Bourbon who would have become Henry V. But after Louis became king, he proved to be more reactionary than Lafayette expected, and the latter found himself the leader of the Opposition to the *juste milieu* in the Chamber of Deputies. His American friend shared with him the feeling of disgust with government measures which were labeled as liberal but which seemed to the Opposition to be reactionary in the extreme. It was this stand which drew Cooper into the finance controversy in the Chamber of Deputies in 1831–32 and into active aid of the cause of Polish freedom during the same years. In both instances, he felt that he was defending the theory and practice of the United States government against, in the first, a direct criticism of the cost of democratic government, and in the second, a tyranny in another country from which the Constitution protected American institutions.

It was this political background which apparently suggested the general themes of his next three novels. What could be more natural for him than to turn the white light of American liberalism on dark corners of the past in which the darker aspects of the present would find analogy? "I had in view," he writes of *The Bravo*, "to exhibit the action of a narrow and exclusive system, by a simple and natural exposure of its influence on the familiar interests of life." The result was the trio of European novels, *The Bravo* (1831), *The Heidenmauer* (1832), and *The Headsman* (1833), all of which were written and published during the latter days of his residence abroad. The scenes were laid in Italy, Switzerland, and the valley of the Rhine, where he had seen for himself surviving monuments of the Middle Ages in the forms of palaces, castles, and monasteries. Contrasting the liberal governments and societies of the Swiss cantons and the Italian free cities with their respective pasts, he drew his own moral in favor of the future of democracy, quite a different one from that of his Scottish rival in romance.

A Letter to His Countrymen (1834) was Cooper's first publication after his return to America on November 5, 1833. It reveals his dismay at conditions of society and politics as he found them, as well as his irritation at the personal criticism which was already being directed toward him by the press. It marks in many ways the principal turning point in his career. His disillusionment is extreme in contrast to his mood five years earlier when he wrote the *Notions*, but for the first time he attempts to reduce his political theories to a generalized statement in other than a fictionalized form.

The primary motive for the tract was its author's desire to defend his personal reputation against the attacks of reviewers. Edward Sherman Gould had contributed to the *New York American* on June 7, 1832, a review of *The Bravo*, in which he not only criticized the social implications in the novel, but expressed the opinion that Cooper had written himself out and was now merely producing romances for the financial return they might bring. The review was sent to Cooper who answered it in a violent mood in the *Albany Daily Advertiser* for April 2, 1833. His resentment was justified, but its expression was tactless and its form irritating. The *New York Courier and Enquirer* and other American journals took up the quarrel. Finally, Cooper decided to review the whole case in a pamphlet. *A Letter to His Countrymen* announced his retirement as a novelist, and for six years he held to his resolution, devoting his attention mainly to critical prose and social satire.

These years produced five volumes of travel, published under the titles of *Gleanings in Europe* and *Sketches of Switzerland*, and *The American Democrat*. In the order of the journeys they describe rather than that of publication, the travel books are *France* (1837), *England* (1837), *Switzerland*, Part I (1836), *Italy* (1838), *Switzerland*, Part II (Paris, Switzerland, and the Rhine valley; 1836). They are ostensibly made up of letters to friends, named in the first two, anonymous in the others; but they actually consist of short topical discussions, of loose unity, presumably based on notes taken during Cooper's residence abroad but later so drastically expanded and amended that no passages from the books can be taken as the record of his opinions at the time of his observations. Cooper's first plan was to write a volume on Europe which might serve as a companion to the *Notions*. "The fragments of travels that are here laid before the reader," he states in the Preface to *Sketches of Switzerland*, Part I, "are parts of a much more extensive work, that it was, originally, the intention of the writer to publish." That work was never written; instead, the travel letters followed each other in haphazard order.

Cooper's main purpose throughout the series is that stated in *A Letter to His Countrymen*: the examination of European institutions and manners, in order to reveal the differences between them and the American which make direct imitation most dangerous to the new country. The works themselves are mere narratives of travel interspersed with comments pointing to this danger. Although the principles which he discusses are themselves political, Cooper's interest in them rests almost wholly in their social applications. His criticism of European society, including the English, reduces itself to a simple formula: European liberal political ideals had advanced far beyond contemporary manners, but the manners themselves had the advantages as well as the liabilities of tradition and were therefore stable enough for the development of culture. In America, the reverse was the case. Whereas European customs must, thought Cooper, eventually be modified to conform to the new ideas, in America well-formulated principles were not yet understood by the mass of the nation and there was no native tradition on which to build. His two attacks, on the disrupting principles threatening a well-ordered society in Europe and on the tardiness of America in recognizing her principles and in applying them to her facts, spring from the same source. It became his obvious duty, he felt, to attempt a logical formulation of ideal social standards for America in terms of what he believed to be basic American principles. What had been implicit in his early novels became explicit in his "primer," *The American Democrat*, in 1838.

The American Democrat is Cooper's most direct and comprehensive formulation of his social and political — and therefore by inference his moral — creed. In it, he defines his matured theory of the American democratic principle, and applies his definition to a variety of American institutions, both in themselves and in comparison with those of Europe. It is presented in the form of an elementary text, but it rests on no authority other than the opinions of the writer. The central principle is the belief in liberty for the individual within a society in which common rights are adequately protected by constitutional checks and balances. The republican form of government, as illustrated in the American system and compared with the monarchical and aristocratic forms of European countries, is analyzed and related to limited ideals of liberty and equality; then the following institutions are discussed: the press, suffrage, slavery, party, and formal religion. Although Cooper was at this time still a member of the Democratic party and was under attack by the Whigs as its spokesman, this book is a vigorous exposé of the egalitarian tendencies of both the Jacksonian Democrats and the Whigs and an effort to systematize what he believed to be the American political inheritance from both Jefferson and the Federalism of his father's views. His book was an effort to recapture and to formulate for a new age what he believed to be the ideals and forms of the original order of American society and government.

Of the other critical prose of the period, the *History of the Navy*

James Fenimore Cooper

of the United States of America (1839) alone demands mention here. Cooper was definitely a "big Navy" man, and his history was undertaken in the interest of this cause. He believed that America's sense of a national being would not be appreciated either at home or abroad until she could build on the foundation of her scattered naval triumphs a strong and regular naval force. As a historian, however, he was no respecter of persons; he told his story as the facts seemed to him to require. Several controversies were the result of his honesty and helped to cloud his later years at the same time that they reawakened his interest in the sea as a source of material for fiction, supplying him with many new story ideas. His later *Lives of Distinguished American Naval Officers* (1846) was both a summing up of his ideas on these controversies and a further use of naval materials. He now singled out the most important actors in the drama and retold their stories.

During this period of critical prose, Cooper wrote only three novels, all of them fictional treatments of his newly formulated doctrines. The first was *The Monikins* (1835), a satirical allegory in which he stressed the contrasting civilizations of two hemispheres. In some respects it anticipates Melville's *Mardi*, in others it harks back to *Gulliver's Travels*. Again the fictional veil is thin. Monkeys or men, these Monikins are Americans, Englishmen, Frenchmen. European civilization fails, he explains, because of caste, corruptions, and insusceptibility to social change; American because of party, vulgarity, and money-madness. But as yet his criticism of his own countrymen is mild compared with that of the Europeans; at heart he still finds America at least theoretically sound.

The other two novels of these years are really one, *Homeward Bound* (1838) and *Home as Found* (1838), the one a romance of the sea, the latter a portrait of Cooperstown very different from that presented in *The Pioneers*. With a long sheet of foolscap in front of him and his pen in hand, he sat down to tell a story in which he planned to record the observations of an American gentleman (himself) on his return with his family from a long residence abroad. The crudities of American society and the purity of

31

American ideals which had been so violated were to have been the substance of the tale. But he made the mistake of opening with a scene on shipboard as the party set sail from England, and a typical romance of a chase, escape, and adventure had to be worked out of his system before the real business of the day could be undertaken in a sequel. It was the second novel, not the first, that he had planned to write, as it was always into social criticism that he was to throw his most deliberate creative effort — whether admitted or implied — from this time forward.

The result was as disastrous to his popularity as had been *The Bravo*. In order to present the case for an American aristocracy of worth, he drew upon the familiar material of his own native town once more, but this time the central character, Edward Effingham, was inescapably a fictionalized portrait of himself. *Home as Found*, in the history of American fiction, is not a bad novel and it marks an advance toward the kind of social fiction that culminated in the work of Sinclair Lewis in that it shows progress in Cooper's ability to build a story with social purpose around a domestic theme; but the realism was too literal for comfort. Neither was the situation helped by Cooper's treatment of the sensitive Three Mile Point controversy in which he was currently involved. In justifying Effingham for asserting his own property rights, as he had himself on Lake Otsego, in defiance of his neighbors, the villagers, Cooper put himself in a very unfavorable light and drew the wrath of the Whig press even more viciously down on his head, as Dorothy Waples has shown.

The close of the period 1838–40 finds Cooper the author of extensive treatises on the national character of America, England, and certain other European countries, a man with a definite social and political creed and a firm base on moral conviction. The novel had for some time ceased to be his central interest; his mission in life seemed rather the reform of the American mind by the rediscovery of national traditions and the battling with what seemed to him the forces of disintegration in the political and social structure of his country. The result was an involvement in controversies on

James Fenimore Cooper

all sides and an expenditure of prodigious effort in libel trials against the Whig press for what he felt to be misrepresentations. Most of these brought him little more than personal vindication on specific points, and all of them have been so thoroughly expounded elsewhere that they do not need to be discussed in detail here. That he was right on most issues does not seem to have mattered; his popularity shrank to a fraction of its former strength, and with it his income. He never regained the popularity which he lost by formulating his theories and applying them to his art and to the civilization of which he was a part.

With his return to Leather-Stocking in 1840, Cooper became once more primarily a novelist and produced what many critics have acclaimed as his masterworks, *The Pathfinder* (1840) and *The Deerslayer* (1841), in the midst of the distress and confusion of the libel suits and in the wake of the popular failure of the Effingham duo. It is obvious that he had decided to try once again to express his view of life in fictional form although there is no second *Letter to His Countrymen* to announce his change of intention. His firm handling of theme, setting, character, and action in these two new episodes in the life of his wilderness hero is, however, sufficient evidence that he had lost none of his old zest and skill and that he had grown both as an artist and as a man of feeling. Recapturing his delight in nature, he brings Natty to life against the background of the country north of Cooperstown on the shores of Lake Ontario where, as a midshipman, the young Cooper had spent the winter of 1808. As sheer romance, the love story of Natty Bumppo and the old game of woodland hide-and-seek with hostile Indians combine to make as good a tale as anything Cooper ever did, and the thoughtless reader might well miss the social and moral themes which give it plot and purpose. Cooper's point in *Home as Found* that happiness depends upon taking one's natural place in the society of one's fellows according to one's native gifts, and that democracy can survive as a social structure only if it is based on an aristocracy of worth, is here unobtrusively but fully illustrated in Mabel Dunham's preference for Jasper Western, her masculine

33

"opposite number," among her suitors, and again and again in such issues as the salt-water sailor Cap's failure in a fresh-water crisis.

Without losing his sense of reality, Leather-Stocking, now re-named "Pathfinder," rises to a new level of idealization and, in a story which uses again much of the old plot of *The Last of the Mohicans*, achieves a serenity and firmness of conviction which reflects Cooper's own emotional and intellectual maturity. There only remained for him to re-create the youth of his hero in the last of the series, *The Deerslayer*, and to give his readers at the same time the beginning of his saga and the fulfillment of its meaning; for Natty as Deerslayer has now become a symbol of the human values toward which Cooper had been reaching, and his story the most "poetic" of the Leather-Stocking tales, in which romance and moral import combine to create what many critics hold to be Cooper at his best.

Once in the saddle again, Cooper's revived narrative power seemed inexhaustible. In the decade remaining to him, 1841–51, he produced sixteen full-length novels, as well as a number of lesser pieces. In most of them his imaginative command of his materials shows little or no decline even though, as his social and political convictions become more and more transformed into moral and religious principles, they also tend to become more reactionary and dogmatic. When, however, his romantic joy of life and his narrative gift are in the ascendant, as they are in these later Leather-Stocking tales and in the sea tales of the same period, his convictions blend with the themes and action of the stories and give them firm structure and forward movement; when ideas take over the center of interest, as they do in many of the other later novels, the result is an inner aesthetic conflict between art and didacticism, and didacticism usually wins.

In *The Two Admirals* (1842) and *The Wing-and-Wing* (1842), Cooper revived his interest in the romance of the sea as he had in that of the forest and achieved something of the serenity and mature mastery of *The Pathfinder* and *The Deerslayer* with the materials of *The Pilot* and the other sea romances. Returning to some of his earlier themes, situations, and characters, he gives them a firmer and altogether more satisfactory treatment. The time of both novels is the middle and late eighteenth century, the scene the Mediterranean, and the historical background the maritime rivalry between Britain and France, a theme derived from but only distantly related to the conflict between these two powers during the Indian and Revolutionary wars which had provided the drama for the earlier sea romances. Now, with the research he had done for his naval history as foundation, he could make even fleet maneuvers romantic, and with the injection of a love story and other elements of the old romantic formula in *The Wing-and-Wing*, he fully recaptured the spell of the sea and succeeded in bringing this second of his major modes to a new artistic maturity.

If these four novels — two of the forest and two of the sea — may be taken as the maximum realization of all the best elements of Cooper's art in their most satisfactory balance, that balance proved to be as precarious in his later years as it had been in the earlier. Beginning with *Wyandotté* in 1843, Cooper entered a new experimental phase of his career, a phase of moral and religious didacticism which had been specifically indicated in his earlier career only by the Puritan novel *The Wept of Wish-ton-Wish* in 1829, but had been present as an undercurrent in all his work.

The novels of this final phase may be divided into two classes: those in which the problems of society are paramount and those in which the solutions of formal religion take over the center of interest. Such a division is, of course, arbitrary, but because the line of thought in this essay has been based on the theory that Cooper's primary concern was always with the conflict between individual integrity and social structure and with the moral versus the anarchic kinds of freedom on both sides of this equation, emphasis in the discussion of these later novels will be on those in which his mature socio-moral rather than his strictly religious thought is uppermost.

Between 1844 and 1846 Cooper published his five novels dealing with his now matured theory of social structure and, in many ways, achieved in them the fullest realization of his ambition to write a novel of manners in the technique of the romance, but only at a sacrifice of his early flamboyancy to a growing sober realism and a sense of the mutability of human destiny. His approach was historical, but he no longer thought of American history as merely a romantic past. He turned to the early days of settlement and to the War for Independence in order to uncover the roots of contemporary society. He had settled his family in the scenes of his boyhood, repaired the old house, and established himself as prototype of the patrician order. In *Home as Found* he had described the condition of society which he had found at Templeton (Cooperstown) by dividing its development into three stages: the first, that of settlement in which "the gentleman, even while he may maintain his character and station, maintains them with that species of good-fellowship and familiarity, that marks the intercourse between the officer and the soldier in an arduous campaign"; the second, in which "we see the struggles for place, the heart-burnings and jealousies of contending families, and the influence of mere money"; the third, in which "men and things come within the control of more general and regular laws." Cooperstown, in William Cooper's day, was in the first stage; his son found it in the second and hoped to move it into the third. To illustrate this process, he took typical landed families of the early days and attempted to tell their histories through several generations.

Afloat and Ashore (1844), with its sequel, is the story of Miles Wallingford, a member of a family that had held Clawbonny, a modest estate on the Hudson, since 1707. Miles succeeded to the property in 1794 at the age of twelve. The "afloat" part of the tale, a good half, is a typical romance of the sea in Cooper's best manner, but modified by the influence of Dana's *Two Years before the Mast* where the action is determined, as it had been in Cooper's version of the narrative of his old sailor friend Ned Myers the year before, more by the biography of its hero than by contrived situations of suspense. But the "ashore" part of the story strikes a new note. Without the asperity of *Home as Found*, it is a more probing study of the ideals, manners, and morals of a type of New York landowner. The plot concerns the courtship of Miles and Lucy Hardinge, member of a neighboring family with somewhat more aristocratic pretensions than those of the Wallingfords. It is not hard to read into this romance, with its idyllic passages and its difficulties and misunderstandings, the social and personal factors which must have operated in the Cooper–De Lancey romance of 1811; and Miles, with his blunt honesty and forthrightness, his recognition of social differences without snobbery or false humility, his love of the sea, and his love for Lucy, is a fair if fictionalized portrait of the youthful Cooper as seen by the elderly. Some of Cooper's most idyllic passages are to be found in these two undeservedly neglected domestic novels of American manners and his two principals are among his most fully and sympathetically created characters. The sea passages also reflect a new realism, with a loss of the trappings but not of the zest of romance. And, most important of all if measured in terms of the intentions and hopes of the author, Cooper has at last presented a full-length and unhurried study of his theories of the individual in democratic society.

The Littlepage novels, *Satanstoe* (1845), *The Chainbearer* (1845), and *The Redskins* (1846), were suggested by the "Anti-Rent War" of 1839–46, but they are a logical consequence of *Afloat and Ashore*, an attempt to follow a family like that of the Wallingfords in detail through four generations, using the techniques of biography and realism rather than a reliance upon plot and action. The Anti-Rent War was a local issue, largely forgotten now by the historians, but important to Cooper because it struck at the heart of his ideas on property rights and therefore of his theory of democracy. The Van Rensselaer patroonship on the Hudson at Albany, dating from 1637 and still in the hands of the same family, was the scene of the disturbances. Most of its tenants had leases in perpetuity, and the annual rent for a hundred acres varied from ten to fourteen bushels of wheat, plus, for farms of over 160 acres, four fat hens and one day's labor with horse and wagon. In addition, a sale of the lease required that a quarter of the sum received be paid to the patroon. At the death of Stephen Van Rensselaer in 1839, unpaid rents had accumulated to large amounts in many cases and the terms of his will required their payment. The tenants, restless for many years under so un-American a land system, used this demand as a reason for general protest. Writs were served and a local war between sheriffs' deputies and farmers resulted. Troops were called out and offenders punished when the tenants, disguised as Indians, resisted; and it was not until 1846 that the Anti-Renters gained their principal points and the patroon system came to an end.

Cooper held no particular brief for the patroon system as such and the differences between it and the more liberal land theories of his father had come to mean less to him than they did in the early days. The real point at issue was the inviolability of private property, however held or administered. The Anti-Renters defied their contracts established in law, and if they were allowed to do so without restraint, the rights of property owners of all kinds would be threatened. Hence the foundations of his theory of democracy were being undermined, further evidence that the new America had lost sight of its principles and was drifting rapidly toward mediocrity and social disintegration. The only way to point out the error was to follow the stages of development of society from the days of settlement to the present, thereby securing the established order by reference to tradition. This he attempted in the Littlepage trilogy, his most detailed fictional treatment of his matured social views and the best picture of life in early New York that has come down to us from this time.

"It is easy to foresee that this country is destined to undergo great and rapid changes," writes Cooper in the person of Cornelius Littlepage, born May 3, 1737, at Satanstoe (Mamaroneck), Westchester County, New York, and subject of His Majesty, King George II. "Without a stage, in a national point of view at least, with scarcely such a thing as a book of memoirs that relates to a life passed within our own limits, and totally without light literature, to give us simulated pictures of our manners and the opinions of the day, I see scarcely a mode by which the next generation can preserve any memorials of the distinctive usages and thoughts of this." Of combined English and Dutch heritage, and of a family that owned land, Corny is representative of the modest aristocracy of the time. Through him, Cooper depicts the experiences and discusses the thoughts and feelings of the cultured class in colonial New York. Courage in adversity, chivalric manliness in love, kindliness toward servants, and Christian faith and charity are the chief components of his character. The text of the story is expressed by Mr. Bulstrode in the form of advice to Corny: "There are two sorts of great worlds; the great vulgar world, which includes all but the very best in taste, principles, and manners, whether it be in a capital or in a country; and the great *respectable* world, which, infinitely less numerous, contains the judicious, the instructed, the intelligent, and on some questions, the good. Now the first form fashion; whereas the last produce something far better and more enduring than fashion." Throughout his life, Corny acts as a member of this privileged class in a society which freely recognized its right to rule.

In *The Chainbearer*, his son Mordaunt carries on the tradition through a period in which this right is challenged by shifting social conditions. "It must not be forgotten," he warns, "that land was a drug in the State of New York in the year 1784, as it is today on the Miami, Ohio, Mississippi, and other inland streams. The proprietors thought but little of their possessions as the means of present support, but rather maintained their settlements than their settlements maintained them; looking forward to another age, and to their posterity, for the rewards of all their trouble and investments." Thus a moral bond was established between landlord and tenant, which reached beyond their own generation. Tenants who did not respect the rights of their landlords had no rights in return. The story deals with the difficulties of holding land through this period of transition, in the face of depleted values and the inroads of squatters from New England, the latter factor providing most of the narrative interest. As a whole, the novel is less satisfactory than its predecessor, although the character of the old Chainbearer himself is one of Cooper's most successful creations.

A generation is skipped in *The Redskins* and the narrative brought down to the current issue in the person of Hugh Roger Littlepage, thereby becoming more topical and dogmatic instead of entering the third stage when men and things are theoretically supposed to "come within the control of more general and regular laws." As long as the author's social purpose could be used mainly to provide motivation and structure, the story could serve its dual role of narrative art plus instruction. Cooper had apparently learned how to master this formula when he had the advantage of historical perspective on his material; but as soon as he attempted contemporary or nearly contemporary realism, his detachment increasingly gave way to his doctrinaire intentions.

The later novels reflect this tendency to shift from social inquiry to dogmatism as he became increasingly disillusioned with his early hopes for a solution of human problems by human means and, through increasing emphasis on moral absolutes, was drawn rapidly, as Howard Mumford Jones and other recent critics have stressed, into religious commitment. With the Littlepage series his identification with his own past was complete; his social philosophy had become a rationalization of his own personality and family traditions and his efforts to stem the current tide of equalitarianism and vulgarity had apparently been fruitless. With the growing feeling in his later years that the world was against him, the consolation of the religious faith with which he was early associated grew upon him. From Mamaroneck he had driven his family on Sundays to Rye in order to attend the Episcopal church. A quarter of a century later, the faith of that church came back to him with a renewed vitality, and, in July of the year of his death, he was confirmed by his brother-in-law Bishop De Lancey.

It would be a mistake to find in this action any material change of heart. He had concluded *The American Democrat* many years before with a note on religion, in which he said: "As reason and revelation both tell us that this state of being is but a preparation for another of a still higher and more spiritual order, all the interests of life are of comparatively little importance, when put in the balance against the future." As little concerned with sects as with political parties, he had refrained from joining any particular church. The Episcopal church had not been finally established in Cooperstown until 1811, the year of his marriage and settlement far away in Westchester County, and he had been brought up under the influence of a variety of more or less itinerant clergy-men. Throughout his writing career he had preferred to preach Protestant ethics in a social context rather than the theological doc-trine of any sect. But when the society about him seemed by its actions to deny his social principles, he was forced back upon a theoretical code of ethics as such, and from there the step to a for-mal theological structure was a short one. Throughout its history, the Church of England had been closely associated with the man-ner of life of the landed gentry and its American counterpart had not departed far from its predominant attitudes. In it, Cooper found a hospitable refuge for his social views not to be discovered in the secular patterns of American life in 1850. Furthermore, his wife's family, with its Tory traditions, was strongly Anglican, and there was a well-established Protestant Episcopal church in Coopers-town when the Cooper family returned from its European adven-tures. James Fenimore Cooper, his wife, and his children are buried in Christ Church churchyard, Cooperstown.

This tendency to shift from a social to a theological basis for ethics is apparent in most of the later novels whether they deal with the frontier once more as in *The Oak Openings* (1848), with the sea as in *Jack Tier* (1848) and *The Sea Lions* (1849), or with a social problem as in his last novel, *The Ways of the Hour* (1850). But it is in *The Crater* (1847), a capsule allegory of the rise and fall of democratic society, that Cooper reaches his fullest statement of faith in the inexorable will of a Trinitarian God. This is the com-plete story of a colony founded on a volcanic reef. Mark, its hero, summarizes at the end both the plot and its meaning: "He would thus recall his shipwreck and desolate condition when suffered first to reach the rocks; the manner in which he was the instrument of causing vegetation to spring up in the barren places; the earth-quake, and the upheaving of the islands from out of the waters; the arrival of his wife and other friends; the commencement and prog-ress of the colony; its blessings, so long as it pursued the right, and its curses, when it began to pursue the wrong." This was the point at which Mark's rule of benevolent dictatorship of worth was un-dermined by an ignorant minority's use of the democratic processes. In despair, he recalls his departure, "leaving it still a settlement surrounded with a sort of earthly paradise, and his return, to find all buried beneath the ocean. Of such is the world and its much-coveted advantages. For a time our efforts seem to create, and to adorn, and to perfect, until we forget our origin and destination, substituting self for that divine Hand which alone can unite the elements of worlds as they float in gases, equally from His mysterious laboratory, and scatter them again into thin air when the works of His hand cease to find favor in His view." Mark's reverie is at once a capitulation of the story, an allegorical interpretation of the history and destiny of both the American people and mankind in general, and a final profession of religious fatalism. Far better than *The Monikins* as social satire, *The Crater* is the novel which, if not his best, is the allegorical statement of the position to which Cooper's complex mind and art had throughout been leading: he had since about 1828 been growing more disillusioned with humanity and its ability to solve moral problems by reason alone. The themes of the ambiguity of right and wrong, the incapacity of man to live up to his ideals, and the vanishing line between reality and illusion, which began to appear in his novels after his return to fiction in 1838 and to dominate them after 1848, were rather the by-products of his own experiences with the press and public than a positive religious awakening. The moral values he had always stressed must be sought in the next world if they cannot be realized in this.

At the same time, English and American fashions in fiction were undergoing radical changes which have only recently been related at all carefully to the changes and experiments in Cooper's development. Scott died in 1832 and *Oliver Twist* and *Twice-Told Tales* both appeared in 1837; by 1848, Thackeray was publishing *Vanity Fair* and Melville his pseudo-travelogues on the South Seas; Cooper's last novel and *Moby Dick* were nearly contemporaneous. We know that Cooper was a wide if not a careful reader, that he knew something of French and German as well as American and English literatures, that he favored fiction, travel narratives, biography, and history, and that he was sufficiently anxious about keeping his readership to alter his techniques and forms, if not his convictions, in order to meet changing current tastes. In turning from time to time to realism, the problem novel, and social allegory and satire, he was obviously experimenting with current literary fashions and techniques, at the same time that his mind and feelings were moving from a simple nationalism to deeper social purpose and then to moral conviction.

Wyandotté in 1843 was the first novel to reflect the full force of his disillusionment and surrender to ambiguities. Here for the first time bad Indians are not all bad, good Indians all good, and virtue always rewarded. A hard-bitten realism had pushed aside the idealization that had sustained his novels through *The Deerslayer* and *The Wing-and-Wing*, a change that was not all loss. One of Cooper's least pleasant novels, it helped to prepare the way for a more realistic treatment of American society and its problems in *Afloat and Ashore* and the Littlepage series and, after the bitterly ironic *Jack Tier* (in many ways, a deliberate reversal of *The Red Rover*), for the symbolism of *The Crater*, *The Oak Openings*, and *The Sea Lions*, novels that raise the problems which were to provide the substance and the meaning of Hawthorne's and Melville's major works but with which Cooper's techniques and comprehension were inadequate to deal effectively. Experimental right up to the end, Cooper's career during the thirty years 1820–50 was the history of American fiction. He had reached the tragic issue of human destiny, but he lacked the literary means to deal fully and finally with it; he left that task to others.

Cooper's achievement goes far beyond romance but stops short of either realism or symbolism; his best work is in the idiom of the literary principles and fashions which were dominant in his own day. His political liberalism came to a focus during his European residence at the midpoint of his career. On his return, he began to do deliberately what he had been doing all along in stumbling and intuitive fashion, to develop an American novel of manners which was to serve as a commentary as well as a record. To provide this extra dimension of interpretation he applied his romantic theory of the imagination, the raising of literal fact to the level of idealized and generalized truth. That truth then became the ethical absolute which guided the construction of each successive novel and unified them all. The novels which appeared in the period 1840–44, from *The Pathfinder* to *Satanstoe*, vary among themselves but share his achievement of a working balance between the real and the ideal in his art. Perhaps, in the final reckoning, Cooper will be best remembered, not only for the Leather-Stocking tales as he prophesied, but for his pioneering in the realistic novel of social purpose which has become, through the later work of Howells, Norris, Dreiser, and Lewis, the dominant mode of the American novel since his time.

Nathaniel Hawthorne

WHEN Hawthorne was born in Salem, Massachusetts, in 1804 the town was already very old by American standards. The Hathornes had been there from the beginning. (Hawthorne added the *w* to the family name when he began to sign his stories.) By the 1690's one of them was prominent enough to be a judge in the witchcraft trials. His descendant's remarks on him in "The Custom House" Introduction to *The Scarlet Letter* mix pride in his prominence and a sense of inherited guilt for his deeds as judge.

Hawthorne is being a little whimsical in "The Custom House," protectively light in his tone, when he takes the judge's guilt on himself and offers to do penance that the family curse may be removed. But there is an undercurrent of seriousness. Salem is a part of him, for good and for ill. The "mere sensuous sympathy of dust for dust" is perhaps all that is needed to bind town and man together. Like William Faulkner in a later century, like Quentin remembering the tales out of the past in *Absalom, Absalom!* Hawthorne admits to being haunted by the figure of the prominent but guilty ancestor who "was present to my boyish imagination, as far back as I can remember."

Later Hathornes were neither so prominent nor so conspicuously guilty. While Salem grew and prospered, they sank into that "dreary and unprosperous condition" Hawthorne hopes, in "The Custom House," may be alleviated by his public assumption of the family guilt. When Captain Nathaniel Hathorne, a shipmaster, died on one of his voyages the year that young Nathaniel was four, the family decline was complete. Left without resources, Elizabeth Manning Hathorne moved with her three children into the nearby home of her brother.

As he grew up, Hawthorne watched Salem decline. The Embargo of 1807 struck the town a heavy blow, and when the end of the War of 1812 made shipping possible again, Salem did not recover its importance as a seaport. The town was repeating the family history, it seemed. It was perhaps too late for both town and family. In his first work of fiction, which Hawthorne compounded of about equal portions of undigested, undistanced personal feelings and experience, and the conventions of the Gothic novel, the central figure, Fanshawe, thinks of himself as nobility in decline. He anticipates, and experiences, an early death. Late in life Hawthorne tried repeatedly to write a romance about an American claimant to a lost great English estate. With a part of himself at least, he was that claimant, as he was also Fanshawe.

When he graduated from Bowdoin in 1825, with *Fanshawe* already complete or nearly so, Hawthorne was determined to become a writer of fiction. Composition was the only subject in which he had excelled in college, or in which he had showed any great interest, and now he proposed to teach himself to write by writing. He spent the next dozen years in the now famous third-floor chamber of his uncle's house on Herbert Street in Salem, reading, writing, projecting volumes of tales refused by publishers, and, during the latter part of the period, publishing regularly in magazines and Christmas gift books or annuals. But the rate of pay for the stories was very low, and though he had increasing success in placing his work, he found himself unable to make even a modest living as a writer of tales.

In 1837 a friend secretly paid for the publication of *Twice-Told Tales.* This brought him a little group of admiring readers but no income. As an expedient, he undertook editorial work in Boston, then got a job in the Boston Custom House, and finally joined the Brook Farm community, hoping, apparently, that in that socialist society he would be able to combine the practical and the creative.

But hard daily labor and social evenings left him neither energy nor time for writing, and after little more than a year there he left without regret and poorer than when he had joined. At the age of thirty-eight Hawthorne married Sophia Peabody of the famous Salem family, and the next several years, spent in the Old Manse in Concord, were the happiest in his life. Here he partly wrote and partly collected from magazines which had published his work earlier the tales and sketches to make a second volume, *Mosses from an Old Manse* (1846). Emerson, Thoreau, and Ellery Channing were friendly neighbors. With Channing Hawthorne boated on the river that flowed beside the house, as he tells us in "The Old Manse." It seemed, for a while, not unfitting to play with the notion that he and Sophia were a "New Adam and Eve."

But he was haunted from the beginning by a sense that this idyll could not last, and his fears, as was so often the case, proved to be well founded. With unpaid bills mounting steadily, and the owner giving notice that he wanted the Old Manse back for his own use, the family was forced to return to Salem, where Hawthorne took the job in the Custom House described in the Introduction to *The Scarlet Letter*. Fired from this position for political reasons, he turned back to his craft and wrote his greatest romance. As he worked on *The Scarlet Letter* (1850), anxiety about money was still severe and grief at the death of his mother was intense, but he never again wrote so rapidly or so surely, or so much from the depths of his sensibility.

In this tale set in Puritan Boston, Hawthorne created four unforgettable characters of American fiction: Hester Prynne, condemned to wear a scarlet A on her breast in token of her sin of adultery; the Reverend Arthur Dimmesdale, revered as saintly by his parishioners but torn by hidden guilt; their child, the " 'Pearl' . . . of great price"; and Roger Chillingworth, Hester's husband, who as he probes into the hearts of those who have wronged him becomes the greatest sinner of them all. The identity of Hester's lover, a secret her ministerial inquisitors cannot force her to reveal, is at last made public in a way the community could not have foreseen and would not have wished.

The Scarlet Letter established Hawthorne's reputation and made it possible, it seemed, for him to devote himself entirely to his writing. Settling in Lenox in the Berkshires, he quickly wrote *The House of the Seven Gables* (1851) and several works for children, a type of writing he found pleasant, easy, and comparatively profitable. Here he became a friend of Herman Melville, who was at work nearby on *Moby Dick*, which he later dedicated to Hawthorne. The cursed Hathornes became the cursed Pyncheons in *The House of the Seven Gables*, declining from wealth and prominence to poverty and eccentricity. Their claim to a great estate cannot be established, for the deed has been lost, as the land in Maine was lost to Hawthorne's family. The many-gabled mansion images the family history: since it will not yield up its secrets for the guilt to be purged, it must be left behind by the new generation.

Mountain scenery and the simple life in the "little red farmhouse" finally palled, and the Hawthornes — there were now three children, Una, Julian, and Rose — returned to Concord to buy The Wayside from Amos Bronson Alcott. Then, when *The Blithedale Romance* (1852), in temper and theme an anti-utopian reflection of the Brook Farm experience, failed to please Hawthorne's newly won public, and when the election of his college classmate and friend Franklin Pierce to the presidency opened the opportunity for a really remunerative political job, he accepted the consulship in Liverpool. The following half-dozen years were uncreative ones. Though he worked sporadically at his writing, it was not until the end of the period that, by a sustained effort, he was able to write his last completed romance, *The Marble Faun* (1860), in which an innocent young man falls into sin and rises into maturity.

When the family returned to America in 1860, Hawthorne had just four troubled years left. The European experience had proved valuable and pleasant, but it had not, as he had hoped it would, made him financially secure. Further, he found himself disliking

Nathaniel Hawthorne

the American climate and missing his English friends. Settling in Concord was, he began to think, a mistake. The Wayside – and Concord itself – did not seem like home to him, and as he thought of the many places the family had lived, he wondered if he could truthfully be said ever to have had a "home." He remodeled the house, modernizing it to please his wife and adding, for himself, the third-floor "tower" study that still disfigures it. Symbolically, Hawthorne was returning to the "dismal chamber" on the third floor of his uncle's house where he had spent a dozen years and from which he had escaped to "open an intercourse with the world."

Working harder and more steadily on his writing now than he ever had for any extended period before, he was unable to bring any work of fiction to completion. Familiar scenes and symbolic images were reused, but in the margins of his manuscripts he wrote himself notes asking "What meaning?" His health began to fail and, haunted by a premonition of early death, he drove himself to write that he might at least leave his family provided for. Though the romances refused to take shape, the sketches of English life that came out as *Our Old Home* (1863) showed that he could still write trenchantly and beautifully on subjects that did not demand exploration of the depths of his imagination.

Provincial Salem and the secluded years of the long apprenticeship were now far in the past, and he had almost succeeded in becoming the "man of society" he had always wanted to be. His publishers pressed him for new work, and recognition of his achievement was widespread and gratifying. Now at least there was no outward reason for his recurrent dream of failure. But his ambivalence of mood increased until everything was Janus-faced. Much that we should like to know about these last years must remain speculative. We do not even know, for instance, what disease he was suffering from, whether physical or psychophysical. Oliver Wendell Holmes examined him but could arrive at no sure diagnosis. The evidence for any conclusion is largely missing, but what there is of it seems to me to point to psychosomatic changes.

One thing seems clear, though, if not the disease that aged him

49

so suddenly and brought death at the age of sixty. The manuscripts of the romances he could not complete suggest that the convictions that had once sustained him, providing a tolerable margin of clarity and meaning in a dark and ambiguous world, were now no longer operative, even if, in some sense, still held. "What meaning?"

When he died in 1864 in Plymouth, New Hampshire, on a trip with former President Pierce intended to benefit his health, he was far from home both literally and symbolically — far, in those days, from The Wayside in Concord, and farther still from that home of the heart's desire, that Eden that had been lost so long ago.

Hawthorne has remained an enigma to his biographers. Those who concentrate on the facts of the outward life tend to present a thoroughly normal and well-adjusted Hawthorne. They show us a man who liked to smoke cigars and drink brandy while playing cards. This Hawthorne may have seemed shy to Emerson but he enjoyed an easy friendship with less intellectual friends like Horatio Bridge and Franklin Pierce. It is quite true that to most of those whose impressions have come down to us he seemed reserved but not unusually withdrawn, thoughtful but certainly not depressed or melancholy. Indeed a good part of the record suggests that many found him ordinarily cheerful and sociable.

But this picture begins to waver and blur as soon as we turn from the remarks of observers to the inner life as revealed in the writing. The well-adjusted Hawthorne, we begin to suspect, is the man he would have liked to be, and no doubt partly succeeded in being, but it is not the man he knew from within. The letters, the *Notebooks*, and the more personal sketches all reveal a quite different man behind the social mask.

With varying degrees of disguise and aesthetic distance from his personal situation, the sketches in particular can take us into the imagination of the man who wrote the major works. "The Devil in Manuscript" is almost autobiography, while Hawthorne appears in "Earth's Holocaust" only as a naive young man who needs to be guided into an understanding of life's complexities. "The Journal of a Solitary Man," which is neither so literally informative as "The

Devil in Manuscript" or so distanced as "Earth's Holocaust," reveals a good deal of the inner Hawthorne whose existence casual observers did not often guess.

The sketch of the "solitary man" reveals not facts so much as attitudes. The years of Hawthorne's "solitary" apprenticeship, after his graduation from college and before his marriage, were not nearly so solitary as they seemed, both at the time and in retrospect. But the important thing is precisely how they *seemed* to the man who wrote so often of alienation. They seemed years of imprisonment in the solitude of self.

Hawthorne pictures the solitary man as "walking in the sunshine . . . yet cold as death." The young unfortunate suffers often from a "deep gloom sometimes thrown over his mind by his reflections on death." He longs to break out of his isolation by travel: perhaps thus he will find something more real than his shadowy existence. But he gets no further from his native village than Hawthorne had gone at the time of writing the sketch. Instead, he spends much of his time looking at himself in the mirror and trying to understand the "pale beauty" he sees there.

There is some aesthetic distance here, to be sure. In part, Hawthorne is contributing to the tradition of the romantic hero as sad clown. But there is also self-revelation. The Hawthorne revealed is not the one family and friends thought they knew but a melancholy young Narcissus who often felt alone even in the midst of company and who was gravely dissatisfied with what he saw in the looking glass. He thought much of death, felt cold and guilty, and wrote "Alice Doane's Appeal."

This Hawthorne blamed himself for his detachment and wrote "The Christmas Banquet." He wished that he could relate to others more easily, that he were not so coldly rational and appraising: he cast cold-hearted scientists in the roles of villains. He worried often about whether being an artist might not have the effect of increasing his alienation. Certainly it required him to study people as objects to be manipulated on his fictional canvas. Might he not come to feel that they were as much *his* creatures as the characters in his book? Should art be thought of as a kind of black magic and the artist as a sort of magician, like the witch of old and the mesmerist of the present? "The Prophetic Pictures" and "The Old Apple Dealer" express his concern with the problem.

This Hawthorne felt guilty about being an artist and determined not to become a mesmerist. Though he toyed, at least once, with the thought that he might enjoy, for a while, being "a spiritualized Paul Pry, hovering invisible round man and woman, witnessing their deeds, searching into their hearts," he countered the temptation by writing so often of the hearth as a redemptive symbol that reference to it became a hallmark of his style. The hearth suggested all that the solitary man and the cold observer of Christmas festivities lacked: warmth and hope and fellow-feeling and the love that held together the family circle. Reunion after isolation came in his works to be both a symbol of and the literal means to salvation. No writer has ever placed a higher value on communion and community.

But he continued to note in himself, and to disapprove, feelings and attitudes he projected in Chillingworth and Rappaccini and Goodman Brown. He noted his tendency not only to study others with cold objectivity but to study himself with almost obsessive interest. He looked into the glass too often and searched too curiously the hearts of others: he wrote "Egotism, or The Bosom Serpent" and "Ethan Brand," condemning both protagonists, the first for his self-concern, the second for treating people as objects of study. Hawthorne had no admiration for detached observers, but he knew one well enough from within to be able to write about the type with authority.

"No human effort, on a grand scale, has ever yet resulted according to the purpose of its projectors. The advantages are always incidental. Man's accidents are God's purposes." Thus Hawthorne dismissed the moral significance of the Civil War. "Chiefly about War Matters," in which these aphorisms occur, is one of his last completed pieces of writing, done when his health was already failing and he was deeply distressed about the war itself. His political position as a Democrat, too, must have made it peculiarly difficult for him to clarify his feelings. We may be tempted to attribute the coldness of the remark, its implied disengagement from the human effort, to conditions of the moment. But the idea was not new to Hawthorne. Years before, writing his campaign biography of Franklin Pierce, he had said the same thing: "There is no instance, in all history, of the human will and intellect having perfected any great moral reform by methods which it adapted to that end . . . " The idea was obviously a useful one in a defense of Pierce, a New Hampshire Democrat who needed the support of the South to be elected, but Hawthorne felt no need to invent it for the occasion. He found himself predisposed toward it by feelings that recurred throughout his life, whenever his supply of hope ran low.

The background of the idea is lighted up by a passage in *The English Notebooks* discussing his reluctance to give the advice his position as American consul in Liverpool seemed to require him to give. "For myself," he wrote, "I had never been in the habit of feeling that I could sufficiently comprehend any particular conjunction of circumstances with human character, to justify me in thrusting in my awkward agency among the intricate and unintelligible machinery of Providence. . . . It is only one-eyed people who love to advise, or have any spontaneous promptitude of action."

Hawthorne believed in Providence even while he found it unintelligible. Confronted with the problem of evil in the form of diseased and suffering English children, he concluded a *Notebook* entry with "Ah, what a mystery!" But he trusted there was a higher purpose, a final meaning in a dark and bewildering world, even if we could not clearly *know* it. "Man's accidents are God's purposes."

Hawthorne in short was a theist who thought of himself as a Christian, but he was skeptical of all claims, whether Puritan or Roman Catholic, to know the details of the divine will. Brought up a Unitarian, he associated himself with no church at all, yet preferred Bunyan to the religious liberals of his day and impressed family and friends as a religious man. He and Melville talked often, and with full mutual understanding, of "final things," but where Melville, like his own Ahab, was compelled to try to strike through the mask of appearance, Hawthorne could better abide the not knowing.

Hawthorne's special mixture of skepticism and faith had much to do with the form of his art as well as his choice of themes. His clearest convictions tended to get expressed in allegory; his dimmer intimations, his hopes and fears, on the other hand, often found expression in tales more mythopoetic than allegorical, closer to modern symbolic fiction than to Bunyan. No less honest and courageous than Melville, he had a different temperament. He found he could live in the darkness with only a little light. Whatever else Hawthorne was, he was not one-eyed. Out of his ironic vision and his sense of paradox came most of his finest work.

Since ours is an age that has found irony, ambiguity, and paradox to be central not only in literature but in life, it is not surprising that Hawthorne has seemed to us one of the most *modern* of nineteenth-century American writers. The bulk and general excellence of the great outburst of Hawthorne criticism of the past decade attest to his relevance for us. It requires no distortion of him to see him not only as foreshadowing Henry James in his concern for "the deeper psychology" but as first cousin to Faulkner and Robert Penn Warren. In all the essentials, "My Kinsman, Major Molineux" is as "modern" a story as "The Bear." Hawthorne's themes, especially, link him with the writing and sensibility of our time.

Alienation is perhaps the theme he handles with greatest power. "Insulation," he sometimes called it — which suggests not only isolation but imperviousness. It is the opposite of that "osmosis of being" that Warren has written of, that ability to respond and relate to others and the world. Its causes are many and complex, its results simple: it puts one outside the "magic circle" or the "magnetic chain" of humanity, where there is neither love nor reality. It is Hawthorne's image of damnation. Reunion, often imaged by the hearth, is his redemptive cure. Anticipating Archibald MacLeish in *J. B.*, he would have his characters "blow on the coal of the heart." Not "knowing" or "using" but "meeting" others — to borrow Martin Buber's terms — would offer a way back into the magic circle to alienated Chillingworth, Ethan Brand, or Rappaccini.

Contemporary critics have shown an even greater interest in Hawthorne's treatment of initiation. Though he wrote only a few stories directly concerned with it, several of them are among his greatest and a number of others touch it tangentially. Stories as rich, yet controlled, in meaning as "My Kinsman" are rare in this or any language. Initiated into life's complexity in a dreamlike evening in a strange city, the young man of the story achieves a difficult maturity. But the protagonist of "Young Goodman Brown" is unable to understand or accept the evil revealed to him in the forest of the soul, loses faith in the reality of the good, and lives the rest of his long life in gloomy alienation. The young couple in "The Maypole of Merrymount" are granted a happier outcome, but Giovanni in "Rappaccini's Daughter" is, like Goodman Brown, unable to accept life's ambiguous mixture of good and evil and so cannot understand his Beatrice or gain the salvation her love would grant.

When such initiations as these have happy outcomes, as in "My Kinsman," we are tempted to see them primarily in psychological terms, as dramatizing the process of maturation. When the results are less happy, so that we have a sense chiefly of the cost of losing innocence, we are likely to read them as versions of the Fall, the myth of the expulsion from the Garden. The psychological and the theological readings are perhaps just different ways of looking at the same archetypal story.

Hawthorne at any rate refused to simplify guilt by reducing it either to merely subjective and irrational "guilt feeling" or to wholly objective and external "sin." He concerned himself instead with guilt feelings that have personal and social causes and cures that are objectively real, not merely subjective or irrational, and that imply the reality of moral obligation. His special way of maintaining the ambiguous connection between the psychological, the moral, and the religious is one of the principal reasons why his works seem so relevant to us.

Moral and religious concerns, in short, are almost always central in Hawthorne's work, but Hawthorne's interest in them is primarily subjective and psychological. But his subjectivism is never solipsist and his psychologism never reductive. Rather, they are signs that his concern with matters moral and religious is existential. Like the Existentialist philosophers who articulate the sensibility of our time, Hawthorne is more concerned with the experienced toothache than with orthodontic theory. Like them he explores the nature of existential guilt, relating it to alienation, reunion, and commitment. Like them too he distrusts the claim of objective reason to be able to arrive at humanly relevant truth: his "empiricists" all end unhappily.

We may call such attitudes romantic rather than existential if we wish. Existential philosophy begins with Kierkegaard, in the romantic movement; but Kierkegaard seems more relevant to many today than John Dewey. Romanticism at this depth is still with us, and perhaps always will be, now that unquestioning certainty about life's "essences" seems unlikely ever to return. Not to be existential in the sense in which Hawthorne was is either to be content with positivism or to assume as unquestionable a fixed and absolute order of truth.

But if the first thing we should notice about Hawthorne is his "modernity," his immediate relevance to us and our concerns, the second thing, if we are to avoid the distortion of seeing in him only our own image, is the way in which he is *not* one of us. It has been said that he was an eighteenth-century gentleman living in the nineteenth century, and the remark has enough truth in it to be useful to us at this point.

His style, for instance, though at its best a wonderfully effective instrument for the expression of his sensibility, is likely to strike us as not nearly so modern as Thoreau's. It was slightly old-fashioned even when he wrote it. It is very deliberate, with measured rhythms, marked by formal decorum. It is a public style and, as we might say, a "rhetorical" one — though of course all styles are rhetorical in one sense or another. It often prefers the abstract or generalized to the concrete or specific word. Compared to what the writers of handbooks, under the influence of modernist literature, have taught us to prefer — the private, informal, concrete, colloquial, imagistic — Hawthorne's style can only be called premodern.

But it is not only style in this narrow sense that marks Hawthorne as a nineteenth-century writer. Apart from that aspect of his writing that we may summarize under the general heading of his symbolism, his whole procedure as a fictionist is pre-modern — which is to say, pre-Flaubert and pre-James. He is one of the most regularly intrusive of intrusive authors. The basic rule of post-Jamesian fiction, reduced by handbook writers to a simple inviolable formula, has been "Don't tell, show!" Hawthorne both tells and shows — tells not simply in his characteristic final moral comment but all the way through.

Ethan Brand, for instance, seeing the absurdity of his situation, bursts into laughter. Hawthorne, having presented the image, then comments: "Laughter, when out of place, mistimed, or bursting forth from a disordered state of feeling, may be the most terrible modulation of the human voice." Hawthorne has lost something in immediacy, and gained something in meaning. Later in the story, in his summary of Brand's career, he does not "show" at all, he merely tells: "Thus Ethan Brand became a fiend. He began to be so from the moment that his moral nature had ceased to keep the pace of improvement with his intellect." "He had lost his hold of the magnetic chain of humanity."

In its insistence that the author never appear in his own pages, that the image alone do all the work, modern fiction has paralleled Imagist poetry. Hawthorne knows nothing of this. For him, fiction was a way of exploring life to find meaning. Not being post-Jamesian, he thought he had a right to bring out and underline the meanings his images revealed. The classic forms of fiction had always permitted this.

If Hawthorne had thought he needed any excuse for his intrusive comments, he might well have said what Faulkner has said of *his* writing, that he wrote "to uplift men's hearts . . . [to] say No to death." Hawthorne wants to strengthen and encourage man, to help him to live in a world in which the ways of Providence are mostly unintelligible.

Since Melville first detected the darkness in Hawthorne's work and praised him for saying No in thunder, a great many sensitive readers have found the dark Hawthorne more impressive than the light. But this is not the way Hawthorne wanted to be, these not the meanings he intended.

The problem is a complex one, but in part it may be somewhat simplified by making two distinctions, the first between the artist and the man, the second between two types of meaning in the art. Hawthorne the artist often did his best writing when he wrote not of what he "believed," or wanted to believe, or thought he should believe, but of the "phantoms" that came unsought and "haunted" him. "The Haunted Mind" can give us the clue here. To the "passive sensibility" halfway between sleep and waking the spectral shapes of shame and death appear: when we get fully awake and the conscious mind takes control, they vanish. Much of Hawthorne's best writing comes out of the haunted mind.

But it is not pleasant or comfortable to be visited by such specters. Hawthorne had to live as a man as well as survive as an artist, and it may well be that one of the reasons he gave up writing short fiction after he had established himself as a writer is that so many of his best early tales *had* come from the depths of the mind — by a process he had no wish to repeat. Hawthorne's desire to be a well-adjusted "man of society" and his disinclination to reveal his inner life in public were in some degree in conflict with his desire to be an artist.

The distinction between the two types of meaning in his art takes us into an area somewhat less conjectural. The distinction I have in mind is that between intended and achieved meaning. Hawthorne hoped that *The Scarlet Letter* might have a happy ending, but the hope he expressed in his first chapter in connection with the rose blooming on the bush beside the prison – that it might lighten his dark tale – did not materialize, even for him. He resolved that his next novel would be a happier one.

The conflict here is only between the hope (or intention? – how consciously had Hawthorne thought out *The Scarlet Letter* before writing it?) of the man, and the achievement of the artist. There is no conflict in the novel, of the type that weakens a work, between intended and achieved meanings. The novel is all of a piece, with a magnificent unity of meaning that emerges equally from what it says and what it shows. But *The House of the Seven Gables* is perhaps not so perfect, for this reason among others. It is almost equally difficult to suppose that the ending was intended to be ironic and for the modern reader to take it any other way. And *The Blithedale Romance* was probably intended to mean only that utopian communities will not succeed unless their members have a change of heart and that frosty old bachelors like Coverdale need girls like Priscilla (or Sophia) to warm their hearts and give them hope. But what it actually means as a work of art is not so simply said, or so hopeful.

We may often, as we have seen, go to the sketches to find out the meanings Hawthorne *intended* to express in the fiction. In the sketches *belief* is generally in control, the phantoms that haunt the mind mostly absent; and Hawthorne's belief maintains a nice balance between the light and the dark. "Earth's Holocaust," for instance, tells us what Hawthorne must have intended to say on his theme of social reform in *Blithedale*. The sketch is one of Hawthorne's finest, and its structure is dramatic, so its meaning is not easily reduced to a brief summary. But a part of its meaning is this: reform is perennially needed, and we may well be grateful for many of the reforms of the past, but reform is superficial and impermanent unless it is accompanied by a change of heart. The source of evil is in the heart of man, not primarily in institutions. The devil laughs when man supposes that lasting progress toward the good can be brought about by merely external and social changes.

But if man's misguided efforts cause laughter in hell, there is still hope, for if man will look deeper for the source of the evil he may find it. There is at any rate a guide for his efforts which he may use if he will. The attempt of the reformers to destroy the Bible as the climax of their enlightened reforms is unavailing. The fire, Hawthorne tells us, is powerless to consume it. Its pages even "assumed a more dazzling whiteness as the finger marks of human imperfection were purified away."

"Sunday at Home" maintains the same kind of balance between the light and the dark, negation and affirmation, that we find in "Earth's Holocaust." But since the language in which Hawthorne defines himself in the sketch as at once gentle skeptic and firm believer seems more dated than the language of the greater sketch, and since the meanings are less solidly embodied in dramatic images, "Sunday at Home" may reveal the balance Hawthorne intended to express better than the greater works do. It is more interesting as a piece of self-revelation than as a work of art.

Hawthorne begins by dissociating himself from the committed believers among his fellow townsmen. While they go to church, he stays at home and peeps at them through the window. He hears the bells but misses the sermon — and feels no loss. He finds aids to faith everywhere, not only in the sound of the bells. Even the sunshine seems to have a special "sabbath" quality about it. This last is no doubt an illusion, but such illusions, he believes, are often "shadows of great truths": "Doubts may flit around me, or seem to close their evil wings, and settle down; but, so long as I imagine that the earth is hallowed, and the light of heaven retains its sanctity, on the Sabbath — while that blessed sunshine lives within me — never can my soul have lost the instinct of its faith. If it have gone astray, it will return again."

The ideas being expressed here may strike us at first as just as archaic as the language. Nineteenth-century "religion of the heart" offers as little appeal today to the neo-orthodox as to the skeptical. But if we look again and note the meaning in the idea of a "hallowed" earth, we may find the notion not simply sentimental. To find the earth itself holy is to find the sources of religious faith in experience. The General Revelation — Nature — will then complement and reinforce the special, unique Revelation of Scripture. The idea is, we are likely to say too quickly, a romantic one; too quickly, because it is not only romantic but Scriptural, as we may see in the Psalms.

The sketch is light in tone and does not pretend to any profundity, but it seems fair to say that Hawthorne is groping here toward a sacramental view of nature. He is no primitivist. He does not suppose that going "back to nature" will cure man's ills or automatically dispel all "evil" doubts. But he does think nature, as the handiwork of God, contains a general revelation of God's purposes and life's meaning, if we will only read it aright.

Religious faith, then, in this sketch, rests on our ability to experience the world in a certain way. And that way of experiencing is dependent on the imagination. When Hawthorne says "so long as I *imagine* that the earth is hallowed," he does not mean "so long as I *pretend*" or "so long as I *make believe*." He means that religion, like art, is visionary. This is the complement to his acknowledgment, in "Earth's Holocaust" and elsewhere, of the authority of a "purified" Scriptural revelation.

"Sunday at Home" maintains the kind of balance Hawthorne always wanted to keep and affirms the light in a way quite typical of him. It reveals a side of Hawthorne that Melville missed — or was not interested in — when he hailed the nay-sayer.

Writing in 1842 to the editor of *Sargent's New Monthly Magazine* about a sketch he hoped to place there, Hawthorne made a statement that, while it applies directly to the piece he had in mind, applies also, less directly and not intentionally, to all his fiction. "Whether it have any interest," he wrote, "must depend entirely on the sort of view taken by the writer, and the mode of execution."

As an artist, Hawthorne knew that in art the question is less *what* than *how*, that in a very important though probably not absolute and exclusive sense, manner is more important than matter, the "fact" unimportant until transformed by "vision." Though he did not normally choose to exercise his talent or test his vision on trifles, he always insisted that the artist's *way of seeing* his subject was the important thing.

This insistence was, of course, both a permanent truth in art and a reflection of the romantic aesthetic, in which the artist is always peculiarly central. Just as clearly, it reflects an idealistic metaphysic. Not the thing known but the knowing, not matter but mind, is the locus of reality for idealism. Here Hawthorne and Emerson agreed. Whether or not Hawthorne should be called a "transcendentalist" depends on how one uses the term — broadly, to point to all varieties of transcendental philosophy, or narrowly, to designate the Concord New Thought. If broadly, then Plato was one of the first transcendentalists, and perhaps the most important; and Hawthorne was a somewhat uneasy and qualified one too. If narrowly, then Hawthorne was still in some respects a Transcendentalist *malgré lui*, but it is important to remember that he thought of himself as not "tinged" with that radicalism.

In any case, however much he may have minimized, or been unaware of, his agreements with his neighbor Emerson, Hawthorne believed that not only the finished work of art but reality itself depended on "the sort of view taken" by artist or man. The best sort of view would, he thought, be that which provided *distance* — in time or space — so that the raw fact as such could not dominate, so that irrelevant multiplicity would be dimmed and softened by distance to allow the pattern, the meaning, to emerge. Long views were best, just *because* the viewer could not see the details so well.

In view of this conviction, it is not hard to see why the past was so useful to him. The past was not only his South Seas, where romance was, but his relevant truth. We may see the consequences of such an aesthetic credo clearly enough in *The Scarlet Letter*. It is not the fact of adultery itself that engages Hawthorne's interest. Adultery might mean anything or nothing. Let it occur before the novel opens and explore its consequences. In Hawthorne's view it was personal guilt, not sin abstractly defined, that was interesting. This was one of the differences between him and his Puritan ancestors.

Nathaniel Hawthorne

Writing the novel, Hawthorne took pains to supply just enough verisimilitude to make it credible. But for the most part he was simply not deeply concerned with merely external reality — except as that reality, perceived as symbol, could take us into the interiors of hearts and minds. That is why writing that must be classified as expository and descriptive (as compared with narrative) bulks so large in the work.

"The Old Apple Dealer" does not have even *The Scarlet Letter*'s minimum of action, but it illuminates what Hawthorne was about in his greatest novel. As a sketch rather than a tale, it is purely descriptive and expository: in it nothing happens except to the speaker, who gains a recognition which alters his point of view. There is even a sense in which the sketch is not "about" anything — or rather, in which it is about "nothing." It is for this reason that any interest it may have must come, as Hawthorne explained to the editor of *Sargent's*, from something other than the intrinsic interest of the subject itself.

The old apple dealer who will be described is, Hawthorne says in the sketch, a purely negative character, featureless, colorless, inactive, hardly alive apparently. He seems an embodiment of torpor, an instance of nonentity. Such a subject is a challenge to the artist, and Hawthorne opens his sketch with a confession of his difficulty. How could one make interesting, or even imaginatively real, a subject intrinsically colorless and featureless? Hawthorne is not sure he can succeed, but he will try, for the very insignificance of the old man gives him a special kind of interest. "The lover of the moral picturesque may sometimes find what he seeks in a character which is nevertheless of too negative a description to be seized upon and represented to the imaginative vision by word painting."

That Hawthorne had indeed found in the old apple dealer what he sought as a lover of the "moral picturesque" is attested by the success of the sketch. For the subject allows Hawthorne to do several things at once. From one point of view, the sketch is about man's nothingness, and the significant qualification of that nothingness. From another, it is about the difficulties, opportunities, and dangers of the artist.

By the end, the difficulties have become opportunities — though Hawthorne does not claim so much — but the dangers remain. Against them Hawthorne issues a final warning that unites the two "subjects" of the sketch, art and life — issues it to himself most clearly, but to all artists by implication. The language of the ending is explicitly religious, but the aesthetic implications of it are clear enough.

Hawthorne had begun his sketch by telling us that without his subject's being aware of his scrutiny, he has "studied the old apple dealer until he has become a naturalized citizen of my inner world." Since what interests one in this "featureless" man is the perfection of his insignificance, if he is to come alive for readers, the artist will have to give him life. By what James would later call "the alchemy of art" he will be brought into being.

Power so great as this brings with it great danger. Hawthorne's metaphor for art in the sketch is witchcraft. Was art a kind of black magic? If the artist can legitimately claim his literary creations as entirely his own, may he not as man similarly conceive of other people as created — and perhaps controlled — by his knowing them? But if we think of other people as objects to be studied and manipulated, as Chillingworth thought of Dimmesdale and Ethan Brand thought of the subjects of his moral experiment, we shall be totally shut out from the saving realities of life. The fate to which the artist, like the scientist, Hawthorne felt, was peculiarly liable was alienation.

The assumption of Godlike knowledge could destroy artist and man equally. Knowledge brings with it the possibility of control, and the artist must achieve control of his subject by controlling his medium; but he will falsify reality if he omits the element of mystery and assumes that he knows the unknowable. One error, then, to which the artist is peculiarly liable, threatens both artist and man. But to see how Hawthorne prepares us to accept his conclusion, which tests art by life's standards and sees life through the eyes of the artist, we must return to Hawthorne's way of bringing the old apple dealer to life in his pages.

Early in the sketch Hawthorne decides that with so negative a subject the only way to describe him is to use negative comparisons, to tell us what he is *not* like. Perhaps in this way he will be able to get at the paradox of a man who seemed completely inactive and stationary, yet whose immobility was composed of continuous minor, almost undetectable, movements. (So "stationary" a man will never "go ahead," never join in "the world's exulting progress.") Then the inspiration comes: what he is most of all *not* like is the steam engine that roars at intervals through the station where the old man sits so quietly. "I have him now. He and the steam fiend are each other's antipodes . . ."

"I have him now." By using contrast the artist has succeeded in conveying to us what he had almost despaired of conveying, the reality of a person who is almost nothing. But as soon as it is made, the claim seems excessive: Hawthorne does not finally "know" the old man at all, nor do we. For he has omitted something from his description, something all-important that he has no way of getting at — the soul. In a superficial sense he has succeeded: insofar as the old man is merely viewed, merely scrutinized, he is a torpid machine in perfect contrast to the active, "progressive" machine. But there is a deeper contrast involved than mere activity or lack of it, and here the artist must confess the limits of his art. "Could I read but a tithe of what is written . . . [in the old man's "mind and heart"] it would be a volume of deeper and more comprehensive import than all that the wisest mortals have given to the world; for the soundless depths of the human soul and of eternity have an opening through your breast. God be praised . . ."

So in the end Hawthorne makes his last confession: whatever his success in describing the old man behavioristically, he did *not* "have" him when he compared him, the stationary machine, to the steam engine, the active machine. Man cannot be fully known in the way we know a machine. This is the deeper sense in which the old man is the antipodes of the engine. To confuse the two is the ultimate error, for both artist and man.

"The Old Apple Dealer" emphasizes the creativity of the artist and the danger such creativity brings with it. The danger is partly that the artist will suppose that he *knows* more than he can possibly know. "Night Sketches: Beneath an Umbrella" dramatizes the danger of the artist's becoming so isolated from reality that his art will be a sort of daydream. Considered together, the two pieces imply that art is both a kind of knowledge — which must never pretend to finality, never lose its sense of mystery — and a kind of dream — which must keep in touch with reality. Art is more like myth than like document, but there are true myths and false myths, and art had better be true.

"Beneath an Umbrella" opens with a long paragraph devoted to describing the pleasures of the unrestricted imagination as it takes one on imaginary travels to exotic lands. "Pleasant is a rainy winter's day, within doors!" the speaker exclaims at the beginning, going on to explain that the "sombre" condition of the world outside the chamber window makes the exercise of unrestrained fancy all the more delightful by contrast. The warm, well-lighted chamber contains the whole world, so long as imagination is active.

Nevertheless, pleasant as daydreaming is, reality *will* break in: "the rain-drops will occasionally be heard to patter against my window panes . . ." As nightfall approaches, "the visions vanish, and will not come again at my bidding." Irresponsible dreaming, it would seem, finally ceases to be even pleasurable: "Then, it being nightfall, a gloomy sense of unreality depresses my spirits, and impels me to venture out, before the clock shall strike bedtime, to satisfy myself that the world is not entirely made up of such shadowy materials as have busied me throughout the day. A dreamer may dwell so long among fantasies, that the things without him will seem as unreal as those within."

About to step outside, the speaker pauses to "contrast the warmth and cheerfulness of my deserted fireside with the drear obscurity and chill discomfort" into which he is about to "plunge." The contrast contains, it becomes clear as the sketch goes on, nearly all of Hawthorne's favorite antinomies: the light and the dark; warmth and coldness, in the human heart as well as externally; faith and doubt; even, implicitly, the heart and the head, if we see here the meanings Hawthorne constantly implies elsewhere when he uses hearth and chamber as heart images. The sketch is rich in meaning. It contains, indeed, in epitome nearly all the central issues of Hawthorne's moral and religious thought, and it significantly illuminates a side of his aesthetic thinking it is easy to overlook.

On the doorstep now, the speaker asks the reader to pardon him if he has "a few misgivings." He is, he thinks, entitled to them, our "poor human nature" being what it is. And in view of what is about to be revealed about reality outside the chamber, the world of fact, as contrasted with the world of feeling and dream he is leaving, we find the misgivings justified. For once he is really outside, he finds himself confronted by "a black, impenetrable nothingness, as though heaven and all its lights were blotted from the system of the universe. It is as if Nature were dead . . ."

A "dead" Nature was of course the specter conjured up by nineteenth-century naturalism, the conception of a purposeless, valueless, colorless world, a "charnel house" world, faced by Ishmael at the end of the chapter on the whiteness of the whale in *Moby Dick*. Melville, we have long known, stared in fascinated horror at this vision of an "alien universe," stared at it more fixedly and with greater philosophic rigor than Hawthorne did. But one of the uses of this sketch is to remind us that Hawthorne was very much aware of what Melville was looking at, even though both his way of looking and what he finally saw were different from Melville's.

Here, for instance, the speaker, though at first plunged into a Slough of Despond, soon finds that there are various kinds of lights in what had at first seemed an unbroken darkness. Some of the lights are deceptive or illusory, especially if they are so bright that they seem utterly to dispel the darkness, but others are real and trustworthy. As the speaker continues his "plunge into the night," he discovers a way of distinguishing the false lights from the true: any light which makes men "forget the impenetrable obscurity that hems them in, and that can be dispelled only by radiance from above," is certain to be illusory.

Like Wallace Stevens a century later, who proposed to create a "skeptical music," Hawthorne is talking here at once about art and about life. He is proposing a life test for art's truth, without at all suggesting that the artist should abdicate, leaving "fact" and Nature in control. The internal world, the chamber of the heart where imagination operates freely, the world of dream, is the peculiar realm of the artist, and Hawthorne returns to it after his excursion into an apparently meaningless external reality has served its purpose. But the internal world is embedded in an external world, which it may ignore only at its peril. The imagination must remain responsible, even while it guards its freedom. No mere daydreaming will do. The romancer, Hawthorne wrote of himself elsewhere, need not aim at "a very minute fidelity" to history and nature, but he "sins unpardonably" if he violates "the truth of the human heart."

Irresponsible daydream, responsible imagination, fact without meaning, or even destructive of meaning — all are present and played against each other in this sketch. The center of Hawthorne's interest is, to be sure, elsewhere, in the moral and religious meanings which, with his usual emphasis, he makes explicit at the end. (Having encountered a figure with a lantern that casts its light in a "circular pattern," Hawthorne concludes, "This figure shall supply me with a moral . . . thus we, night wanderers through a stormy and dismal world, if we bear the lamp of Faith, enkindled at a celestial fire, it will surely lead us home to that heaven whence its radiance was borrowed.")

But the aesthetic meanings are here too, implicitly. No over-reading is required to see them. It was as a "dreamer," with insufficient experience of the world, Hawthorne says several times elsewhere, that he produced his tales and sketches during his apprentice years. But even while he dreamed and created, he was dissatisfied with dreaming. He wanted to test his dreams against a reality he could not control, to determine their truth.

When, in the Preface to *The House of the Seven Gables*, Hawthorne made his famous distinction between the novel and the romance, he was not at all intending to assign "truth" to the novel and mere "fantasy," or escapist dreaming, to the romance. He was distinguishing between "fact" (which the novel deals with) and "truth" (which is the province of the romance), and at the same time suggesting an orientation in which "fact" is external and "truth" internal. So far as he was defending, implicitly, the validity of his own practice as a romancer, he was implying a "mere" before "fact." (He was ambivalent about this, as he so often was on other matters, to be sure. He thought Emerson *too* idealistic, and he greatly admired the "beef and ale" realism of Trollope.)

The romantic artist creates, Hawthorne thought, by transforming fact into symbol, that is, into *meaningful* fact. Facts that he cannot see as meaningful may be disregarded. He is at liberty to manipulate his materials, to shape them freely into meaningful patterns, so long as he does not violate the truth of the human heart. Hawthorne felt that he himself could pursue his desired truth best by a combination of looking within and exercising the kind of imaginative sympathy that had been both his subject and his method in "The Old Apple Dealer." In a very suggestive metaphor in the Preface to *The Snow Image and Other Twice-Told Tales* in 1851, he defined his role as artist as that of "a person, who has been burrowing, to his utmost ability, into the depths of our common nature, for the purposes of psychological romance — and who pursues his researches in that dusky region, as he needs must, as well by the tact of sympathy as by the light of observation . . ."

After 1850 Hawthorne wrote no more tales or sketches and consistently belittled the ones he had written. He wondered, once, what he had ever meant by these "blasted allegories." Yet several of his earliest tales are among his best. "My Kinsman, Major Molineux," first printed in 1832, is surely one of the finest short stories in the language. Again and again in recent years critics have turned back to it and found new meanings — and no wonder, for its images are archetypal.

The vehicle for its themes is the journey from country to city, from simplicity and innocence to complexity and experience. Young Robin makes the journey to enlist the aid of a powerful kinsman, who will, he hopes, help him to "rise in the world." Armed only with a club, his innocence, and his native shrewdness, he is mysteriously baffled in his search for Major Molineux. He finds the city a bewildering and threatening place. Everything is ambiguous. Cruelty appears in the guise of patriotism and lust calls out in a "sweet voice" that seems to speak "Gospel truth." Symbols of authority have no power and epiphanies of meaning go unrecognized. To those already initiated, he is the object of ridicule, but he cannot discover the reason for the laughter that follows him through the streets as though he were having a bad dream.

When he finally rests beside a church after his long "evening of ambiguity and weariness," he sees, inside, a Bible illuminated by a ray of moonlight. He has remembered his father in their country home "holding the Scriptures in the golden light that fell from the western clouds." Nature and Scripture, General and Special Revelation, are united here, Hawthorne suggests, in presenting a way out of Robin's impasse. But Robin himself does not make the connection. Fortunately, a kindly stranger appears at this point, offers helpful advice, and finally tells Robin that "perhaps, as you are a shrewd youth, you may rise in the world without the help of your kinsman, Major Molineux." But this hope is offered only after Robin has taken his place in mankind's brotherhood in guilt by joining in the mob's ridicule of his Tory kinsman, thus repudiating the father-figure.

The reader feels that Robin may indeed rise, though not by means of his club, his innocence, or his shrewdness. His club has of course only made him ridiculous: one does not force one's way through moral and psychological initiations. His innocence is more fancied than real. Of it one might say what Hawthorne wrote in "Fancy's Show Box," that "Man must not disclaim his brotherhood, even with the guiltiest . . . Penitence must kneel." His shrewdness, if it is without love, can only alienate him, as a merely intellectual development made Ethan Brand lose his hold of "the magnetic chain of humanity." The kindly stranger is being gently ironic when he refers to Robin's shrewdness.

The ultimate reason why Robin's shrewdness is not enough for him to rely on is that man, as Hawthorne made clear in "The Old Apple Dealer," is not a machine. He has a soul. He therefore cannot be understood, Hawthorne believes, by empirical reason or observation alone. At the very center of his being there is a mystery, which will always remain a mystery, never be "solved," for, in Gabriel Marcel's terms, it is a mystery and not a problem. In the last analysis, what baffled Robin in his quest, before the kindly stranger came to his aid, is the same thing that made Hawthorne confess failure in his effort wholly to capture in words the essence of the old apple dealer.

The moonlit Bible in the church in "My Kinsman" may be related to the man with the lantern and to the "radiance from above" in "Beneath an Umbrella." The tin lantern is an analogue of the "lamp of Faith" which will lead us home to heaven just because its radiance is not of our creation but "borrowed" from heaven itself. There are two tests, apparently, for the validity of the various lights that appear in a dark world, their source and their effect. About the test by effect, Hawthorne is explicit: if a light is bright enough to seem to make the darkness disappear entirely, it is false — its effect depends upon a bedazzling of the eyes. The test by source he leaves to implication in his conclusion, but the implication is clear enough. The stranger's light will lead him home to his fireside because it was kindled there. "Just so" our faith will lead us back to its source. The light cast by the fire on the family hearth is our best analogue of the supernatural light that must guide us to an ultimate home. It images the light that art cannot picture more directly.

The sketch and the story reinforce each other on this matter. If Robin is not to become another Goodman Brown, overwhelmed by the discovery of evil, he must salvage something of his childhood faith. The vision of the moonlit Bible in the church and the appearance of the stranger who comes to his aid combine to suggest that he will do so once he ceases to rely solely on himself to save himself — on his innocence, his strength, and his shrewdness. Justification by faith, not by works, is implied — by a mature faith, a tested and tried faith that does not deny the darkness or ignore the complexity of the world.

If Robin's adventures in town had ended before he arrived at the church and met the friendly stranger, his story would have been one of simple loss with no compensating gain — a fall with no rise, an initiation into evil with no accompanying redefinition of the good. But Robin at the end has not been destroyed by the loss of his innocence. Indeed, he seems to be the better for it.

Could his case be taken as a paradigm for mankind? Could the Fall of man be conceived as fortunate? On the whole, most of the time, Hawthorne thought so; or at least hoped so. But part of the time he could not summon so much hope. And he was aware of dangers involved in pursuing a line of thought that might seem to suggest that sin was beneficial. Taking as instructive myth what his ancestors had taken as literal history, he turned the subject around and around, examining it from every angle.

Of his four completed novels, only the last treats the subject directly. *The Marble Faun* is Hawthorne's theological novel. But *The Blithedale Romance* explicitly examines the possibility of undoing the Fall, and *The House of the Seven Gables* retells the story as enacted by a family over generations. Only *The Scarlet Letter* is not concerned with it. It simply assumes it. But even it adumbrates the familiar pattern: a clear fall into sin, followed by an ambiguous rise.

The Scarlet Letter is the perfect expression of what Roy Male has called "Hawthorne's tragic vision." There is light in this story as well as darkness, clarity as well as ambiguity — a symbolic rose in the first chapter as well as a cemetery and a prison. But the "radiance from above" never reaches the center of the action to save, to rescue, to guide home. The saintly Mr. Wilson walks by the scaffold carrying a lantern like that carried by the man of faith in "Beneath an Umbrella," but the light he sheds about him has no such effect on Dimmesdale as the stranger's light has on the speaker in the sketch. Hester's dark glossy hair shines in the sunlight as though it were surmounted by a halo, making her almost an image of "the divine maternity"; but the Puritans look at her only as an adulteress, and the reader is likely to feel that she is only a suffering woman. Though the novel shows us good coming out of evil, it shows it coming only at a tragic cost.

Hester, the "woman taken in adultery," rises to saintliness as she becomes an "angel of mercy" to the community, but her dreams of a new order of society can find no expression in her life and resignation is all she has to take the place of happiness. Few of us would envy her "rise." Or Dimmesdale's. In a novel constructed of ironic reversals, the apparently saintly minister first falls into a life of utter falsehood, then finally — too late, too late — rises toward integrity and truth until, in the final scaffold scene, the allusions to the death of Christ on the cross seem not wholly ironic. But there is no joy for Dimmesdale either, any more than there is for Hester. And though his faith is always assumed, it seems to have as its only consequence an intensification of his feeling of guilt. He is first cousin to Roderick Elliston in "Egotism," the man with the snake in his stomach, so tormented by his morbid symptoms that he cannot forget himself.

The novel ends in a kind of gloomy Good Friday. The minister accepts the justice of his crucifixion, blesses his persecutors, and warns Hester not to expect fulfillment of their love in another life. The faith that earlier had chiefly served to increase his torment now seems to afford him little basis for hope that his life has not been wasted. The light that feebly penetrates the gloom of the ending is of uncertain source — not from the hearth, certainly, and only obscurely "from above." The tombstone that serves the two graves of lovers separated in death as they were in life is lit "only by one ever-glowing point of light gloomier than the shadow." And what the dark light reveals as it strikes the words on the stone is the ambiguity not only of Hester's symbolic A (adulteress? angel?) but of the still dominant colors, red and black.

The red has been associated with nature and life and beauty — the rose beside the prison, Hester's vivid coloring, her beautiful needlework — but also with sin. Black has been associated with both sin and death — the prison and the cemetery. Hester and Arthur have not been able to escape the consequences of their past. There is very little here to relieve what Hawthorne calls in his first chapter "the darkening close of a tale of human frailty and sorrow." No wonder he resolved to make his next novel a happier one.

The chief problem facing the critic of *The House of the Seven Gables* today is presented precisely by his happy ending. Almost all modern readers have found it unconvincing, for a number of reasons. Phoebe and Holgrave fall in love, for one thing, rather abruptly. We see too little of them as lovers to believe fully in the reality of their love, and so in its redemptive power, as we must if we are to find Hawthorne's theme fully achieved. Then too, we may have trouble believing in their love because we have trouble believing in *them*. The portrayal of Phoebe is likely to strike us as a little sentimental: she moves too quickly from being an attractive country girl to being a symbol of Grace. Holgrave is better. Certainly he is very interesting theoretically as a portrait of the young American, pragmatic, oriented toward the future, full of energy and boundless hope, confident that he can control his destiny, a self-reliant secular utopian in effect. Yet for most readers he seems to have proved more interesting as a symbol than convincing as a character.

The marriage of Phoebe and Holgrave is the symbolic union of heart and head. Hawthorne associates the conservatism of the heart not only with the feminine but with both Nature and Grace. The ringlets of Phoebe's shining hair and the curves of her figure are related to the cycles of Nature's annual death and renewal exhibited in the elm that overshadows the house. The radicalism of the head, of reason, that leads Holgrave to expect uninterrupted progress, is associated equally with the fact of decline and the dream of easy progress without suffering. Rejecting the paradox of life through death suggested by the flowers growing in an angle of the rotting roof, rationalism oversimplifies history in its reading of both past and future. For all his "futurism," Holgrave is in a sense more closely linked to the past than Phoebe is, for without her influence he would perpetuate the very errors that led to the long Pyncheon decline.

The Pyncheons have lived by the merely reasonable standards of a secular morality. For the sake of the world's goods, power and money, they have violated the heart's higher laws. The result has been self-defeating. Living by reason alone, they have planned and schemed shrewdly, but time and nature have defeated them. Clifford's mind is ruined and the dead judge sitting in the dark chamber will never execute his plans. Though he is at first morally neutral, Holgrave falsifies history, which is better expressed by images of circles than by straight lines, whether the lines are pictured as pointing downward or upward, suggesting uninterrupted decline or uninterrupted progress. He might have learned his lesson from the ancient elm, if he had been more sensitive to its meanings, as earlier Pyncheons might have learned the same lesson from "Alice's posies," but it takes his love for Phoebe to teach him what Clifford intuitively knows, that history neither endlessly repeats itself nor marches straight onward from novelty to novelty, but moves in an "ascending spiral curve."

But the heart can read such revelations, provided equally by Nature and Scripture, better than the mind, so it is not surprising that this first cousin to idealistic Aylmer and empirical Giovanni should need Phoebe to teach him. That he is so quickly taught is the surprising thing. One of the reasons the ending strikes the reader as unconvincing is that Holgrave puts up so little resistance to Phoebe's truths. The escape from the house and what it has stood for seems at last too easy.

What Hawthorne *meant* to suggest by his ending, though, is pretty clear, whether it works with us or not. The basic pattern is one of life, death, and resurrection or renewal. Within this cyclical pattern love acts redemptively, but not in the sense of removing one from the downward phase of the cycle. If love has its way, the inherited fortune and the fine new house in the suburbs will not bring about a pointless repetition of tragic Pyncheon history. We may legitimately hope that the circles of history include an upward movement to form a "spiral curve."

Just how difficult Hawthorne found it to maintain even so chastened a hope becomes apparent in his next novel. *The Blithedale Romance* assumes the Fall of man and examines the hope of undoing it, of returning to an unspoiled Eden or Arcadia by creating a pilot model of a better world. Blithedale is a socialistic colony in which the conditions that have prevailed since the Fall should prevail no more. It aspires to be a true community in which men will work together for the common good. The law of love will be put into effect in a practical way for perhaps the first time in human history. Man will no longer be shut in the prison of self.

But the project does not work out that way. This is Hawthorne's most hopeless novel. *The Scarlet Letter* was tragic, but this is simply cold. Coverdale, the narrator, is glad that he *once* hoped for a better world, but since experience has destroyed the hope, in effect he is saying that innocence is a happy state while it lasts, before the plunge into experience destroys it. The colonists at Blithedale were not united for the common good. Instead, each used the project for his own selfish purposes. Furthermore, the group as a whole found itself in a state of competition with the surrounding larger community. Not love and sharing and truth were dominant here but competition, mutual distrust, and masquerading.

Two patterns of imagery carry a great burden of the meaning in the novel, and both have the same effect thematically. Fire images suggest that warmth of the heart, that mutuality of hope that, if it could have been maintained (if indeed it was ever as real as it once seemed), *might* have made the venture succeed. But the great blazing fire on the hearth that warmed the hearts as well as the bodies of the colonists on the first night of Coverdale's stay burned out quickly: it was built merely of brushwood. Only ashes remain now, as Coverdale looks back at the experience, to remind him of generous hopes once entertained.

The other chief line of the dual image pattern is made up of various types of veils and disguises. As Hawthorne had said of Dimmesdale in *The Scarlet Letter* that at least one clear truth emerged from his complex and tragic story, "Be true! Be true!" so here he feels that if the colonists cannot "be true" with one another, cannot take off their several veils and disguises, there can be no real community. From the "Veiled Lady" of the opening chapter, who would *like* to take off her veil; to Coverdale, whose name suggests covering the valley of the heart and who spends much of his time observing people from behind a screen of leaves or window curtains; to Old Moodie, with the patch over his eye and his false name; to Westervelt with his false teeth and Zenobia with her artificial flowers — all the chief characters are in some way masked. Until they take off their masks, revealing themselves to each other in love and truth, no such venture as theirs can succeed, Hawthorne implies. Since instead of unveiling themselves they masquerade throughout the novel, there is no real hope in their enterprise, generous and idealistic though it once seemed.

But of course if, as Hawthorne was to write later about the Civil War, "No human effort . . . has ever yet resulted according to the purpose of its projectors," then the venture was doomed from the start, whether or not the reformers managed to take off their veils. Hawthorne does not resolve this ambiguity, and it is one of the sources of our sense that this is his most hopeless novel. If we take the veils to mean only that which hides man from man, then there may be hope that a sufficient number of personal conversions may ultimately result in a better world: what no merely external changes can do, an inner change may effect. Utopianism may be mistaken, but individuals do change, and if enough of them change . . .

With this reading, the final meaning of the novel is not far from the meaning of "Earth's Holocaust." A better world required better people, a change in the *heart*: "unless they hit upon some method of purifying that foul cavern, forth from it will reissue all the shapes of wrong and misery — the same old shapes or worse ones — which they have taken such a vast deal of trouble to consume to ashes."

But perhaps what is ultimately veiled is an intolerable reality. If so, this "exploded scheme for beginning the life of Paradise anew," this effort to reverse man's mythic history and undo the Fall, was doomed before it began, before Coverdale "plunged into the heart of the pitiless snow-storm, in quest of a better life." At times the "wintry snow-storm roaring in the chimney" at Blithedale seems more real to Coverdale than the "chill mockery of a fire" that is all his memory retains to keep hope alive. The outside darkness and cold may *be* reality, the brushwood fire itself a kind of veiling delusion, necessary if we are to have hope but none the less false.

Such a reading would make the meaning of the novel equivalent to what the meaning of "Beneath an Umbrella" would have been if the speaker had stopped just outside his door, with the discovery of a Nature seemingly dead, and had not gone on through the dark to find at last a true light. Dream and reality, the light and the darkness were, finally, not utterly at odds in the sketch. In the novel they may be. Neither Coverdale, at any rate, nor the reader can quite dispose of the suspicion that they are.

By the time Hawthorne came, a few years later, to write his last completed novel, he was ready to confront directly the subject he had treated implicitly so often before. *The Marble Faun* is, as the dark mysterious Miriam says, "the story of the fall of man." In it Donatello, who has grown up in innocence in a kind of rural Eden or Arcadia, is, like Robin before him, introduced to sin in the city. Like Robin, too, who had joined in the cruel laughter of the mob, Donatello is corrupted by what he encounters among art students in Rome. He commits a murder, though his intentions are obscure and his provocation great. Like Robin, finally, he is matured by the experience, brought from an innocence that was only half human at best to a condition in which he shares mankind's nature and lot.

Was the Fall then "fortunate"? Miriam poses the question and implies a hopeful answer: " 'The story of the fall of man! Is it not repeated in our romance of Monte Beni? And may we follow the analogy yet further? Was that very sin — into which Adam precipitated himself and all his race, — was it the destined means by which, over a long pathway of toil and sorrow, we are to attain a higher, brighter, and profounder happiness, than our lost birthright gave?' "

We must suppose, I think, that Hawthorne intended his reader to answer Miriam's question in the affirmative and that he further intended this answer to be the largest meaning of his novel. But if this was his intention, he was only partially successful in embodying it. Hilda, the blonde New England maiden, comes down from the tower of her spotless innocence, to be sure, to marry the

coolly detached sculptor Kenyon, and he is presumably human-
ized by his love for her. But this union of heart and head is not
much more convincing as a symbol of redemptive possibilities than
the similar marriage of Phoebe and Holgrave in *The House of the
Seven Gables*; and for the two chief actors in the plot — Kenyon
and Hilda are onlookers, affected by what they see — there is no
promise of happiness. Donatello, the archetypal man, ends in
prison, isolated not only from Miriam but from mankind by his
sin. Only in some figurative or purely spiritual sense has he been
drawn into Hawthorne's *brotherhood* of sin. And for Miriam, the
most thoroughly created and felt character in the novel, there is
even less assurance of happiness than Hawthorne granted Hester.

In short, though the intended meaning of the novel may be rea-
sonably clear — a qualified affirmation, of the kind consistent with
a tragic but not hopeless view of life — the achieved meaning is obscure. We end convinced of the loss of innocence, and of the present reality of the "long pathway of toil and sorrow," but the evidence that this pathway may lead to "a higher, brighter, and
profounder happiness" falls far short of being convincing — to us,
and, I suspect, to Hawthorne himself at this stage in his life.

The qualified happy ending of "My Kinsman" was much more
convincing, and the ending of "Roger Malvin's Burial" is clearer.
The meaning of the latter tale is comparable to what we may take
to be the intended meaning in the novel, that suffering and sacrifice are the only means to redemptive reunion with God and man,
but there is nothing in the tale, as there is in the novel, to make us
doubt the validity of that meaning. In *The Marble Faun* Hawthorne leaned principally upon Hilda with her spotless heart to
provide hope. She proved a weak reed.

Hawthorne has never been wholly out of favor since the publication of *The Scarlet Letter*, but in the half century following his
death he seemed much more old-fashioned than he does now. In a
period of literary realism his symbolic and allegorical fiction seemed
to need defense: it was not clear that it was a valid way of writing.
Even James patronized him and could generally think of no better

way of praising the pieces he liked best than to call them "charm-ing."

Both literary, and philosophical and religious, changes since James's day have made it quite unnecessary to apologize for or de-fend either Hawthorne's mode of writing or his vision. When he failed, as of course he often did, it was sometimes because he had, for the time being, succeeded too well in becoming the "man of society" he always wanted to be — had too successfully adjusted himself to his age, come to share both its mode of feeling and its opinions too uncritically. His blonde maidens are a case in point. Reflecting the mid-century idealization of woman and wholly in-consistent with his own otherwise persistent and consistent idea of mankind's brotherhood in guilt, they remain, fortunately, on the fringes of the action in *The Scarlet Letter* but weaken *The House of the Seven Gables* when they move into center in the person of Phoebe.

But even his failures are more interesting than most writers' suc-cesses. His probings into the nature and consequences of guilt and alienation sometimes struck earlier generations as morbid, but we have been prepared to understand them by Camus and Sartre and Kafka. His explorations of the possibilities of redemptive reunion need no defense in an age when philosophers have popularized the term *engagement*.

The scene in *The House of the Seven Gables* when Clifford at-tempts to join the procession in the street by jumping through the arched window suggests both Existential philosophy and anti-realist fictional practice. Hawthorne's terms *head* and *heart* may sound a little old-fashioned, but his constant implication that the realities they stand for must interpenetrate and balance each other is as modern as psychoanalysis. His characteristic way of treating moral matters with the kind of ambiguity that makes both the psy-chological and the moral or religious perspectives on them rele-vant, the two perspectives quite distinct yet neither canceling the other, is likely to seem a major virtue to an age determined to as-sert the reality of man's freedom and responsibility, yet almost overwhelmingly conscious of the mechanisms of conditioning.

Nathaniel Hawthorne

We are prepared today even for his special blend and alternation of light and darkness. Tillich and the religious Existentialists have taught us enough about the dynamics of faith to enable us to respond naturally to a writer who explored the darkness to the very limits of the town searching for a trustworthy light. Few nineteenth-century American writers today seem so likely to reward rereading as Hawthorne.

Herman Melville

HERMAN MELVILLE was born in 1819, died in 1891, and has been adopted by the twentieth century as a writer peculiarly its own. Heir to the great tradition of romantic literature, he wrote realistically of life at sea and became a popular storyteller who responded to the cultural conflicts of the mid-nineteenth century with such shrewd and passionate ambivalence that his own age eventually found him incomprehensible and left his writings for a later generation to interpret in almost as many ways as there are readers. From the outbreak of the American Civil War until the end of World War I he was an almost completely forgotten writer. Now he is one of his country's most widely read, frequently discussed, and greatly admired authors.

The familiar image of Melville today is that of all his surviving portraits — bearded, formal, and reserved, as though he were holding himself aloof from a world of getting and spending and wasted powers. It is easy to imagine him as the author of the book which puzzles and challenges his latest critic. It is less easy to imagine him as the boy who went to sea in order to escape the boredom of rural school teaching, who signed himself up for a whaling voyage on Christmas Day because he could not get a respectable job as a legal scrivener, who deserted his ship to live among cannibals, and who was to date his intellectual development from his twenty-fifth year and write *Moby Dick* at the age of thirty-one. There is a mystery about the man as well as about his works which teases and excites the imagination.

For a century, until recent scholarly investigations, the actual events of his life were so obscure that readers of his autobiographical romances were unable to tell whether specific statements were fact or fiction. He was born to adversity on August 1, 1819, in New York City, where his father was a well-to-do importer whose business was severely damaged by the scarcity of foreign exchange during America's first postwar depression. After eleven years of struggle Allan Melville moved his family (by then consisting of his wife, Maria Gansevoort Melville, and their eight children, of whom Herman was the third child and the second of four boys) to Albany, where Herman attended the Academy for two short years of formal education before his father's death forced him to find employment in a bank. Less than two more years of schooling, before he reached the age of eighteen, prepared him for the simple duties of elementary school teaching and the literary career he was to follow — although, like Benjamin Franklin before him, he engaged in a considerable amount of self-education by joining a young men's literary and debating society and contributing to the local newspaper in the village of Lansingburgh to which his widowed mother had moved.

In the summer of 1839 the attraction which the sea held for both the Melville and the Gansevoort members of his family induced him to make a trial voyage to Liverpool as a merchant sailor, and during the following summer he tried his inland fortune by traveling west to the lead mines around Galena, Illinois, where an uncle had settled. Another severe financial depression, however, had preceded as well as driven him westward, and he was forced to return to New York and shave his whiskers in order to look like a Christian (as his older brother put it) while vainly attempting to impose his abominable handwriting upon some lawyer in need of a clerk. Something like the desperation he was later to attribute to Ishmael, the narrator of *Moby Dick* — a damp, drizzly November of the soul — caused him to join a whaling voyage to the South Pacific, for a whaler in those days was the last refuge for criminals and castaways. But Melville was free, white, and twenty-one — a sturdy, energetic young man of five feet nine and a half whose blue eyes could twinkle with humor beneath his father's high brow and waving brown hair. Desperate though he may have been in committing himself to an undefined voyage of three years or more, he was still interested in adventure when he sailed out of New Bedford on the new ship *Acushnet* on Sunday, January 3, 1841.

His voyage took him to Rio, around Cape Horn, up the coast of South America to the Galápagos Islands, and for cruises along the Line before Melville and a friend found conditions intolerable and deserted in the Marquesas on July 9, 1842. By mistake they took refuge in the valley of the Typees, who were notorious as a tribe of cannibals, and Melville remained in captivity for a month before being rescued by an Australian whaler, the *Lucy Ann*. An ailing captain, drunken mate, and mutinous crew made conditions worse on the *Lucy Ann* than they had been on the *Acushnet*; and when the vessel put into Papeete, on September 20, Melville refused further duty. He was placed under shore arrest and brought to trial but allowed to escape after his ship sailed on October 15. With one of his shipmates he then went to the neighboring island of Moorea, or Eimeo, where the two men remained as wandering beachcombers until November 3 when the master of the *Charles and Henry*, out of Nantucket, hired Melville as a harpooner for the run to the next port. After an uneventful voyage he was discharged in Lahaina, in the Hawaiian Islands, on May 2, 1843, and made his way to Honolulu where he decided to settle down as a clerk in a drygoods store for at least a year. The promise of a quick voyage home, however, persuaded him to sign on board the U.S. frigate *United States* on August 17. But it was not until early October of the following year that the ship reached Boston and Melville was discharged and allowed to rejoin his family in Lansingburgh, where they welcomed him with relief and listened with enthusiasm to the stories of his adventures.

Out of these stories grew his first book, *Typee: A Peep at Polynesian Life*, to give it its American title — which might have some relationship to the spirit in which it was composed. For Melville seems already to have been the good storyteller who was later to astound Mrs. Nathaniel Hawthorne with his vividness, and his sisters and their friends were good listeners. They thrilled to his dangers and could be easily teased by ambiguous references to South Sea maidens who were as charming as any from Lansingburgh or Boston but whose impulses (as everybody knew) were considerably less inhibited. Furthermore, the Typees were widely known as man-eaters, and although Melville had never known a human being to pass their lips he was not averse to taking advantage of their reputation for the sake of suspense. From the very beginning Melville played a game with his audience as he strung out his stories to book length with picturesque descriptions, details from memory, and other details gathered from reference books.

The game was continued, in another way and by force of circumstances, when his older brother, appointed to a diplomatic post in London, took the manuscript with him to England and submitted it to John Murray whose imprint could be expected to guarantee the success of an American edition. Murray was willing to accept it for his Home and Colonial Library (which was advertised to consist of books as exciting as fiction, but all true) if he and his readers could be assured of its authenticity. Gansevoort Melville gave his personal assurance that his younger brother was not "a practised writer," as Murray suspected, but a genuine sailor, and Herman undertook to provide three new chapters and additional revisions and details which enabled the book to be published as a sober two-volume *Narrative of a Four Months' Residence among the Natives of a Valley of the Marquesas Islands* on February 27 and April 1, 1846. In the interim, on March 17, it was published in New York under its more lively American title. It was an immediate success in both countries, and Melville was so assured of the fact in advance that he began working at once on its sequel.

He had learned something from his publishers, and *Omoo*, the sequel, was a more carefully calculated narrative. It was less teasing than *Typee*, more straightforward and convincing as a narrative of real experience, more coherent in its tone of humorous realism; and its characters, especially the narrator's companion Dr. Long Ghost, seemed drawn for a popular comic illustrator. Yet in substance it was the same sort of book *Typee* had been—a combination of memory, imagination, and research in which the author used the same device of extending each week of his real adventures into a month in order to be plausible about what might have happened to him. Because its factual background has been better established by scholars, *Omoo* in fact gives a better indication than *Typee* of the nature of young Melville's literary imagination. All he wrote was focused upon the actuality of experience, but he wrote less about what had happened to him than about what he might have experienced had he participated more fully in the events he knew about. Both books were products of that area of consciousness where memory and imagination blend and are controlled only by the desire to tell a good but convincing tale.

In the meantime, before *Omoo* was completed in December 1846 and published in the following spring, Melville was being attacked from two sides—quietly for his romance and vociferously for his realism. John Murray continued to be suspicious of *Typee* and kept insisting upon documentary proof of its veracity. So Melville was triumphant when his fellow deserter from the *Acushnet*, Richard Tobias Greene, appeared and offered to authenticate the narrative up to the time of his earlier escape from the Typees. "The Story of Toby" was added to subsequent editions of the book and also published by Murray as a separate pamphlet. The other objection was met by suppressing certain of the realistic details in later editions. Melville had been quite candid in his criticisms of the behavior of missionaries and the social effects of their activities in the South Seas and had commented with a sailor's matter-of-factness upon the customary behavior of native females on visiting ships. The storm raised against him, in the United States, as a "traducer of missions" led to the publication of a second, expurgated, edition of his book by his American publisher, Wiley and Putnam, and his transfer to the Harpers for the publication of *Omoo* and his later novels.

His next book and first actual novel, however, was to be a problem. He had based *Typee* upon his experiences in the Marquesas and *Omoo* upon those in Tahiti, and although he had deliberately excluded any account of the whale fishery from these books he had no pattern, at the moment, for using the material which was later to go into *Moby Dick*. He was telling, with great success, a continued story of adventure while exploiting the novelty of the South Seas (which had not before been treated in fiction), and he had no more adventures of the same sort to recount. His voyage on the *Charles and Henry* had been uneventful and unprovocative. He would have to invent a series of incidents which, for the first time, would be entirely unrelated to any core of personal experience. He may have been doubtful of his ability to do so, for before he went back to his writing he rallied his friends and visited Washington in an attempt to get a job in the Treasury Department. When the attempt failed he took up his pen again with more forced energy than persuasiveness.

The impulse behind Melville's energy at this time was matrimonial. He had been courting Elizabeth Shaw, daughter of the chief justice of Massachusetts and one of his sisters' friends who had listened to him tell the tales of *Typee*, and he wanted to settle in a larger place than Lansingburgh. He had been spending an increasing amount of time in New York City, becoming acquainted with the complexities of the publishing world and finding congenial associates in the literary circle gathered around the scholarly editor Evert Duyckinck. In turn, Duyckinck found him a promising contributor of comic articles to *Yankee Doodle* and serious reviews to the new *Literary World*. Removal to the city made sense for a man who was being compelled to become a professional writer. Accordingly, after his marriage on August 4, 1847, he borrowed money to buy a house large enough for his whole family — his wife and his mother, his four unmarried sisters, his younger brother Allan and his bride, and his youngest brother Thomas who at the age of seventeen had already been two years away from home on a whaler. There, at 103 Fourth Avenue, he settled down in late September to throw himself with enthusiasm into the world of literature and begin working again on the manuscript of his third book.

The new book, eventually called *Mardi*, was to be neither a popular nor an artistic success, but its composition provides an extraordinary illustration of the growth of an artist's mind. The basic reason for its failure is structural, because it represents an unresolved conflict between Melville's conscious effort to find a unifying narrative corresponding to the picaresque sort he had been using and his unconscious compulsion to relate his writing to his own experiences which were now predominantly literary and intellectual. For the unschooled author began reading widely and avidly during this period, and his writing reflected his reading — Dante and Rabelais, Spenser and other Elizabethans, Robert Burton and Sir Thomas Browne, La Motte-Fouqué and other German romancers, Coleridge and the English romantics, and philosophers from Seneca to David Hartley. The early chapters in which he attempted to invent adventures like those in *Typee* and *Omoo* soon gave way to a more romantic but still adventurous interlude and this in turn to a sort of satiric travelogue in which a group of type characters discoursed, according to type, on the world around them as it was portrayed with increasingly purposeful symbolism in the form of a South Sea archipelago called Mardi. The narrator's original companion (corresponding to Toby and Long Ghost) was abandoned entirely after the romantic interlude, when the author departed completely from the pattern of his earlier books, but a certain connection was kept between the interlude and the travelogue by making the beautiful maiden introduced in the first the object of a quest in the second.

Incoherent though all this seems and is, there was a certain imaginative focal point for it within Melville's immediate experience. Books had become more exciting to him than cannibals and whales, and he was actually recording, while trying to do something else, his adventures among books. The quest reflected La Motte-Fouqué's quest in *Undine* and in *Sintram and His Companions*, Spenser's Red Crosse Knight's quest for Holinesse, and the Rabelaisian quest for the Oracle of the Bottle. His use of allegory came from these writers, especially Spenser, and others – including the compilers of popular books on the meaning of flowers. His eccentricities of manner and style were often those of Burton's *Anatomy of Melancholy* and of Sir Thomas Browne. And one of the companions on the quest was specifically created to express his new philosophical interests. The result, inevitably, was chaos, but the apparent chaos was the turbulent effect of a vigorous mind exploring a new world which it was to conquer and control.

The tendency toward control, in fact, is evident in *Mardi* itself. For as the book progressed Melville's mind became more critical and speculative than it had been in the first half of the narrative. He had made his quest an allegorical search for happiness in which the hero was led forward by pure desire and driven from behind by the threat of danger from the consequences of a past action. And he had evidently decided from the beginning that happiness was not to be found in the sensuous temptations of anything like Spenser's Bower of Bliss. But at some point in his writing the quest quit being a casual narrative device holding together his random thoughts and opinions and acquired, instead, an intellectual seriousness. Religion especially interested him as a potential source of happiness, but not the institutionalized religion which he examined and rejected in the book as he had already rejected it in his actual observations on missionaries in the South Seas. Yet he allowed his philosophical companion to take refuge in the allegorical island of Serenia, where the dictates of reason and of Christian charity were one; and eventually his historian and poet were also directed there, while his representative ruler renounced all thought of happiness and returned to his turbulent country. But the hero and narrator, Taji, was more romantic: his was an endless quest as he pursued his intangible goal, followed by the specters of his past, "over an endless sea."

This was the book as Melville thought he had completed it on the eve of the French Revolution in the spring of 1848. But the intellectual development revealed in it was not yet complete. For when news of the events in Europe reached him Melville's imagination was stirred, as it had never been before, by the signs of immediate social change, and he increased the size of his book one-sixth by the insertion of some twenty-three chapters of political allegory. These referred to the revolutions in France (Franko) and other parts of Europe (Porpheero), to the Chartist movement and the international and fiscal policies of England (Dominora), to the problems created by slavery and by geographical expansion in the United States (Vivenza), and to various other matters ranging from the potato famine in Ireland to conditions in India. They reveal an extraordinary perceptiveness, in depth, to the long-range significance of contemporary events; and perhaps the most interesting of these chapters, from this point of view, are those in which he anticipated the social consequences attendant on the closing of the American frontier and on the California gold rush which had not yet occurred at the time he wrote. The young man who had so recently moved to the city and entered the larger world of the mind had acquired an unusual amount of knowledge, understanding, and vision in a remarkably short time.

Melville had also acquired something else while writing *Mardi* which he did not recognize or appreciate. He knew before the book was published in March 1849 (by Bentley, in London, for Murray had refused it) that it would be a failure, and financial necessity compelled him to return at once to his old successful vein — the autobiographical romance. The richest of its novelties, his South Sea adventures, had been exhausted, except for the whaling materials, but he still had the events of his trip to Liverpool which he worked into *Redburn: His First Voyage* and completed by the end of June. He always spoke of it as a book he despised and may actually have done so. He knew that so many men had written of their youthful experiences before the mast that the subject was hackneyed, and he knew, too, that he could not afford to put into this book the sort of intellectual and literary excitement which had damned *Mardi* as a commercial venture. But he did not know that the emotions he felt while writing could be projected into the past or into a fiction in a way that would give his words a vitality which he himself did not associate with the intentional context of meaning.

Herman Melville

With *Redburn* Melville became a novelist — so persuasively so, in fact, that many later readers have had difficulty accepting the evidence that he himself was some four years older than his hero when he first went to sea and that the most memorable parts of the book are pure fiction. It is true that most of the characters in the novel were Melville's actual companions, some under their real names, on his first voyage. But Jackson, the most memorable of them because of his strange hold over the crew and his dramatic death, was alive at the end of a trip which included no casualties of any sort. Melville himself was by no means the timid, under-sized innocent who serves as the narrator, nor did the ship carry immigrants or the plague on its return voyage. Yet the personality of the narrator and the circumstantial accounts of the outbreak of a virulent disease in a crowded steerage seem to reflect an emotional involvement which makes the book more convincing than either *Typee* or *Omoo*.

The probability is that Melville was more deeply involved in *Redburn* than in his earlier books but that it was the involvement of the moment, not of the past through memory. Wellingborough Redburn may have been not at all like Herman Melville but he could very easily be an older brother's affectionate representation of Thomas Melville who had gone to sea at the age of fifteen, who had recently returned and left again on a voyage to China, and who was so much on Herman's mind that *Redburn* was dedicated to him. And if Melville's own return from Liverpool had not been on a plague ship crowded with immigrants, he was nevertheless writing the latter part of his book while the blue cholera was creating panic in New York after having been brought there by an immigrant ship the preceding December. The unregulated conditions on board such ships were notorious, and Melville knew the slums from which their passengers came. A man whose imagination and emotions could be deeply stirred by contemporary events (as Melville's had been when he wrote the political chapters of *Mardi*) may readily have undertaken, out of a sort of indignant humanitarianism, to make the public realize that it was suffering from its own indifference to the welfare of the less fortunate. "For the whole world is the patrimony of the whole world," he wrote with reference to the agitated question of whether "multitudes of foreign poor should be landed on our American shores"; "there is no telling who does not own a stone in the Great Wall of China." *Redburn* is a convincing book because the emotions which controlled it were genuine, profound, and pervasive enough to affect its style: the writing in the first part reflects the simplicity of his involvement in a boy's point of view, whereas that of the last half has the detachment of an observer who realizes the significance of what he is writing about.

But Melville had no time, at the moment, to realize the significance of his literary achievement. He was heavily in debt and turned at once to a book based on his naval experience, writing *White Jacket* at the rate of nearly three thousand words a day during July and August while reading proofs on *Redburn*. Once again he used real people, drawn out of his memory, as characters, but most of the events of the voyage around Cape Horn were fictitious. He borrowed freely from various sources the numerous comic incidents which were sprinkled through it, but what he called its "man-of-warish" style was a holdover from the indignant humanitarianism of *Redburn*. Some of his indignation was undoubtedly a reflection of his past resentment against the arbitrary restraints and cruelties of naval life, and his brutal ship's surgeon, though perhaps real enough, belonged to a literary tradition that went back to Smollett. But the abolition of flogging was being agitated at the time he wrote, and the pervasive theme of his emphasis upon it as an unnecessarily cruel but all-too-usual punishment was in the interest of reform. Both in *White Jacket* and in *Redburn* he exhibited the naturalistic impulse to portray vividly the evils of society in the hope that legislative action would be taken against them.

Yet *White Jacket* was a deeper book than its predecessor had been. Its subtitle labeled it "The World in a Man-of-War" and its concluding chapter drew an elaborate analogy between the frigate and the earth, sailing through space with clean decks and dark storerooms of secrets beneath the "lie" of its surface. For Melville had found the microcosm of his man-of-war, despite its friendly companionship of the foretop and its occasional comedy, a cruel world of arbitrary power and discipline, motiveless malice, ruthlessness, and brutality. Above all, it was a world of constraint, in which men had to swing their hammocks without "spreaders," turn on signal when they were allowed to sleep on the crowded deck, and go sleepless because precedent and convention required the storing of gear in the daytime. It was a world of absolute command from above and of mystery and subterranean darkness below. Perhaps Melville felt the constraint to an unusual degree while writing, for he had sacrificed his customary summer vacation to the book and was working through the August heat in a city so panic-stricken from the cholera that people were afraid to go outdoors or eat their customary food. Physically as well as financially, the world was pressing in upon him, and he must have felt it. At any rate, there was an incipient violence in the emotion underlying *White Jacket* which suggested that at any moment its author might break loose.

Whatever the constraint Melville may have felt during the summer was relieved in October 1849, when he decided to go abroad in an effort to get better terms for *White Jacket* than he had been able to get, by correspondence with his English publisher, for *Redburn*. He also planned to collect material for a historical novel based upon the real life of an American Revolutionary patriot who had been captured by the British and had lived for forty years in England as an exile. But the trip was to have unexpected consequences. For one thing, it renewed his sea memories. The captain of his ship gave him a private stateroom with a porthole through which he could gaze at the ocean, and he was also allowed the freedom of the rigging so that he could recapture all the old emotions of being at the masthead. For another, it proved to be an exciting intellectual experience. Two of his fellow passengers, George J. Adler and Frank Taylor, were young men of philosophical inclinations with whom he could discuss the subject which had so interested him in the concluding chapter of *White Jacket* — "Fixed Fate, Free-will, Fore-knowledge absolute." Their interest in German

Transcendentalism appealed to the man who had become acquainted with Emerson, for the first time, only eight months before and had been surprised to find in him deep thoughts rather than "myths and oracular gibberish." He was to talk with them, on every occasion he could make, even after the voyage was over and he was in London and Paris.

By the time Melville returned home, on February 1, 1850, he seems to have laid aside his plan for the historical novel. At any rate, by May 1 he had seen *White Jacket* through the press and was able to write Richard Henry Dana, Jr., that he was "half way" in a book which he referred to as "the 'whaling voyage.'" And on June 27 he promised the completed volume to his English publisher "in the later part of the coming autumn" and described it specifically but with some exaggeration as "a romance of adventure, founded upon certain wild legends in the Southern Sperm Whale Fisheries and illustrated by the author's own personal experience, of two years and more, as a harpooneer." In the middle of July he was ready for a vacation and left for Pittsfield, Massachusetts, where Evert Duyckinck visited him in early August and wrote that "Melville has a new book mostly done — a romantic, fanciful and literal and most enjoyable presentment of the Whale Fishery — something quite new."

These early references to the book which was to become *Moby Dick* are of unusual interest because they introduce the most teasing question which arises in any effort to follow the development of Melville's creative imagination: How did it happen that he was to spend a year of agonized composition upon a "mostly done" manuscript and transform it from a romance with autobiographical overtones into the powerfully dramatic novel it became? He seems to have had no intention, when he went on his vacation, of doing more than filling out his narrative with realistic details gathered from books of reference he had collected for that purpose. But once again the emotions of immediate experience were to project themselves into his fiction, transform it, and give it — this time — not only the vitality of his own life but the tensions of the century in which he lived.

Herman Melville

The trigger action for his explosion into greatness was that of a single day, August 5, 1850, during his vacation when one of his neighbors arranged an expedition and dinner party for all the literary celebrities of the region – the New Englanders who summered in the Berkshires and Melville and the New York guests he had invited up for a visit. The expedition was to the top of Monument Mountain where Melville, Nathaniel Hawthorne, and Oliver Wendell Holmes were made gay by the elevation and champagne and brought back to sobriety by the New York critic Cornelius Mathews, who insisted upon making the occasion literary by reading William Cullen Bryant's solemn poem about the Indian lovers who had leaped to their death from the projecting ledge on which Melville had been performing sailor's antics. Holmes's satiric impulses were aroused, and the result was a literary quarrel which continued throughout the "well moistened" dinner party later. It focused upon the theory of the influence of climate upon genius and the question whether America would produce a literature as elevated as its mountains and as spacious as its plains. The New Englanders (as Holmes's Phi Beta Kappa poem *Astraea* of a few days later was to show) were skeptical of the New Yorkers' enthusiasm.

Melville's part in the argument seems to have been more mischievous than serious, but he was impressed by it and even more impressed by his first meeting with Hawthorne. His aunt had given him a copy of *Mosses from an Old Manse* at the beginning of his vacation, but he had not yet read it. Now, having met the author, he read it with the extraordinary enthusiasm he expressed in the belated review he wrote for the *Literary World* before his New York friends went home. Hawthorne proved the greatness of American literature, he contended, under the anonymous signature of "A Virginian spending July in Vermont"; but it was a greatness of heart and mind, observable in Hawthorne's willingness to present the "blackness" of truth – the same dark "background against which Shakespeare plays his grandest conceits" and which "appeals to that Calvinistic sense of Innate Depravity and Original Sin, from whose visitations, in some shape or other, no deeply thinking mind is always and wholly free." In Hawthorne and his *Mosses* Melville

95

found an attitude of mind which courageously reflected all his doubts concerning the transcendental idealism and optimism that had interested him during his recent voyage and had affected his reading since.

The impression made by Hawthorne was so great that Melville cultivated his acquaintance assiduously during the following months and eventually dedicated *Moby Dick* to him. Yet he did not become a wholehearted convert to his new friend's "black" skepticism. He was himself a man of greater vitality, more of a man of action, than Hawthorne; and although the two shared an interest in the Gothic romance, Hawthorne's interest was in the Gothic atmosphere whereas Melville's was in the romantic hero — the Byronic wandering outlaw of his own dark mind. Furthermore, Melville had borrowed *Sartor Resartus* at the time he finished collecting his whaling library for the revision of his book, and he found in Carlyle's transcendentalized version of the romantic hero a character who was as "deep-diving" as Emerson but who had proved himself susceptible to Hawthorne's pessimism and capable of defying it. In one of his stories in the *Mosses*, "Earth's Holocaust," Hawthorne had set forth allegorically his belief that evil could not be destroyed because it was constantly being re-created by "the all-engendering heart of man." Melville was inclined to agree. But the best "strong positive illustration" Melville found of the "blackness in Hawthorne" was in the story of "Young Goodman Brown" and his allegorical but unanswered cry for "Faith." In Carlyle's book Melville found a hero who could live in such a spiritual state of "starless, Tartarean black" that he could hear the Devil say "thou art fatherless, outcast, and the Universe is mine" but who still had the courage and the energy to say "*I* am not thine, but Free, and forever hate thee!" Whether he was as sensible as Young Goodman Brown (who went into a lethargy when he was made to suspect, either by a dream or by a real experience, that the world was the Devil's) might be questionable. But he was more heroic and, to Melville's mind, more admirable.

Melville's literary interests, in short, reveal the tensions that existed in his mind at the time he began what otherwise might have been the routine job of revising his manuscript. They were vital tensions, not only in terms of his own sensitivity but in their profound effect upon Western civilization during the nineteenth century — tensions set up by the conflict between the will to believe and the need to be shown, between transcendentalism and empiricism in philosophy, between religion and science, between faith and skepticism. These were not tensions to be resolved, as so many of Melville's contemporaries tried to resolve them, for no satisfactory resolution has yet proved possible. Melville, at his deepest and most complex creative level, made no attempt to resolve the conflict. Instead, he dramatized it. And it may be that the ambiguity and ambivalence inherent in the dramatic Shakespearean qualities of *Moby Dick* are responsible for the fact that it has a greater appeal to the puzzled and questioning twentieth century than do the writings of Melville's contemporaries who were more explicitly concerned with the same tensions.

In any event, Shakespeare was an important element in the literary and intellectual ferment which went into the making of *Moby Dick*. Melville had become excited about him at the time he discovered transcendentalism, in February 1849, when he wrote Evert Duyckinck that "if another Messiah ever comes twill be in Shakspeare's person." And he kept looking, in his review of the *Mosses*, if not for another Messiah at least for another Shakespeare — perhaps "this day being born on the banks of the Ohio." Hawthorne had "approached" him, for a nineteenth-century Shakespeare would not be an Elizabethan dramatist but a part of his "times" with "correspondent coloring." There is no doubt but that Melville was excited by the company and the literary debate of August 5, 1850, and it may have been that this excitement was intensified by a feeling of challenge. Within a few days he was to denounce the "absolute and unconditional adoration of Shakspeare" and his "unapproachability" as one of "our Anglo-Saxon superstitions." Might not he himself be another man "to carry republican progressiveness into Literature as well as into Life" by writing a novel that had the quality of Shakespearean tragedy?

However this might be, his novel began to change from a story

97

of the whale fishery to a story of "the Whale." Captain Ahab (named for a man who had "done evil in the sight of the Lord") remained the protagonist in his narrative, but his antagonist was neither the worthy mate Starbuck nor any member of his exotic crew. It was the great white whale with a humped back and hieroglyphics on his brow, known throughout the fishery as Moby Dick and notorious for the viciousness with which he had turned upon the men who had hunted and attempted to destroy him. Ahab himself had been his victim on a previous voyage when the whale had sheared off his leg and started a train of cause and effect that resulted in his further mutilation by its splintered substitute. And Ahab, a queer "grand, ungodly, god-like man," had embarked on a voyage of revenge which would follow the paths of the migrating leviathan throughout the vast Pacific until he and the whole ship's crew were destroyed and the narrator alone was left to tell the tale. In order to make the voyage plausible Melville had to draw upon the whole body of available whaling lore in extraordinary detail. He also had to make his captain, from the narrator's point of view, mad.

But the power of the book does not come from the realistic fantasy of the voyage or from the obsessed madness of the traditional Gothic or romantic protagonist who is half hero and half villain. On the contrary, it comes from the fact that Ahab is one of the few characters in literature genuinely "formed for noble tragedies." Like Lear, he is a noble individual whose only flaw is a single mistake in judgment. And like Hamlet, at least as Coleridge interpreted him, his mistake is that of a disordered judgment — that of a man with a "craving after the indefinite" who "looks upon external things as hieroglyphics" and whose mind, with its "everlasting broodings," is "unseated from its healthy relation" and "constantly occupied with the world within, and abstracted from the world without — giving substance to shadows, and throwing a mist over all commonplace actualities." For to Ahab "all visible objects" were "but as pasteboard masks" from behind which "some unknown but still reasoning thing puts forth the mouldings of its features." To him the white whale was the emblem of "outrageous strength, with inscrutable malice sinewing it"; and it was "that inscrutable thing" which he hated, and he was determined to "wreak that hate upon him."

Whether Ahab's attitude should be interpreted in psychological or philosophical terms is an important question with respect to Melville's biography. The narrator, Ishmael, uses psychological terms in his accounts of the phases Ahab goes through while "deliriously transferring" his idea of evil to the whale as an object which would visibly personify it and make it practically assailable. Ahab himself, of course, sounds like Carlyle's hero asserting his individual freedom and defying the Devil's claim to the universe. The weight of the evidence, derived from the book and from letters written at the same time, appears to favor a rather close identification of the author's point of view with that of the narrator. Melville's conscious fable in *Moby Dick* seems to lead to the conclusion that a belief in the emblematic nature of the universe is a form of madness. His rational judgment apparently concurred with that of Hawthorne: the white whale was a natural beast, and the evil in him was a product of the "all-engendering heart" or mind of Ahab. But, for the moment, Melville's personal philosophy is not relevant to an interpretation of *Moby Dick* as a work of literature. "Dramatically regarded," as he himself put it, "all men tragically great are made so through a certain morbidness." The important point is that Ahab's "morbidness," whether a sane conviction or a mad obsession, was the tragic flaw in his character which directed his heroic behavior toward destruction.

Yet if one goes beyond superficial interpretation into an attempt to explain the strange power of *Moby Dick*, Melville's personal beliefs do become important and his chapter on "The Whiteness of the Whale" becomes particularly relevant. For here he collects evidence for the existence of a sort of knowledge which is more intuitive than the rational empiricism used by Ishmael to explain "crazy Ahab" in the immediately preceding chapter. The inference to be drawn is that Melville was not wholly convinced of the validity of the fable his rational mind constructed in order to provide himself with a plot of the sort he found and admired in Hawthorne. The conflict between transcendentalism and empiricism was not something which he merely observed and then dramatized. It was something that he experienced and felt deeply within himself. Ahab, who sometimes doubted whether there was anything beyond the "wall" of the emblematic material universe, was only slightly more mad than the storyteller who condemned him but sometimes doubted whether the material world of experience provided the ultimate form of knowledge. Melville could easily imagine within himself the rage to believe, the madness, he attributed to his hero as a "tragic flaw."

In fact, if one explores the creative level which lies beneath an artist's identification with the intellectual and emotional conflicts of his age, there is abundant evidence of a deeply rooted desire in Melville to be as heroically mad as Ahab. Such evidence is to be found in his imagery. The image of the fatherless outcast had been a controlling one in his earlier books. He had been the deserter in *Typee*, the runaway in *Omoo*, the escaped captive in *Mardi*, the orphan in *Redburn*, and the poor sailor denied a charitable daub of paint in *White Jacket*. And in *Moby Dick* he was Ishmael, the homeless wanderer. The image, of course, was that of his own life from the time he left school at his father's death until he married, bought a house, and established himself in New York. But in *White Jacket*, as we have seen, a new and conflicting image began to emerge and become dominant — that of constraint and subterranean mystery, with emotional overtones of incipient violence. The loss of his wandering bachelor's freedom, his crowded household, his serious financial problems, and the peculiar cooped-up desperation of his writing *Redburn* and *White Jacket* during the plague may have all contributed to its emergence. But its origin probably was in something deeper — in the feeling of growth, so vividly expressed in a letter to Hawthorne in June 1851, which made him believe that what he was most moved to write was banned and that all his books were "botches." He felt himself one of those "deep men" who had something "eating in them" and frustrating them. It was time for him to deny his fatherless, outcast state and assert his freedom, like Carlyle's hero, with his "whole Me." Looking at all the things that hemmed him in, he might well suspect that "there's naught beyond" but still cry with Ahab "How can the prisoner reach outside except by thrusting through the wall?"

The imagery of constraint, frustration, and the obscure mystery of frustration is so pervasive in *Moby Dick* that one is almost compelled to believe that the secret of its vitality lies somewhere in Melville's own heroic attempt, by using all the resources of language and invention he could command, to thrust through the wall of frustrations he could not fully understand. "I have a sort of sea-feeling," he had written Evert Duyckinck in December 1850, when the ground was covered with snow. "My room seems a ship's cabin; and at nights when I wake up and hear the wind shrieking, I almost fancy there is too much sail on the house, and I had better go on the roof and rig in the chimney." And at the end of the following June, when the book was half through the press, he wrote Hawthorne of his disgust "with the heat and dust of the babylonish brick-kiln of New York" and his return to the country "to feel the grass — and end the book reclining on it." It was only natural, perhaps, that he should have also written Hawthorne that the book was baptized (like Ahab's harpoon) in the name of the Devil, for there was a great deal of Ahab's passion in Melville while he wrote.

Moby Dick was completed shortly before its author's thirty-second birthday and published in London on October 18, 1851, and in New York about four weeks later. Hawthorne understood the fable, and his understanding gave Melville, for a moment, "a sense of unspeakable security" and an awareness of more pervasive allegorical implications than he had intended. But the book was not a success. Although the reviews were better, the sales were no greater than those of *Mardi*. Once again Melville had to face the fact that if he poured his whole self into a book it was almost certainly doomed to commercial failure.

While he was writing *Moby Dick* Melville's way of life was drastically changed. He had bought a house, Arrowhead, and a hundred and fifty acres of ground in the Berkshires, and he had set himself up as a farmer. There his second son was born during the autumn of 1851, and there, during the winter, he contemplated his next literary project. Hawthorne's appreciation of *Moby Dick* in November had stirred his ambition: "Leviathan is not the biggest fish," he had written; " — I have heard of Krakens." But by January 1852 he apparently faced the fact that he would make very little money from the sort of books he wanted to write and decided that, if dollars damned him, he would go ahead and be damned. He would try to do something that would be popular. And so he wrote Mrs. Hawthorne (who had surprised him by liking the whaling story) that he would not again send her "a bowl of salt water" but "a rural bowl of milk." He offered the new book to his English publisher, Richard Bentley, soon afterward; and when Bentley cited his losses on the earlier books as an argument in favor of a contract for half-profits instead of a substantial advance, Melville suggested that he "let bygones be bygones" and publish the new work under an assumed name such as "Guy Winthrop." For it was "very much more calculated for popularity than anything you have yet published of mine — being a regular romance, with a mysterious plot to it, and stirring passions at work, and withall, representing a new and elevated aspect of American life."

By this time, April 16, 1852, the rapidly written book was completed and in type at his American publisher's, and it is difficult to understand how its author could have written about it in such terms. For this "rural bowl of milk" was *Pierre; or, The Ambiguities*, surely the most perverse of Melville's novels in its unrestrained imagination, about which Bentley worried, and its offensiveness to the "many sensitive readers" with whom he was concerned. It was probably planned as a sort of satiric variation on the *Moby Dick* fable in a situation and setting which would have a greater appeal to feminine readers. Its hero, Pierre Glendinning, was a sophomoric version of Captain Ahab who also had his vision of the absolute and acted accordingly. But Pierre's intuition was of good rather than evil — of an absolute morality superior to that of the everyday world which surrounded even his idyllic existence with an affectionate widowed mother on a large country estate. It led him, when he became convinced that a strange dark girl in the vicinity was his illegitimate half-sister, to pretend marriage with her in order that she might have the Glendinning name without disturbing his mother's devotion to his father's memory. And it also led him to disinheritance, to a fantastic existence in New York City as a writer among a group of Transcendental Apostles, and to a tragic end which was more melodramatic than that of Captain Ahab.

Melville may have persuaded himself while trying (in vain) to sell the book to Bentley that he had managed to combine genial satire with the mysterious plot and passions of the Gothic romances which had so interested him during the early stages of writing *Moby Dick*. But if he did he was ignoring the fact that the major — and, from a commercial point of view, the most damning — ambiguity in *Pierre* reflected his compulsive desire to resolve the emotional and intellectual conflict which had made *Moby Dick* so effectively dramatic. Did Pierre Glendinning deserve any sympathy at all for his immature behavior while pursuing some ideal of absolute morality? Was there any validity in the sort of evidence for intuitive knowledge that Melville had assembled the year before for his chapter on "The Whiteness of the Whale"? Or was a person who believed in the transcendental absolute simply fooling himself? By presenting Ahab dramatically as an obsessed madman, he had made the answer to such questions as these a matter of opinion rather than one for investigation; and he had expressed his own rational opinion in the fable of the book. But the questions continued to haunt him.

For Pierre was not mad. He was very young and very foolish but in no sense neurotic, obsessed, or crazy. And Melville could not resist the impulse to explore the psychology of his behavior, following "the endless, winding way" (as he put it) of "the flowing river in the cave of man" wherever it might lead in a manner that would not be permitted in a "mere novel." He did it with an honesty and a subtlety which resulted in the first genuine psychological novel in American literature. But the way led him to the ruinous theme of incest. At the beginning he had made the dark Isabel beautiful in order to keep Pierre from seeming too perfect and immaculate: his hero would have been less ready to "champion the right," Melville observed, had he not been invited to do so by beauty rather than ugliness. His intention had been to make her beauty one of those "mere contingent things" of which Pierre would be unaware while it served the artistic purpose of keeping the "heavenly fire" of his enthusiasm within a plausible vessel of human "clay." But Melville's years at sea and in strange lands had given him a greater understanding of human frailty than of Victorian proprieties, and he allowed the "contingent" attraction of Isabel to develop beyond the limits of discretion before the book reached its melodramatic conclusion. Once more he had gone too far in putting too much serious thought into a book designed for popular consumption.

He had also gone beyond simple indiscretion. For *Pierre* shows signs of strains and tensions quite different from those in *Moby Dick*. It contains less ambivalence and more indications of conflicting purpose. The superficial romanticism of its idyllic episodes and mysterious plot was calculated to make it a popular novel, but the serious probing into psychological depths represented the kind of speculation that had been widely condemned in *Mardi* and *Moby Dick*. The amused detachment with which Pierre was treated as a "sophomore" probably represented an effort to achieve the "genialities" Melville admired in Hawthorne, but the amusement sometimes became sardonic. He drew upon his own early background to a considerable extent for the details of Pierre's, but as he approached the present a touch of bitterness crept in. His picture of Pierre at his writing plank was a comic portrayal, in Carlylese, of a desperate attempt to write the great American novel; but it was based so much upon the grim conditions under which he himself had been writing during the past three years that the comedy had to be forced and exaggerated in order to avoid the risk of self-pity. The serious elements in the book are many and varied, but they all serve to create the total effect of an author who was attempting the light touch with an uncontrollably heavy hand.

More than ever, perhaps, Melville was feeling the spiritual claustrophobia which had become evident in the summer of 1849. The image of the vault is frequent in *Pierre*, and the statue of Laocoön appears, near the middle of the book, in a niche off the stairs leading to Mrs. Glendinning's chamber. One of the most memorable incidents in the story is the section in which Pierre, in a dream, identifies himself with Enceladus, imprisoned in the earth with only the stumps of his once audacious arms, striving in vain to assault the heavens. Melville's comment on this section indicates clearly that Pierre could and did use his knowledge of old fables to elucidate his own dreams and that he found this one "most repulsively fateful and foreboding" only because he failed to wrest from it its ultimate meaning: "Whoso storms the sky gives best proof he came from thither! But whatso crawls contented in the moat before that crystal fort, shows it was born within that slime, and there forever will abide." Pierre never learned to strike the "stubborn rock" of fable "and force even aridity itself to quench his painful thirst" for self-knowledge. But Melville did. And what he learned, while writing *Pierre*, helps explain the mystery of some of his writings which were to come later.

Commercially as well as artistically *Pierre* was Melville's greatest failure. The reviewers were unanimous in condemning it, and fewer than three hundred copies were to be sold during the entire year following its publication. The wise old judge who was his father-in-law became worried as soon as he read the book. He knew that Melville was a popular writer only when he wrote about ships and sailors, and so he persuaded the young man to go with him on a trip to Nantucket where he was holding court in early July 1852. He planned to have Herman meet some of the people connected with whaling in New Bedford and Nantucket and then have a refreshing vacation at Martha's Vineyard and the Elizabeth Islands. Melville was willing to go and also to keep his eyes open for fresh literary material.

But what he found was not what Judge Shaw probably hoped for. No suggestion of adventure — either of escape or of bold defiance — came his way and fired his imagination. Instead of being impressed by the daring seafaring men of Nantucket he was impressed by the patient women of the island who waited, so often in vain, for their husbands' return from distant lands and seas. The story he brought back with him, well documented, was that of a certain Agatha Robertson whose husband had deserted her for seventeen years and then returned and deserted her again with no reproach from Agatha. The whole story and the incidents connected with it, he felt, were "instinct with significance"; but he hesitated about writing it and tried in vain to get Hawthorne to do so before he decided, with the beginning of his winter writing season in December 1852, to undertake it himself. There is no evidence that Melville ever wrote or even made a fair beginning of the Agatha story, but his interest in it and his unproductive winter are both significant in view of his preoccupation with the theme of patience when he did begin to write again.

During this period of nonproductivity his family decided that writing was bad for him and that he should apply to the new Democratic president, Hawthorne's friend and classmate, Franklin Pierce, for a diplomatic post abroad. They enlisted the help of so many friends and made such a case for the desirability of a change in occupation for him that they created a lasting impression of a nervous breakdown from "too much excitement of the imagination." But they failed to get him an appointment and failed to divert him from the profession of writing. On the contrary, Melville decided, during that winter, to turn more professional than he had ever been before. He agreed to become a contributor to the new *Putnam's Monthly Magazine* at five dollars a page (the highest price paid any of its contributors), and *Putnam's* introduced him to its readers in the issue of February 1853 as the first of "Our Young Authors." His first contribution, which, however, did not appear until November and December, was "Bartleby, the Scrivener; A Story of Wall-Street," not only the first of his short stories but one of the most interesting and revealing of all the documents in the history of Melville's imaginative life.

In the first place, "Bartleby" is a classic but unusual fable of patience — unusual because it tells of a patience which has within itself the tensions of both acceptance and defiance. Its hero is not active, like Captain Ahab or even Pierre. He is completely passive. But he is as defiant as either. He makes no attempt to storm the sky, but he does not crawl in the slime. He would simply "prefer not to" crawl or to conform to any of the expectations of him. His force of character is great but entirely negative. Furthermore, there seems to be little question but that this was a fable deliberately created by Melville in a search for self-knowledge. For the patience of Bartleby was much closer to that of his own temperament than was anything he could find in the story of Agatha or the women of Nantucket. Various real incidents may have contributed to the substance of the fable, but the powerful center of its invention seems to have been a soul-searching speculation about "what might have been." Suppose Melville had obtained and accepted a job as a lawyer's clerk instead of defiantly going to sea and writing such defiant books as *Mardi, Moby Dick,* and *Pierre.* What might his fate have been? Melville looked in his heart and wrote that it would be pretty much the same as Pierre's — death in the Tombs.

"Bartleby" is a story extraordinarily rich in its suggestiveness, but, next to its soul-searching quality, its most interesting characteristic is its conscious use of a dominant image — as though Melville, like Pierre, had been directed by his most haunting dreams to a fable that was capable of revealing his condition. The wall that Ahab saw in Moby Dick is everywhere in this "Story of Wall-Street." Bartleby faces it in his employer's office and in the exercise yard of the Tombs, and he dies quietly at its base. Pierre's dream of Enceladus was of a no more profound symbol of confinement. It was a symbol that had crept gradually into Melville's writings, probably without his awareness, but this time he used it as consciously as he might have done had he been attempting to exorcise it. He did not succeed. But as he continued to write short stories he continued to be conscious of his own feeling of frustration, to seek its possible cause, and to use his search as a device for giving meaning to the fables he created.

One such story was the otherwise trivial "Cock-a-Doodle-Doo!" published in *Harper's Monthly Magazine* for December, in which he explained the behavior of a character similar to Bartleby in terms of pride. But he had more ambitious plans for the winter and did not continue this kind of analysis. Despite the failure of *Pierre* the Harpers were eager for another novel from him, and on December 7, 1853, they gave him an advance of $300 for a work on "Tortoises or Tortoise-Hunting" which he hoped to complete in January. He knew the Galápagos Islands well enough, from experience and through reading, to provide the background; but unfortunately he had no story, and the best he could find was that of a Chola woman who was left alone on desolate Norfolk Isle when her husband and brother died in a fishing accident. Her experience should have appealed to whatever had haunted him in the Agatha story, but he could make nothing of it. "She but showed us her soul's lid, and the strange ciphers thereon engraved," he said; "all within, with pride's timidity, was withheld." He seems to have turned to Spenser and other poets for suggestions and inspiration for an allegorical narrative of patience, but when the Harpers' publishing house burned, shortly after he received his advance, and he thought their book-publishing activities would be suspended, he lost his incentive for proceeding with a difficult job. He turned his material into a series of ten sketches and sold them to *Putnam's* for serial publication, as "The Encantadas," in the spring. The whole affair was unfortunate because the Harpers were offended and Melville lost the encouragement and support of his publishers when his creative energies were at their lowest ebb.

The little additional writing Melville managed before the spring planting season touched upon the theme of frustration in economic terms. It consisted of two pairs of contrasting sketches, "The Two Temples" and "Poor Man's Pudding and Rich Man's Crumbs," and the first was particularly effective in the use it made of the imprisonment image when the poor man who was excluded from the congregation of a wealthy church became locked in the bell tower. It was rejected by *Putnam's*, however, on the grounds that it might disturb the magazine's "church readers"; and if Melville had any deep or serious impulse to find further social and economic symbols for the "wall" around him he repressed it. Instead, he turned in the late spring to the historical novel he had planned in 1849. *Israel Potter; or, Fifty Years of Exile* was published serially in *Putnam's* and in book form (by Putnam rather than the Harpers) in the spring of 1855. Actually, he had little personal reason to get wrought up over the world's economic distinctions. He was making a living from his farm, his bank balance was increasing, and, although he satirized the mercenary spirit of Benjamin Franklin in *Israel Potter* and the cruel salesmanship of "The Lightning Rod Man," he presented the readers of *Harper's* for July 1854 with "The Happy Failure" — a man who had worked on an invention for as long as Melville himself had worked at writing and found kindness in his heart only when his device failed.

Yet Melville did not seriously consider himself a failure, as a writer or in any other way, and during the following winter he undertook one of the most ambitious and impressive of all his literary projects. It was to be the story of a South American slave ship, bound from Valparaiso to Callao, on which the slaves revolted, killed the owner, and forced the captain to promise to take them to Africa. Based upon a real story told by a New England ship's captain, Amasa Delano, it was focused on Captain Delano's gradual realization of the situation when the South American vessel appealed to him for help. It was one Melville could handle by developing its "significances" as he had developed those in *Moby Dick*, and it quite evidently appealed strongly to his imagination. Here was all he needed to enable him to project his deepest feelings out of himself and into the characters of a fiction — the Spanish captain, Don Benito Cereno, surrounded by an ominous crowd of blacks whose leader played the role of a devoted servant but was always prepared to cut his master's throat; and the New England captain who was aware that there was something beyond the wall of his perception and to whom the mystery could be unveiled in a dramatic climax. Here were the ships and the sea that Melville knew so well, the material for the plausibly grotesque symbolism he loved, and a number of technical legal documents he could expound upon. It did not have the dramatic possibilities of *Moby Dick*, but it had the potentialities of a great novel in the Gothic tradition, historically true in fact and so close to Melville's own experience in setting that he could let his imagination control it without the risk of implausible fantasy.

He proposed the book to *Putnam's* in March 1855, but the magazine had just acquired a new publisher whose new reader advised him to "decline any novel from Melville which is not extremely good." And the advice was apparently taken, at the worst of all possible times. For Melville was still estranged from the Harpers, and he had just experienced what his wife called "his first attack of severe rheumatism in his back—so that he was helpless." He also must have been deeply discouraged because in April he sent to the magazine the portion of the book he had written, complete with legal documents but without explanation. The reader complained of the "great pity that he did not work it up as a connected tale instead of putting the dreary documents at the end" but advised its acceptance on the grounds that it was Melville's "best style of subject" although he continued to fret that he "does everything too hurriedly now." After many delays it was published as a long short story, "Benito Cereno," and only a careful comparison of Melville's version of the "dreary documents at the end" with their originals gives a clue to the full substance of the novel Melville might have written had either he or his publishers possessed greater confidence in his energy and talents.

But he continued to write, and his writings show that he continued to search his own consciousness for fables of frustration. Marriage was one explanation he seems to have considered in "The Paradise of Bachelors and the Tartarus of Maids" in *Harper's* for April—although the allegory of gestation he introduced into the second part suggests that Elizabeth's pregnancy (with their second daughter, and fourth and last child) was more in his mind than marriage itself. "The Bell Tower" in the August *Putnam's*, however, was more serious, because it seems to have been closely connected in his mind with "Benito Cereno" and because it seems to be an introspective consideration of his own literary career. More flamboyant in style than any of his other stories, it was a parable of an overambitious architect who was destroyed by a flaw in his own work; and, for once, Melville made his meaning plain: "So the creator was killed by the creature. So the bell was too heavy for the tower. So the bell's main weakness was where man's blood had flawed it. And so pride went before the fall."

Herman Melville

From the point of view of popular success, his own work had been weakest when he put his human "blood" in it, and his pride was going rapidly before the crippling illness from which he suffered all summer. "I and My Chimney" (which was accepted by *Putnam's* in September but not published until the following March) is almost certainly a humorous account of the physical examination of his injured back rather than of his mental condition as some traditions have maintained. And it is this preoccupation with physical frustration which helps explain the peculiarities of *The Confidence Man* — the last piece of prose fiction he was to publish during his lifetime — which he wrote during the winter of 1855-56. The book is a double-bitted satire, attacking gullibility in its first part and cynicism in its last, and its imagery reflects and perhaps explains its attitude and tone. The parts first composed (including the story of China Aster interpolated in the latter part) are bitter, and they are also pervaded by the imagery of illness, disability, and twisted bones. The last part, written after Melville had begun to recover, has more of the tone of Shakespearean comedy with its hero in motley, an Autolycus playing the role of Touchstone. Melville in fact had returned to Shakespeare and had found in him, as the introductory sketch for the collection of *Piazza Tales* (published before *The Confidence Man* was completed) indicates, a means of relief and escape from bitterness. But the dramatic intensity which Shakespeare had inspired in *Moby Dick* was gone.

Melville, at the age of thirty-seven, seemed worn out. He had sold the productive half of his farm in the spring of 1856, and his family was worried about his health. Judge Shaw agreed to finance a trip to Europe and the Holy Land, and Melville left on October 11 for Scotland, England (where he saw Hawthorne), and the Mediterranean; he returned on May 20, 1857, with restored energy and the full notebook that his father-in-law doubtless hoped for. But he was not to return to writing. The firm of Dix and Edwards, which had been the most recent of his publishers, had been dissolved; and although he was invited to contribute to the new *Atlantic Monthly* he was persuaded that lecturing would be more profitable. Accordingly, for three years, he traveled the lecture circuit, going as far south as Tennessee and as far west as Chicago and Wisconsin, talking about "Roman Statuary," "The South Seas," and "Traveling — Its Pleasures and Pains." But he was not successful on the platform, and soon after the beginning of his third season he gave it up and decided to make a trip around the world on a sailing ship captained by his younger brother Tom.

He had amused himself by writing verses before he left, and he left behind a volume of poems for Elizabeth to publish if she could. Neither the volume nor the trip, however, materialized. The ship was indefinitely delayed in San Francisco, and Melville was homesick enough to hurry home by steamer. After the outbreak of the Civil War he tried in vain for a commission in the Navy and eventually managed to sell the rest of his Pittsfield property and move to New York City where he continued to write verses about the progress of the war. By the end of the hostilities he had almost enough to make a volume, and he filled it out and published, through the Harpers in 1866, *Battle-Pieces and Aspects of the War* with a prose supplement advocating peaceful reconciliation with the South. Although there was no question about his firm Union sympathies, the poems and the supplement were sufficiently detached from the strong political feelings of the day to make him properly eligible, during a period of reform, for appointment to a position he had been seeking for some years — that of deputy inspector in the New York Custom House. He received it in the early winter of 1866 and held it for nearly twenty years.

During these years Melville continued to be quietly but unprofessionally interested in writing. Poetry seemed to be the best means he found for occupying his mind, and the quantity of it increased as he filled the numerous quarter sheets he could conveniently carry around in his coat pocket. In 1870 he began buying books again (a sure symptom, in him, of literary activity) and in 1875 his secret could no longer be kept: "pray do not mention to any one that he is writing poetry," Elizabeth wrote her mother after revealing it; " — you know how such things spread and he would be very angry if he knew I had spoken of it." Yet within the confidence of the family his uncle Peter Gansevoort heard the report and generously offered to subsidize the publication of Melville's most ambitious work — a narrative poem of about eighteen thousand lines called *Clarel: A Poem and Pilgrimage in the Holy Land.*

Clarel was supposed to be a philosophical poem, based on Melville's own pilgrimage of nineteen years before, dealing with a young man's search for religious faith. But its imaginative design is that of a novel. The plot centers on a wandering pilgrimage undertaken by Clarel and a group of companions while he is waiting for his sweetheart Ruth to pass through a period of mourning for the death of her father. The time is between the symbolic dates of Epiphany and Ash Wednesday, and the climax occurs when Clarel returns to Jerusalem and finds that Ruth, too, has died and that such wisdom and faith as he has acquired must be subject to the test of deep and bitter emotion. And within this framework of design Melville placed the most extraordinary and interesting group of characters he had ever created: the mysterious hunchbacked Roman, Celio; Nathan, the Puritan Zionist from Illinois; the American recluse, Vine, who resembled Hawthorne; Nehemiah, the gentle, saintly version of Captain Ahab who had learned to accept the universe; the misanthropic Swede, Mortmain; Ungar, the embittered Confederate, with American Indian blood; the smoothly armored Anglican priest, Derwent; the eager believer, Rolfe, who is more bronzed in body than in mind and may have been an ironic partial portrait of Melville himself; and a score or more of others representing many nationalities and beliefs. Melville's interest in people and his knowledge of mankind had obviously increased enormously since he had quit writing fiction.

More significantly, though, he had become less interested in absolute truth and the means of attaining it than he had been in his youth. The conflict which had created the dramatic tension in *Moby Dick* had, in the course of a quarter century, become for him almost conventionally symbolized in the controversy between religion and science; and, although he used this at length in his poem, it no longer seriously bothered him. The psychological interests which had emerged in *Pierre* had become stronger and more diverse. He was more interested in the kinds of people who could hold such a variety of beliefs with such great ranges of intensity. Human beings would always find symbols for their emotions of faith and despair, he decided, and inspiration, observation, and introspection were simply different means of obtaining emotional satisfaction instead of being conflicting ways to "truth."

In the light of this change in the direction of Melville's imaginative development it seems a pity that he did not write his poetry early and his novels late in life. For *Clarel*, fascinating though it is in many respects, is not a great or even a good poem. The major characters are entirely too discursive, and their discourse is often hard to follow in the jingling octosyllabics in which most of it is composed. It was less designed for popularity, in fact, than any other of Melville's works; and when it appeared, in two volumes, on June 3, 1876, it was almost completely ignored.

Yet a return to print had a stimulating effect on Melville, and although he was almost a completely forgotten author he spent a good deal of time during the last years of his life gathering his literary resources. He had poems from his last years in the Berkshires, poems from his trip abroad that he called "Fruit of Travel Long Ago," and other poems called "Sea Pieces" that he had written from time to time. He was also experimenting and was to continue to experiment with prose sketches of picturesque individuals and appropriate poems to go with them. Near the end of his life he was to publish two small volumes of verse in limited editions of twenty-five copies for his friends (*John Marr and Other Sailors* in 1888, and *Timoleon* in 1891) and was to collect and organize for publication at least two more. The best of the poems are those that preserve or seem to preserve the fresh emotions of some special occasion or the retrospective pieces (such as "After the Pleasure Party," among the longer ones) of a man who continued to be puzzled by the many mysteries of life but had become content to make the best of his own. Yet his final burst of creative energy and one of the finest works of his imagination was not in the form of poetry but in the prose fiction he had completely neglected for over a generation.

Billy Budd, Sailor differs from Melville's earlier novels because it was a mature and successfully controlled outgrowth of the inquisitiveness about human behavior which made *Clarel* so remarkable. It developed out of one of his experiments in combining prose and verse, such as the one he published as "John Marr" — an introductory sketch of a remarkably handsome young sailor who was condemned to be hanged as the ringleader of an incipient mutiny and who expressed his last sentiments in a ballad composed on the eve of the execution. But Billy, as he crept into Melville's imagination with all the physical signs of noble birth, seems to have been difficult to sketch. He appears to have first been imagined as guilty and then as innocent of the charge, and the conception of innocence was the germ from which the story grew. Why should an innocent man be hanged? The best inference to be drawn from the surviving working manuscript is that Melville's first impulse was to answer that he was a victim of another man's wickedness. He had personally known, if the record of *White Jacket* can be trusted, a ship's master-at-arms with an evil sadistic genius beneath a bland exterior, and he was acutely aware of the power for evil that a malicious person in such a position might possess. Out of his memory and still-indignant awareness he created the character of John Claggart who was to accuse the innocent Billy of a crime and be killed by a spontaneous blow from the speechless sailor. And for this, under the Articles of War, Billy had to be hanged.

Yet Melville had learned that the world was far too complex to be pictured in black and white. Evil and goodness might exist side by side, as he made clear in the almost allegorical exaggeration of these qualities in Claggart and Billy, but reality was in between. Billy had not struck "through the mask" of anything (as Ahab had tried to do) by hitting Claggart. Justice was not absolute, as Pierre had believed, but man-made. Billy had to be hanged not as a matter of course but by decision of court-martial. And Melville also had within his experience a court-martial such as Billy would have had to endure: his cousin, Guert Gansevoort, had presided over such a one under the direction of Captain Alexander Mackenzie of the brig *Somers* in 1842 and had hanged the son of the secretary of war on a similar charge. The affair had created a scandal which was being revived at the time Melville was working on the *Billy Budd* manuscript and it was still a family mystery that Guert should have been almost broken by his action while insisting that it "was *approved* of God." Here was a mystery that appealed to the mature Melville more than the mystery of Iago.

So, as his manuscript went through its various later stages of painful revision, he created the character of Captain Vere, master of H.M.S. *Indomitable* (or *Bellipotent*, as he finally decided to call it) during the Napoleonic wars, who resembled both Guert Gansevoort and Captain Mackenzie and was a wise and good man who loved Billy as a son but forced a reluctant court to condemn him to death. He talked privately with Billy to such effect that Billy died with the words "God bless Captain Vere" on his lips. But the captain was not blessed. He was haunted. He himself died murmuring the words — though not in accents of remorse — "Billy Budd, Billy Budd."

Billy Budd has almost as many meanings to as many readers as *Moby Dick*, and perhaps for the same reasons. It has the hidden ambivalence of any work of art which grows by accretion rather than by design, the ambiguity that is found in any intelligent and honest attempt to solve a profound problem of human behavior, and the power which an author only manages to get into a book when he succeeds in capturing in his own person the major tensions of his age. For the problem that bothered Melville in *Billy Budd* was not the problem of knowledge that had worried him in his youth. It was the problem of man. Is he a social being, responsible to the welfare of the society to which he belongs? Or is he an independent moral individual, responsible to his private awareness of guilt and innocence? This was the dilemma Captain Vere faced when, in Melville's fiction, the preservation of discipline in the British fleet was absolutely requisite to the preservation of England's freedom. Melville's solution was to make him behave as a social being but pay a penalty by suffering the private agonies of his private conscience.

The problem, however, was not a fictitious one. When Melville finished the last revision of his manuscript, on April 19, five months before his death in 1891, society had become far more complex than it had been when he dealt with the validity of individual awareness in *Moby Dick* forty years before. *Billy Budd* was not to be published until 1924, many years after its author's death. But the problem with which it dealt has not lessened with the passing years. Man's relationship to his private self and to the society in which he dwells is still the greatest source of tension of modern times. And one of Herman Melville's strong claims to greatness is that his imaginative development kept abreast of the times — despite neglect and adversity and more than one failure, the acuteness and depth of his sensitivity never failed.

His strongest claim, however, may be based upon an imagination which reached ahead of its times and provided for posterity a unique literary mirror in which it could examine itself. *Moby Dick* is like no other novel of the nineteenth century. Part drama and part personal narrative, it permits a hero to have the stage and compel that willing suspension of disbelief which is the essence of dramatic art. But, when belief becomes too great a strain, it permits escape through the person of a narrator who is sometimes a detached observer, skeptical commentator, or active participant in the action and sometimes an amusing, scholarly, and reminiscent author. Most twentieth-century intellectuals are part Ahab and part Ishmael — using symbols to master an overwhelming naturalistic universe while suspecting that the effort might be neurotic — and to them the form and rhetoric of *Moby Dick* has a powerful appeal. Melville's sensitivity to man's suspicion of his private self is the source of his greatest fascination to modern minds.

Mark Twain

꙰Most Americans regard Mark Twain with special affection. They know him as a shaggy man who told stories of boy adventures so like their own or those they would like to have had that they become intimately a part of personal experience. His cheerful irreverence and unhurried pace seem antidotes for attitudes to which they necessarily but unwillingly surrender. His is the image of what they like to think Americans have been or can be: humorously perceptive, undeceived by sham, successful in spite of circumstance because of distinctive personal characteristics.

More often than not they smile approvingly at his portrayal of man as "a museum of diseases, a home of impurities," who "begins as dirt and departs as stench," created for no apparent purpose except the nourishment and entertainment of microbes. The words seem bold and appropriately bitter, iconoclastically vulgar but, for all of that, funny. Evolution failed when man appeared, for his is the only bad heart in all the animal kingdom; only he is capable of malice, vindictiveness, drunkenness; when he is not cruel, he is stupid, like a sheep. It does seem such a pity, commented Mark Twain, that Noah and his companions did not miss their boat. And he tempts readers toward the compulsive nightmare of our time by wondering if a device might not be invented which could exterminate man by withdrawing all oxygen from the air for two minutes.

They admire Mark Twain's hardheaded exposures of human venality, but respond also to his unembarrassed sentiment, his compassion and simple humility. What any man sees in the human race, he once admitted, "is merely himself in the deep and private honesty of his own heart." Everything human is pathetic: "The secret source of Humor itself is not joy but sorrow. There is no humor in heaven." He would have agreed with Robert Frost that earth is the right place for love, but would have added that it is inevitably also the place for stumbling and then forgetting the hurt by recalling or inventing other, older, and less disreputable times.

No wonder then that Ernest Hemingway found all American literature to begin with Mark Twain. His escape to adventure, to the past, to humor which moves through and beyond reality, is not unlike Hemingway's escape from thinking through the simpler pleasures of wine, women, and manly exercise. Not only is Mark Twain's simple declarative style a parent of Hemingway's style; not only is his boy's-eye view of the world like Hemingway's view, like Willa Cather's, Sherwood Anderson's, even J. D. Salinger's; the publication of *The Mysterious Stranger* in 1916 reveals him mastered by the same cluster of opinions which produced the retreat to older times of Henry Adams, as well as the despair of the "lost generation" of Hemingway and Scott Fitzgerald, and the wasted land of T. S. Eliot.

It was as difficult to convince people of his time as it is to convince people of ours that Mark Twain never really existed except as a character, costumed and carefully rehearsed, cannily a crowd-pleaser. For in both a literary and psychological sense the shambling but perceptive humorist remembered as Mark Twain is a mask, a controlled, drawling, and whimsical voice, a posturing and flamboyant figure, behind which exists the man, Samuel Langhorne Clemens, who with the help of circumstance and receptive wit created him. Some would explain them, the image and the man, as twins, and Clemens as a man divided, but this is not in any real sense true. The image is partly self-portrait and, indeed, partly self-defense, but shrewdly retouched until the character who is Mark Twain becomes Clemens' most successful achievement, and the voice of Mark Twain speaks in a special literary relation to its creator.

It is probably true that the two became as confused in Clemens' mind as they have in the minds of people who have talked about Mark Twain, but the distinction is radical. Which is which or who did what to whom remains an important critical puzzle. To simplify more than is appropriate, it can be suggested that Mark Twain was a character who inserted himself, sometimes with joyous abandon, into almost everything which Samuel Clemens wrote. He was irrepressible but self-conscious, alert to his responsibilities as diagnostic spokesman for his time and as representative of much which wove itself into the pattern of contemporary notions of success. But failure to remember that Mark Twain was a medium through whom stories were told, and that he was only in an indirect sense their author, is to fall into the attractively baited trap which opens even more invitingly before commentators on such other American writers as Whitman, Thoreau, and Hemingway, whose masks are more subtle and less clearly designated.

Which spoke when cannot always be determined, nor is the distinction in every case important, except that in some of the writings, and many of them the best, the burden of being Mark Twain is discarded and a voice speaks directly, undistorted by comic pose or anger. Either could have admitted, as one of them did, that his books were like water and the books of great geniuses like wine, but it was surely Mark Twain who supplied the twister to remind us that "everyone drinks water." Part of his character was that of a man among litterateurs, a journalist who detested, he said, novels and poetry, but who liked history, biography, curious facts, and strange happenings.

But it has not been necessary for Americans to read Mark Twain in order to remember him with affection. Probably more people know of Tom Sawyer's slick method of getting a fence whitewashed than have read the book in which it appears. Hollywood versions of Tom and Huck, of the prince who became a pauper, or of the Yankee from Connecticut who brought American know-how to King Arthur's court have reached millions of viewers, as originally filmed or as adapted for television. A popular comedian has danced and sung his way through a celluloid Camelot. A spectacular Negro boxer has played the runaway slave whose simple loyalty confuses, then converts, Huck Finn. Tom Sawyer has tripped barefooted through a musical comedy, and plans have been considered for a musical adaptation of *Innocents Abroad*. More than one actor has found it profitable to dress and drawl as Mark Twain did, and to hold an audience laughter-bound by retelling some of the tales he told.

Mark Twain's laconic, soft speech, whimsical understatements, and outrageous exaggerations made him a platform favorite and pampered after-dinner speaker for more than forty years, and his witticisms were passed by word of mouth and faithfully recorded in newspapers. He saw to that, for he was in every best sense a showman who kept himself and his books effectively before the public. His heavy shock of hair, once red, but soon an eye-catching white, made him seem larger than he was, an illusion which it pleased him later in life to reinforce by dressing summer and winter in white serge or flannel. He learned early how to attract and hold attention, and he used the knowledge well. One way or another, he was the best known and most successfully published author of his generation.

He saw to that also, for — within limits — he was the canny businessman he liked to think himself. His lectures sold his books, and his books helped pack his lectures. As a publisher, he took pride in gauging public taste so well that each book supplied a popular demand. Many were not issued until subscription agents throughout the country had sold in advance enough copies to make them surely profitable. And subscription books in the late nineteenth century were gaudily attractive books, usually handsomely bound and illustrated — the kind almost anyone would be proud to have on his table, particularly when the author had just been or would soon be in town for a lecture.

For these reasons, though not only for these, Mark Twain's books found themselves in a preferred position in thousands of American homes. At the end of the century, he offered a twenty-two-volume Autograph Edition of his works, which found its way into thousands more, and into libraries, even small town and county libraries which could not afford to buy it but received it as a gift when house shelves became crowded or when it was replaced by the new, twenty-five-volume Underwood Edition a few years later. Shortly before Mark Twain's death in 1910 the Author's National Edition began to appear, and then, in the 1920's, the "definitive edition" in thirty-seven volumes. Few authors, perhaps not even Balzac or Dickens, achieved greater shelf space during their lifetime.

Such success has seemed appropriate, for it fit precisely to patterns which Americans have thought peculiarly their own. Mark Twain was a poor boy who by reason of native skill rose to wealth and fame. He was kin to Daniel Boone or Andrew Jackson because he had known the rigors of our frontier. Abraham Lincoln's rise from log cabin to President created a norm of which his career was a verifying variation — indeed, Howells called him the Lincoln of our literature. He had worked with his hands, like Andrew Carnegie, and then had a large house and servants. These things testified to the validity of what Emerson had said of the divine sufficiency of the individual. Here in truth was the powerful, uneducated democratic personality for whom Whitman had called. Mark Twain walked with kings and capitalists, but never lost the common touch. In his mansion at Hartford, his residence on Fifth Avenue, or his country place at Stormfield, he still remembered old times and old friends.

This popular image was never completely an accurate likeness, but is sufficiently well drawn to remain attractive. Samuel Langhorne Clemens was born on November 30, 1835, on the Missouri frontier, in a straggling log village called Florida, to which his parents had come from their former home among the hills of Tennessee. His father was a local magistrate and small merchant, originally from Virginia, who had studied law in Kentucky and there met and married auburn-haired Jane Lampton, descended from settlers who had followed Daniel Boone across the mountains. One among thousands of Americans who in the early decades of the nineteenth century moved westward to seek opportunities in newly opened lands, John Marshall Clemens did not prosper in the hamlet in which his third son was born, and so, when Samuel was four years old, moved to Hannibal, a larger town with a population of almost five hundred, on the banks of the Mississippi River.

There, beside this river, Samuel Clemens grew through boyhood much as Tom Sawyer did, fascinated by the life which swarmed over its mile-wide surface or which sought refuge or sustenance on its shores. Through this frontier region passed the picturesque, sometimes mendacious or menacing, pilgrims of restlessly expanding America, up or down the river or across it toward the western plains. Young Samuel must have watched, as any boy might, admiringly, but fearfully also. He saw men maimed or killed in waterfront brawls, Negroes chained like animals for transportation to richer slave markets to the south. He had nightmares and walked in his sleep, and always remembered these things, the rude ways and tremendous talk, and the terror.

Better things were remembered also, like giant rafts and trading scows piled with produce or sweet-smelling timber, coming from or going where a boy could only guess. Gallant river steamers left wake behind in which small boys swimming or in boats could ride excitedly. Below the village lay wooded Holliday Hill, unrivaled for play at Robin Hood or pirate, and near its summit a cave tempted to exploration. Away from its boisterous riverfront, the village was "a heavenly place for a boy," he said, providing immunities and graces which he never forgot: hunting and fishing, a swimming hole, an inevitable graveyard, truant days at Glasscock's Island, and yearnings toward the better freedom of Tom Blankenship, the town drunkard's son, to whom truancy brought no penalties of conscience or recrimination.

But these days were soon over, for when Samuel was twelve years old, his father died, and the boy was apprenticed to local printers, and then — partaking of a tradition which Benjamin Franklin had established a century before — worked as compositor and pressman for his older brother Orion, who managed a not completely successful newspaper in Hannibal. There was room in its pages for humorous features which young Samuel composed, set in type, and printed over the flamboyant signature of "W. Spaminodas Adrastas Blab" and for miscellaneous items which he collected for "Our Assistant's Column." He even ventured verse, addressing one poem over the signature of "Rambler" ambiguously to "Miss Katie in H——l." The appropriation of so time-worn a pseudonym seems less indicative of literary consciousness than descriptive of desire. Samuel Clemens was not yet a rambler, though he wanted to be, for — again like Franklin — he chaffed under the discipline of a brother, or anyone else.

By the time he was seventeen he was able to think of himself as something more than a local writer. In May 1852 "The Dandy Frightening the Squatter" appeared in the *Carpet-Bag*, a sportsman's magazine in Boston, signed "S.L.C." Done in the slapstick tradition of native humor such as was being written or was soon to be written by pseudonymous favorites like Sam Slick, Orpheus C. Kerr, and Artemus Ward, it anticipates much of the later manner of Mark Twain: it celebrates the laconic shrewdness of the frontiersman; is told with some of the exaggerated flourishes of the western tall tale, seasoned with caricaturing strokes which may have been learned, even indirectly, from Dickens; and is laid in Hannibal on the Mississippi River. Comparison of its tone and language with Nathaniel Hawthorne's *The Blithedale Romance* or Herman Melville's *Pierre*, which also appeared in that year, suggests some of the things which, for better or worse, were happening or about to happen to writing in the United States.

But wanderlust soon hit young Samuel Clemens, so that he became in fact a rambler. At eighteen he left little Hannibal for St. Louis, the largest town in Missouri, where he saved his wages carefully until he could strike out beyond the limits of his western state, to discover whether a young man's fortune might not be more quickly made in larger cities to the east. He traveled first, by steamboat and rail, through Chicago and Buffalo, to New York, where he worked briefly as a job printer, until he moved southward to become a compositor in Philadelphia and later Washington, then again to Philadelphia, then west to Muscatine, Iowa, to set type for his almost equally peripatetic brother. Soon he was back in St. Louis, and then once more, for two years this time, joined his brother, now in Keokuk, Iowa.

Two years, however, was a long time for a rambler to remain in one place, and his fortune certainly was not being made. He spent the winter of 1856-57 in Cincinnati, but this was a way stop, for he had hit on the notion that a young man almost twenty-two might do well and have fun besides exploring opportunities for riches in South America, along the lush banks of the Amazon. So it was that in April 1857 — the date is a turning point — he started down the Mississippi toward New Orleans, on his first step toward fame. What happened then — his meeting with the veteran steamboat pilot Horace Bixby, his own apprentice pilot days, his four years of life on the Mississippi — has often been told, and never better than by Clemens himself as he later remembered these years and threw about them the color of romance which only made more persuasive the realism of his detail.

But the abortive trip to South America is remembered for other reasons also, for to make it Samuel Clemens entered into a professional engagement of a kind which later would bring him worldwide acclaim. At Keokuk he shaped the first piece of the pattern which would make continued wanderings possible, even profitable, by arranging with the editor of the *Evening Post* that Samuel Clemens, rambler, would supply reports as regularly as possible on what he saw and did on his ramblings. Only three now appeared, probably because Clemens was deep in the more exciting business of learning to pilot a steamboat. Signed "Thomas Jefferson Snodgrass," they were desperately, self-consciously humorous, hardly distinguishable in language or tone from the work of any other journeyman journalist.

Snodgrass was a name always infinitely funny to Clemens. He used it again in writings in California; more than thirty years later in *The American Claimant* he presented two characters, "Zylobalsamum Snodgrass" and "Spinal Meningitis Snodgrass"; and in *Tom Sawyer Abroad* he spoke of the "celebrated author . . . Snodgrass." While steamboating on the Mississippi from 1857 to 1861, a licensed pilot by the spring of 1859, he is said to have contributed letters signed "Quintius Curtius Snodgrass" to the New Orleans *Daily Crescent*, and is said also to have written a burlesque of the pontifical river lore which a retired steamboat captain named Isaiah Sellers printed in a New Orleans paper over the signature of "Mark Twain." A favorite but unverifiable tradition insists that Captain Sellers was so hurt by the ridicule and Samuel Clemens so conscience-stricken at the wound he had given that a few years later the younger man adopted the old captain's pseudonym — which, as everyone knows, is the leadsman's cry to the pilot when water which is safe, but barely safe, lies ahead.

When in 1861 the Civil War cut across the Mississippi so that river traffic from north to south or south to north was no longer possible, steamboating ceased to be a profitable occupation, and Samuel Clemens was without work. He took only a minor part in the war between the states: one not very dependable account suggests that he was detailed for river duty; the New Orleans Snodgrass letters suggest that he had some connection with militia drill in that city; and Mark Twain later delighted readers of the *Atlantic Monthly* with a humorous "Private History of a Campaign That Failed," which tells how he and a few companions formed themselves into an irregular company which searched vainly for a unit of the Confederate Army to which it might become attached. Whatever his service, it was brief and with the rebellious southern forces — a circumstance which is supposed to have made the later northernized Mark Twain extraordinarily circumspect in speaking of it.

In the summer of 1861 Clemens went farther west, with his brother Orion who had been rewarded for activity in Abraham Lincoln's campaign for the presidency by appointment as secretary of the newly opened Nevada Territory. Orion Clemens, never greatly successful, had little money, but brother Samuel, after profitable years as a river pilot, apparently had his pockets full and provided stage fare for both, traveling himself as unpaid secretary to the new secretary of the territory. The story of their journey across the plains and experiences in Carson City is later recounted in *Roughing It*, in which, as Huck Finn said of him on another occasion, "Mr. Mark Twain . . . he told the truth, mainly." Here we learn of his adventures in staking out timber claims near Lake Tahoe, only carelessly to leave his campfire unattended so that much of the forest went up in flames. He tells of money invested in silver mines, as he and Orion were caught up in a wild seeking for wealth. Once he was a millionaire for ten days when he found a rich mine, but lost it through carelessness again. Stories of Samuel Clemens in Nevada, variously told by himself or by people who knew him, make up a large share of the public image of Mark Twain. A loose, shambling man, with unruly hair, who lounged about the frontier town in corduroys and shirt sleeves, swapping stories and listening to the way men spoke, he was ready, we are told, to take his chance with the best or worst at poker or in wildcat speculation.

Before he had been in Nevada a year, however, he was back at his old trade as a writer for newspapers, contributing burlesque sketches over the signature of "Josh" to the *Territorial Enterprise* in Virginia City. There he lived freely among friends like fiery Steve Gillis, a printer whose escapades were to keep them both in trouble. The unrestraint of that remarkable frontier paper stimulated Clemens to such journalistic hoaxes as "The Petrified Man" and "The Dutch Nick Massacre," which to his joy were copied as true in eastern papers. Here he first met Artemus Ward and spent convivial evenings with the popular humorist, who advised him how Mark Twain — for Clemens was now using that name — might extend his reputation. Already known as the Washoe Giant, the wild humorist of the Sage Brush Hills, famed as far as California, Samuel Clemens was ambitious for something more.

But then he ran afoul of an anti-dueling statute when he challenged a rival newspaperman, and he and loyal Steve Gillis beat their way in the spring of 1864 to California, where a range of hills stood between them and Nevada jails. Clemens worked briefly as a reporter on the *San Francisco Call*, but it was "fearful drudgery," he said, "an awful slavery for a lazy man," so he left regular employment to free-lance for the *Golden Era* and Bret Harte's *Cali-*

fornian. Then he became San Francisco correspondent for his former paper in Virginia City, until he ran headlong against the law again when Steve Gillis was arrested for barroom brawling and released on bail which Clemens supplied. Then when dapper Steve skipped over the mountains back to Nevada, his protector thought it appropriate to leave also.

This time he took flight to the Sierras, where he stayed on Jackass Hill with Steve Gillis' brother Jim, a teller of tales who was to receive later renown as Bret Harte's "Truthful James." Here, at Angel's Camp, he heard old Ross Coon tell of "The Celebrated Jumping Frog of Calaveras County." Clemens wrote it down, this "villainous, backwoods sketch," in just the rhythm of dialect in which Ross Coon told it, and he sent it east for place in a book of yarns to which Artemus Ward had asked him to contribute. By fortunate mischance it arrived too late for burial in Ward's collection. Instead, it was pirated by the *New York Evening Post* and became an immediate favorite, copied in newspapers all across the country, even in California to give its author prestige there as an eastern writer. For all the good it did him — he made nothing from it.

At just this time, in 1865, the Pacific Steamboat Company began regular passenger service between San Francisco and Honolulu, and Clemens took the trip, paying for it with letters to the *Sacramento Union*, thus setting to final form the pattern which four years later was to establish Mark Twain's reputation with *Innocents Abroad*. These Sandwich Island letters are exuberant, and sometimes vulgar. With him traveled an imaginary, completely irrepressible companion named Mr. Brown, whose sweetheart, he boasted, was so elegant that she picked her nose with a fork. When passengers became seasick, "Brown was there, ever kind and thoughtful, passing from one to the other and saying, 'That's all right — that's all right you know — it'll clean you out like a jog, and then you won't feel so awful and smell so ridiculous.'" It was good for Mark Twain to have someone to hide behind, and good especially for Samuel Clemens who could disguise timidities doubly removed.

Mark Twain

Mark Twain liked these lovely Pacific islands: "I would rather smell Honolulu at sunset," he wrote, "than the old Police court-room in San Francisco." And he liked the islanders who "always squat on their hams and who knows but they may be the original 'ham sandwiches.' " He liked their customs, especially the "demoralizing *hula hula*" which was forbidden "save at night, with closed doors . . . by permission of the authorities and the payment of ten dollars for the same." Sometimes he became almost lyrical about the beauties of the islands, but when he did, Mr. Brown pulled him up short to remind him that there were also in Honolulu "more 'sentipedes' and scorpions and spiders and mosquitoes and missionaries" than anywhere else in the world.

Clemens had now found the work which suited him best: he could ramble as he pleased and pay his way by being informative and funny, and donning masks which might excuse irresponsibility. In December 1866 he signed with the *Alta California*, the West's most prominent paper, as its "travelling correspondent . . . not stinted as to place, time or direction," who would circle the globe and write letters as he went. The first step in the journey was to New York, the long way around, by boat, and with the ebullient Mr. Brown beside him. The letters written then are more lively than any he had done before, and without the restraints in concession to taste of his later travel accounts. Here he presents the jovial Captain Wakeman, whose tall tales, profanity, and Biblical lore were to live again in Captain Blakely in *Roughing It* and in Captain Stormfield who made a voyage to heaven. There is sentimentality in the account of a runaway couple married at sea, and slapstick aplenty in Mr. Brown's further inelegant concern with seasick passengers, but there is compassion also as Mark Twain writes of the misery of cholera in Nicaragua, and anger as he snarls at gouging Floridians.

When he arrives in New York, the letters take on fresh vigor, and reveal much which is sometimes said to be characteristic of an older Mark Twain. The "overgrown metropolis" had changed mightily since he had seen it thirteen years before when he was a "pure and sinless sprout." He looked with indignation now on the squalor of her slums where the "criminally, sinfully, wickedly poor" lived amid filth and refuse, victims of their "good, kind-hearted, fat, benevolent" neighbors. His social investigations came to climax when he was arrested for disorderly conduct and spent the night in jail, enraged as he talked with tramps, prostitutes, and former soldiers, pawns at the mercy of society's whim. It is not necessary to turn to a later Mark Twain for records of pessimism which damns the whole human race. It is solidly a part of him at thirty. Sin bothered him, even when he was being funny about it.

In New York he saw to the publication of his first book, *The Celebrated Jumping Frog of Calaveras County and Other Sketches*, just as he set out again to continue his wanderings, not around the world, but on an excursion to the Mediterranean and Near East on the steamship *Quaker City*. The letters which he sent back then, to the California paper and also to Horace Greeley's *Tribune* in New York, reached a public ripe for appreciation of his confident assumption that many hallowed shrines of the Old World did not measure to American standards. And such was public response to what he wrote that, when he returned to New York a few months later, the wild mustang of the western plains discovered himself a literary lion, sought by magazines, newspapers, lecture audiences, and publishers.

Caught up by currents of popularity, Samuel Clemens from this time forward was swept from one success to another. He had struck his bonanza, not in silver as he had once dreamed, but in selling his jocund alter ego in print and from the platform. He met and, after dogged courtship, married Olivia Langdon, daughter of a wealthy New York industrialist. With money advanced by his future father-in-law, he bought a share in a newspaper in Buffalo. The rambler finally would settle down, not permanently as an editor, for that occupation soon palled, but in a magnificent house which royalties and lecture fees would allow him to build in Hartford. He was through, he said, "with literature and all that bosh."

But when *The Innocents Abroad; or, The New Pilgrim's Progress* appeared in 1869, revised from the *Quaker City* letters (with Mr. Brown's offensive commentary, for example, deleted), review-

ers found it "fresh, racy, and sparkling as a glass of champagne."
The satire was alert, informed, sophisticated, and sidesplittingly
funny. The accent was of western humor, but the subject, a favorite among men of good will since the Enlightenment of the century
before, spoke of the decay of transatlantic institutions and their
shoddiness beside the energetic freshness of the New World. Traveling American innocents haggled through native bazaars, delight-
edly conscious that every language but their own was ridiculous,
and unconscious completely of their own outlandishness. Venice
was magnificent, though her boatmen were picturesquely absurd,
but the Arno at Florence was darkened by blood shed by the Me-
dici on its shores. The Holy Land was hot and dirty, filled with
beggars and larcenous dragomans — when confronted by a boat-
man at Galilee who demanded exorbitant fare, one of the pilgrims
remarked, "No wonder Jesus walked." Because he was clever or
because he was by nurture one of them, Clemens touched attitudes
shared by many of his countrymen, even to admitting preference
for copies of masterpieces because they were brighter than the
originals.

To many readers *The Innocents Abroad* remains Clemens' sec-
ond-best book, finding place in their affection behind *The Adventures of Huckleberry Finn* and just ahead of, or side by side
with, *Life on the Mississippi*. As if anticipating Henry James, it
takes a fresh look at the transatlantic world and the stature of
Americans when measured against its requirements. Without
James's subtlety, conscious art, or depth of penetration, it discovers faults on both sides so that it becomes a book which cosmopo-
lites and chauvinists can equally admire. The hearty and headlong
inelegance of the earlier, more carelessly devised travel letters has
been pruned from it, and not only because Mark Twain was sur-
rendering to prudish and Victorian notions of propriety. In sub-
mitting to the demands of public taste, Clemens was also learning
something of the possibilities of converting a casual colloquialism
to art.

Roughing It, in 1871, was also greatly successful, suited, said one
commentator, "to the wants of the rich, the poor, the sad, the gay,"

and a sure recipe for laughter. Again it was a book of traveling, the kind that Mark Twain was always to write best, in which one story after another was strung along a journey overland or on water. Every ingredient was here — the tall tale, the straight-faced shocker, melodrama in adventure, insight into raw life among men unrestrained by convention, folklore and animal lore. The effect was of improvisation, for narrative must flow, Clemens later said, as a stream flows, diverted by every boulder, but proceeding briskly, interestingly, on its course.

Such motion did not characterize *The Gilded Age*, published in 1873, which he wrote in collaboration with his Hartford neighbor, Charles Dudley Warner. For the opening chapters Clemens drew on recollections of frontier life to produce situations not unlike those we associate with *Tobacco Road* or *Li'l Abner*, where back-country people dream expansively of fortunes they have neither energy nor ability to acquire. Colonel Beriah Sellers is a hill-town Mr. Micawber, but drawn from memory of people, even relatives, whom Samuel Clemens had known. Some of the river scenes are beautifully realized. And as the locale shifts to Washington and New York, the novel touches with satirical humor on political corruption, the American jury system, and the mania for speculation, so that it became a best seller and gave title to the age which it reviewed. But artistically it was not a success, for the narrative finally collapses under the weight of plot and counterplot, and is not remembered as one of Mark Twain's best.

Given a story to tell, Clemens was almost always able to tell it well. As raconteur he had come to maturity in *Innocents Abroad*. But the invention of stories did not come easily to him. As he approached forty, he felt written out. He collected miscellaneous writings in *Sketches Old and New* and, with an eye on the market, tried to fit further adventures of the popular Colonel Sellers into a new book which failed to go well but which he published many years later, in 1891, as *The American Claimant*. He labored over a boy's story based on his early life in Hannibal, but that did not go well either.

Finally, at the suggestion of a friend, he recalled his years of steamboating and wrote, with hardly any posturing at all, of "Old Times on the Mississippi" in seven installments for the *Atlantic Monthly* in 1875. Eight years later he was to add thirty-nine chapters to make the book called *Life on the Mississippi*, but the added material, arduously compiled, recaptures little of the charm of these earlier portions. In them the viewpoint is consistently that of a boy bound by the spell of the Mississippi who becomes a pilot and learns her secrets. It is a story of an initiation. Seen from the pilothouse, the river loses much of her glamour; beneath her beauty, painted by sun and shaded by clouds, lurked an implacable menace of snags, hidden reefs, and treacherously changing shores. The face of the water was a wonderful book, he said, which he was never to forget, and piloting was a profession Clemens loved more than any he followed again: "a pilot in those days was the only unfettered and entirely independent human being that lived on the earth."

On the river he became "personally and familiarly acquainted with about all the different types of human nature to be found in fiction, biography, or history." He never read of or met anyone again without "warm personal interest in him, for the reason that I had known him before — met him on the river." But for all its attention to remembered detail, "Old Times on the Mississippi" was not in strictest sense realistic. Its narrator seldom looked aside to notice people not admitted to the pilothouse, like the sharpers, gamblers, and painted women who plied a profitable trade on Mississippi steamers, but kept his eyes on the river and his mind on the discipline she demanded from men who knew her charm but also her mystery and menace, who were skilled, not only in finding their own way among her dangers, but in guiding others safely through. Thus a reminiscent account becomes more than re-creation of times that are gone and will not return because steamboating, like the whaling of which Melville wrote in *Moby Dick*, was the product of a way of life which was past. It speaks of appearance as opposed to reality, of innocence and experience, of man's duty in a world of perils, and also of a conception of the function of literature.

The Mississippi River appeared triumphantly again in *The Adventures of Tom Sawyer* which in 1876 placed Mark Twain once more at the head of best-seller lists. Probably no more continuingly popular book has ever appeared in the United States. On first reading it seems loose and shambling — as Mark Twain was loose and shambling. Episodes designed "to pleasantly remind adults of what they once were themselves" often remain longer in memory than the plot of murder and pursuit which must have been intended to hold younger readers. But there is artistry in it also, beyond the artistry of the raconteur who engraved minor realisms about provincial society for all time. Perhaps because he worked long over it, this first independent novel, published when its author was forty, is better constructed than any he was to write again. And its structure reveals levels of meaning which Mark Twain may not have known were there.

The story is divided into three almost exactly equal parts. There are ten chapters in the first part, ten in the second, and thirteen in the climactic third. The first part is separated from the second and the second from the third, each by an interchapter. Within each of the three parts events are detailed carefully, time moves slowly, incident by incident, day by day. In the interchapters time is accelerated, and weeks go by within a few pages. Each of the parts is different from the others in tone, in the kind of adventures in which Tom involves himself, and in the relationship of these adventures to the unifying theme of the whole.

The first ten chapters reveal boys engaged in characteristic play, stealing jam, playing hookey, swapping treasured belongings, until finally they visit a graveyard at midnight and there inadvertently witness a murder. Time has been chronicled exactly, from Friday afternoon to Monday night, but then in the first interchapter, Muff Potter is arrested for the crime which the boys know he did not commit, and two weeks pass. The second part, Chapters 12 through 21, is divided into two major episodes, the Jackson Island adventure and the last day at school. Again time slows down, the boys are again at play, but no longer at simple play of boys among themselves for their own ends: it is directed now against adults, as if in revolt against what the world holds for boys who grow, as Tom has grown, beyond simple innocence to knowledge and, indirectly, participation in evil. After the second interchapter in which summer days are quickened by the boys' guilty knowledge of Muff's innocence, the plot moves to a cluttered climax. In the last thirteen chapters the boys begin to act tentatively as adults act. Tom gives evidence in court, he and Huck stalk Injun Joe in a serious, common-sense manner, and they search for treasure which is real and not an imagined product of boyish play. But then Tom shucks off responsibility and goes to a picnic, leaving matter-of-fact Huck to watch for the murderer. And Huck does discover him but only to frighten him into hiding from which he may emerge to strike again. No adult or even adult-like action succeeds in *The Adventures of Tom Sawyer*. In the first part, Aunt Polly is foiled in efforts to have Tom whitewash a fence. In the second part, grownups arrange a funeral for boys who are not dead and the schoolmaster loses his toupee. Now, as the story draws to an end, bumbling adult planning goes astray, and Tom and Becky are lost in the cave for hours before search for them begins. But adult search does not find them, any more than adult efforts do away with the evil which is Injun Joe. Tom's imaginative exploration at the end of a string brings them to safety. Even when adults seal the mouth of the cave, it is not to capture the murderer, but to prevent a recurrence of Tom's kind of adventuring. This notion of the excellence of simple innocence, imaginative and irrepressible, and superior to adult methods of confronting the world, was one to which Mark Twain would often return.

After several years of miscellaneous publication, which included the popular, now forgotten, *Punch, Brothers, Punch and Other Sketches* in 1878 and a second account of European travel, *A Tramp Abroad*, in 1880, Clemens turned to the theme again in *The Prince and the Pauper*, in 1882, but with less success. The account of Tom Canty's adventures in the court of Edward VI was again addressed to boys and girls, tested by readings of the manuscript to the Clemens children and the children of friends, but it was addressed also to adults as an expression of its author's continuing assurance that, for all its shortcomings, democracy as practiced in the United States was superior to any other manner of living anywhere. It is the kind of melodramatic story which Tom Sawyer might have told, of a poor boy who became heir to a king and of a prince who learned humility through mixing with common men.

"My idea," Clemens told one of his friends, "is to afford a realistic sense of the severity of the laws of that day by inflicting some of their penalties upon the king himself." Poverty which brutalizes and restrictive statutes which force men to thievery are ridiculed, as well as superstition and meaningless ritual. The language of old England, with which Mark Twain had experimented in the surreptitiously printed, mildly ribald *1601, or Conversation as It Was by the Fireside in the Time of the Tudors*, two years before, comes in for a full share of burlesque. When Tom's nose "itcheth cruelly," he asks, "What is the custom and usage of this emergence?" He fills his pockets with nuts and uses the Royal Seal to crack them. When Henry VIII dies and his funeral is delayed to an appropriate ceremonial time in the future, the boy observes, "'Tis strange folly. Will he keep?" Hardly any of the kinds of humor which the public had come to expect from Mark Twain, or of sagacious insight into the frailties of man, is left out of *The Prince and the Pauper*.

In spite of this and largely, Clemens thought, because he had changed to a new publisher, unexperienced in selling copies in great number by subscription, *The Prince and the Pauper* did not do as well commercially as Mark Twain's previous books. So Clemens established his own publishing house and launched it in 1885 with another boy's book which he was careful to link in the public mind to his earlier, encouragingly popular account of young life by the Mississippi by identifying its hero in a subtitle as "Tom Sawyer's comrade." But *The Adventures of Huckleberry Finn* made no such immediate impression as its predecessor. At Concord in Massachusetts, still the mecca of genteel New England cultural aspiration, it was banished from the local library as presenting a bad example for youth. Years later, it was blacklisted in Denver, Omaha, and even Brooklyn. When chapters from it appeared in the *Century Magazine*, some readers found it indefensibly coarse, "destitute of a single redeeming quality."

But *The Adventures of Huckleberry Finn* has outlived almost every criticism of those who have spoken against it to become a native classic thrust forward exultantly in the face of any who still dare inquire, "Who reads an American book?" — its health endangered only by a smothering swarm of commentators who threaten to maim it with excessive kind attention. Except perhaps for *Moby Dick*, no American book has recently been opened with more tender explicatory care or by critics to whom we are better prepared to listen. The river on which or beside which the action develops is a great brown god to T. S. Eliot; and Lionel Trilling reminds us of the "subtle, implicit moral meaning of the great river" as he translates Emerson to contemporary idiom by explaining that "Against the money-god stands the river-god, whose comments are silent," that Huck is "the servant of the river-god," and that Mr. Eliot is right in saying "The river is within us."

Other commentators call attention to the social criticism, the satire, the savagery in this book of boy adventures; to its language so cleanly direct and simply natural that reasons for Hemingway's admiration for it come to mind; to its structure which is at one time or to one critic great art, at another fumbling improvisation; to the recurrent imagery, so like what E. M. Forster pointed to in writings of Marcel Proust and called repetition by variation. Its mythic quality is explained as reinforced by elements of popular lore and superstition or by parallels with primitive initiation rites. The once familiar three-part division of the blackface minstrel show, a genuinely indigenous art form, has been superimposed on *The Adventures of Huckleberry Finn* to reveal instructive similarities. Various interpretations of its theme, some inevitably religious, have been patiently explored. Its endlessness, as if the adventures might have gone on forever, has been persuasively held forth as similar to other distinctively American contrivances which emphasize process rather than product, like the skyscraper, jazz, the comic strip, chewing gum, and *Moby Dick.*

These things are all probably true, if only because attentive readers have discovered them. An encompassing and synthesizing rightness reveals itself now in the casual career of Samuel Clemens who drifted from one occupation to another, managing by accident of birth and qualities which moralists cannot always hold up for emulation to have been at many right places at exactly the right time. His was indeed a pioneer talent, and sometimes so unused to itself that it postured boisterously, almost always ready to break into laughter if response to what was said proved it ridiculous. Its melancholy, even when invaded by the mockery of burlesque, was related to that of home-starved men who sang sad songs on lonesome prairies or rivers, in forests or mountain camps. Its sentimentality was like theirs, ready to retreat to guffaw when detected. The aggressive playfulness which delighted in hoaxes and practical joking changed in almost classic pattern to anger like that of gods — or of simple men — when the joke is turned against them.

Clemens had known backcountry America and the overland push toward great fortunes in the gold-filled, silver-lined West. He had known, better than he learned to know anything else, her great arterial river through which the lifeblood of middle America had once flowed. And he had known men in these places, of all kinds, and then known riches and the company of well-fed, respectable people whom he also recognized as types known before. He had listened to men talk, boastfully or in anger, had heard their tales and their blandishments, and had learned to speak as they spoke. For his ultimate discovery was linguistic, the creation of a language which was simple, supple, and sustained, in what Richard Chase has called "a joyous exorcism of traditional literary English." No one had ever written like him before. What is more difficult to remember is that no one ever effectively will again because, to say it very simply, his models were not in literature but in life. Even he, when he tried to write something like something he had written before, succeeded only in producing books which were amusing because written in Mark Twain's manner.

Mark Twain

The Adventures of Huckleberry Finn is the story of a boy who will not accept the kinds of freedom the world is able to offer, and so flees from them, one after another, to become to many readers a symbol of man's inevitable, restless flight. It is instructive to recall that it appeared in the same year that Clemens' friend William Dean Howells presented in *The Rise of Silas Lapham* another simple protagonist who retreated when confronted by perplexities, and a year before Henry James, who approached maturity through avenues almost completely different from those which Clemens followed, revealed in both *The Princess Casamassima* and *The Bostonians* the struggle of honest young provincials forced to reject promises offered by society. Each played variations on a familiar American theme, which Emerson had expressed, which Whitman approached, and Melville also, and which has reappeared often again. It poses what has been called the inescapable dilemma of democracy — to what degree may each single and separate person live as an unencumbered individual and to what extent must he submit to distortions of personality required by society? If Clemens presented it better than most, by endowing it with qualities of myth interwoven with fantasy, realism, satire, and superstition, it was not because his convictions were different. It was because he had mastered a language supple enough to reveal the honest observations of an attractive boy and the ambiguous aspirations of many kinds of men whom he came upon, and also the subtly ominous but compelling spirit which in this book is a river.

Huckleberry Finn's solution of the problem of freedom is direct and unworldly: having tested society, he will have none of it, for civilization finally makes culprits of all men. Huck is a simple boy, with little education and great confidence in omens. One measure of his character is its proneness to deceit which, though not always successful, is instinctive, as if it were a trait shared with other wild things, relating him to nature, in opposition to the tradition-grounded, book-learned imaginative deceptions of Tom Sawyer. The dilatory adventures of Huck and his Negro companion, both natural men enslaved, have even reminded some readers of the more consciously directed explorations in Faulkner's "The Bear" of Ike

McCaslin and his part-Negro, part-Indian guide, if only because they suggest more than can easily be explained. American fictions, we are told, are filled with white boys who are influenced by darker companions.

Young Huck had become something of a hero to the inhabitants of the little river village because of his help to Tom Sawyer in tracking down Injun Joe. He had been adopted by the Widow Douglas, washed, dressed in clean clothes, and sent to school. With Tom he shared the incredible wealth of one dollar a day for each of them derived as income from the treasure they had discovered in *The Adventures of Tom Sawyer*. But Huck is not happy. Tom's make-believe is incomprehensible to him. The religion of retribution which Miss Watson, the widow's sister, teaches makes no sense at all. The religion of love which the widow suggests is better, but he will not commit himself. When his scapegrace father returns and carries Huck across the river to a desolate log house, the boy accepts the abduction with relief because, though he fears his father's beatings and drunken rages, he is freed from restraints of tight clothing, school, and regular hours, and from the preaching and the puzzling tangle of ideas which confuse village life. But the bondage of life with his father chaffs also, so he steals down the river at night to Jackson Island, where he meets the Negro Jim, Miss Watson's slave, who had run away because his Christian owner was going to sell him.

Thus the first eleven chapters of *The Adventures of Huckleberry Finn* tell of adventures on land, with Huck bewildered or miserable or in flight. The next twenty chapters detail adventures on the river or beside the river, in a pattern of withdrawal and return, as Huck and Jim float with their raft toward what they hope will be freedom for both. On the river or its shores many kinds of men are encountered, most of them evil or stupid or mean: cutthroats, murderers, cheats, liars, swindlers, cowards, slave hunters, dupes and hypocrites of every variety. Even the isolation from society which life on a raft might be thought to afford is violated, for malevolence also intrudes there in grotesque guises. Nor is the movement of the great brown river to be trusted. It carries Jim beyond freedom to capture again by respectable, benevolent people whose conscience is untroubled by human slavery.

The final twelve chapters take place again on land. Tom Sawyer once more appears, filled with romance-bred notions of how Jim might be freed. And Huck joins in the laborious nonsense, for he admires Tom, if he does not understand him — often on the river when confronted with crisis or cleverly, he thought, surmounting difficulties, he wished Tom had been there to aid or commend him. But the boys' make-believe at rescue becomes a travesty, for Miss Watson had granted Jim his freedom — he was no longer a slave. The narrative ends hurriedly, as if embarrassed to linger while loose ends were tied. Huck's father is dead — Jim had known that since the first stage of their journey but in kindness had withheld the knowledge. One threat to Huck's freedom is gone, but another remains, for good people again pity the brave pariah boy and offer to adopt him. But Huck will not have it: "I can't stand it," he said. "I been there before."

Much has been made of these last chapters, in condemnation or approval. To some readers they certify Clemens' inability to control plot, to others they reveal a compulsive attraction toward elaborate inventions such as Tom Sawyer loved, but to still others they are exactly right, supplying an inevitable rounding out of tale and theme. And much has been made of the development of Huck's character, his initiation, or his disillusionment with the world and its ways, and especially the change in his attitude toward the Negro Jim whom he finally recognizes as a fellow being, more decent and honest than most of the white people who hold him and his kind in slavery. A few find special charm in the assumption that Huck does not develop in any fundamental sense at all, because as a child of nature he is changeless. But to all, it is Huck and his view of the world which secure for this book its high place among American writings.

For one of the things to notice about *The Adventures of Huckleberry Finn* is that Mark Twain is not the narrator. Huck makes that plain in the first paragraph: Mr. Mark Twain had written of him in *The Adventures of Tom Sawyer*, he said, but this would be his own story. And the first-person narrative which follows allows Huck to misspell and mispronounce words in a manner which could delight admirers of Mark Twain, and to act sometimes in a manner which he thought would have delighted Tom Sawyer, but it is his voice which speaks, authentically and without posturing. Sometimes Mark Twain's accents are heard, as compellingly humorous as ever, tempting attention away from the boy who, with no humor at all, struggles to make himself understood. But Huck is finally the better witness, infinitely better than Tom Sawyer whose vision is blurred by boyish trickery very different from Huck's protective deceit.

Boyish Tom, however, seems to have been Samuel Clemens' favorite. He wrote of him again in *Tom Sawyer Abroad* in 1894 and in *Tom Sawyer Detective* in 1896, contrived books, imitative of earlier successes, and crowded with imagined adventure rather than experience. Yet, with boyhood behind him, even Tom was not to be envied. Clemens once thought of writing of the two boys as adults who return to their river village. "Huck comes back sixty years old, from nobody knows where — and crazy." He imagines himself a boy again and watches everyone who passes to find the face of one of his boyhood friends. Then Tom returns, from years of "wandering in the world," and they talk of old times. "Both are desolate, life has been a failure, all that was lovable, all that was beautiful was under the sod."

But if old times in backcountry America were idyllically best, older times in Europe certainly were not. Far too many of his countrymen, Clemens thought, were beguiled by romantic notions popularized by Sir Walter Scott, which made overgrown Tom Sawyers of them all. Scott was "so juvenile, so artificial, so shoddy," not once "recognizably sincere and in earnest." His characters were "bloodless shams," "milk-and-water humbugs," "squalid shadows." Nor were American romancers, bred under Scott's influence, appreciably better. Among the most persistently anthologized of Clemens' short pieces is the humorously perceptive dissection of "Fenimore Cooper's Literary Offenses" in which he finds that "in the restricted space of two-thirds of a page, Cooper has scored 114 offenses against literary art out of a possible 115." He speaks of Cooper's "crass stupidities," his lack of attention to detail, and his curious box of stage properties which contained such hackneyed devices as the broken twig: "It is a restful chapter in any book of his when somebody doesn't step on a twig and alarm all the reds and whites for two hundred yards around. . . . In fact, the Leather-Stocking Series ought to have been called the Broken Twig Series." Surely, Clemens reasoned, history could be presented without such twaddle.

So Clemens wrote of the adventures of a sturdy, practical nineteenth-century mechanic who is knocked unconscious by a blow on the head and awakes to find himself under a tree near Camelot, amid a landscape "as lovely as a dream and as lonesome as Sunday." But *A Connecticut Yankee in King Arthur's Court*, published in 1889, was double-edged in satirical intention. The Yankee proves himself a better man than the magician Merlin and he overcomes the best of knights in single or multiple combat. He provides what he called "a new deal" for downtrodden common people, transforming Arthur's England into a technically efficient going concern in which gunpowder and mechanical skills triumph over superstition, injustice, and oppression. But "this Yankee of mine," explained Clemens, "is a perfect ignoramus; he is boss of a machine shop, he can build a locomotive or a Colt's revolver, he can put up and run a telegraph line, but he's an ignoramus nevertheless."

A Connecticut Yankee has been called Mark Twain's finest possibility, combining satire, the tall tale, humor, democracy, religion, and the damned human race. Loosely picaresque and brightly anecdotal, it was an attempt, Clemens explained, "to imagine and after a fashion set forth, the hard condition of life for the laboring and defenseless poor in bygone times in England, and incidentally contrast those conditions with those under which civil and ecclesiastical pets of privilege and high fortune lived in those times." But what finally emerges from beneath the contrast between Yankee ingenuity and medieval superstition is the portrait of an American. He is unlearned, with "neither the refinement nor the weakness of a college education," but quick-witted and completely, even devastatingly successful. Consciously created or not, it is the image of Samuel Clemens and of many of his friends. And it explains something of the nature of the literature which he and his fellows produced.

Meanwhile Clemens had thought for years that he might write a comic story about Siamese twins, one of whom was good, the other a rake, imagining that sidesplitting situations could result when, for example, the rake drank to excess and the teetotaler twin became intoxicated. Perhaps no idea was more grotesquely unfavorable for fiction, and Clemens never developed it fully, partly because, as he said, "A man who is not born with the novel-writing gift has a troublesome time of it when he tries to write a novel. . . . He has no clear idea of his story; in fact he has no story. He has merely some people in his mind, and an incident or two, also a locality . . . and he trusts that he can plunge those people into those incidents with interesting results."

When he did put shreds of this tale together in *Those Extraordinary Twins*, he pretended jocosely to reveal something of his casual literary method, particularly in dealing with characters who became lost amid the intricacies of plot. One female character named Rowena, for example, began splendidly but failed to keep up: "I must simply give her the grand bounce," he said. "It grieved me to do it, for after associating with her so much I had come to kind of like her after a fashion, notwithstanding she was such an ass, and said such stupid, irritating things, and was so nauseatingly sentimental." So he sent her "out into the back yard after supper to see the fireworks," and "she fell down a well and got drowned." The method seemed perhaps abrupt, "but I thought maybe the reader wouldn't notice it, because I changed the subject right away to something else. Anyway it loosened Rowena up from where she was stuck and got her out of the way, and that was the main thing."

Successful once, he resolved to try the stratagem again with two boys who were no longer useful ("they went out one night to stone a cat and fell down the well and got drowned") and with two supernumerary old ladies ("they went out one night to visit the sick and fell down a well and got drowned"). "I was going to drown some of the others, but I gave up the idea, partly because I believed that if I kept it up I would attract attention, and perhaps sympathy with those people, and partly because it was not a large well and would not hold any more anyway."

This was pure Mark Twain, in mood and language which many people liked best. Part of the fun was that what he said was so true or seemed so true in revelation of the shambling way he really wrote or liked to have people think he wrote stories. And the laugh was on him, or seemed to be, at the same time that it mocked conventional or sentimental writers who had no convenient wells in their back yards. Almost everybody agreed that Mark Twain made most sense when he was funniest. He could double people over with laughter as he pointed to their shortcomings or his own or those of people not quite so clever as they. The laughter was cleansing, but quieting also, for surely such amusing peccadilloes needed no correction.

Those Extraordinary Twins appeared in 1894 as an appendix to *The Tragedy of Pudd'nhead Wilson*, a better story which unaccountably had grown from it. Using the same device of the changeling which had provided the plot for *The Prince and the Pauper*, he told now of two children born on the same day in the Driscoll home at Dawson's Landing, one the son of the white master of the house, the other of a mulatto slave named Roxana, who switched the babies in their cradles so that her tainted son was brought up as Thomas à Becket Driscoll, heir to estates, while Tom, the white boy, became a slave. The bogus Tom grew to be a wastrel, a thief, and finally a murderer. When his mother threatened to expose him if he did not change his ways, he sold her to a slave trader.

The mulatto Roxana dominates the book, sentimentally perhaps, but illustrating again qualities of nobility like those which Huck discovered in the Negro Jim. But her attitudes on race are ambiguous and have puzzled people who would relate them to Huck's attitude or Jim's. When her son proved himself in every respect bad, she told him, "It's de nigger in you, dat's what it is. Thirty-one parts o' you is white, en only one part nigger, en dat po' little one part is yo' soul. 'Taint wuth savin', 'taint wuth totin' out in a shovel en throwin' in de gutter." Perhaps it is a mistake to expect consistency in a writer like Clemens. Or perhaps the greater mistake is to think that any one book of his can be used as commentary on any other.

Potentially more significant is the title character, a lawyer fond of philosophical maxims, but considered queer, a Pudd'nhead, by the rest of the community because he fails to conform to village standards. Among his strange hobbies is that of taking fingerprints, and he had years before made prints of the baby boys before they were changed about. When the trial for the murder which the bogus Tom had committed is held and Italian twins (the remnant of the Siamese twin idea) are blamed for it because they have the misfortune of being foreigners and strangers in the village, Pudd'nhead defends them, dramatically revealing by means of his prints that the true murderer is Roxana's villainous son.

The Tragedy of Pudd'nhead Wilson is filled with familiar failings, false starts, and rambling excursions. The title makes us wonder why it is Pudd'nhead's tragedy. But it contains excellencies also, of a kind which Sherwood Anderson was to use in writing about village people, and which have earned for it a reputation as "the most extraordinary book in American literature," filled with intolerable insights into evil. Even distorted by drollery, it penetrates toward recognition of social ills not unlike those which William Faulkner was later to probe. Beneath the burlesque which peoples the sleepy village of Dawson's Landing with representatives of decayed gentry bearing such exuberant names as Percy Northumberland Driscoll and Cecil Burleigh Essex runs a vein of satire which allows recognition of these people as ancestors of the Sartorises and Compsons. Pudd'nhead himself might have sat as model for Faulkner's Gavin Stevens, who comments on tradition-ridden life in Yoknapatawpha County. The octoroon who masquerades as white can be thought of as a tentative foreshadowing of Joe Christmas in *Light in August* or Sutpen's half-caste son in *Absalom, Absalom!*

Its failure is literary, the failure of words, not of ideas. Mark

Twain is telling a story according to a familiar pattern, incident strung on incident as if they might go on forever. Humor, pathos, sentiment, anger, and burlesque rub shoulders with intimacy bred of long acquaintance. *Pudd'nhead Wilson* is serious in intention, for all its belly-laughs and tears. It faces up to problems made by the venality of man. Seldom is it more plainly evident that Mark Twain's eyes rarely twinkle when he laughs. A social conscience here is plainly showing. Scorn looks boldly out from behind the burlesque. But the words do not come true, as Huck's words did or as Clemens' did when he remembered apprentice days on the river. He is saying what he wants to say, but in accents which ring false because they speak now as people expected him to speak.

Perhaps it is even possible to suppose that Mark Twain, who was responsible for so much of Clemens' incomparable contemporary success, became finally an encumbrance. As Stephen Crane once said, two hundred pages is a very long stretch in which to be funny. And the stretch is more enervating when the humorist understands that what he writes about is not of itself funny, but only seems so because of the way he writes about it. Man was more likely than not to be mean and do wrong — this even Huck knew, who was not humorous at all. Clemens seems to have known it also, and for a long time.

But Clemens had never kept his observations on the venality of man completely in focus, not even in *The Adventures of Huckleberry Finn*. Whether his seasoning of humor and relaxed excursions into anecdote are uniformly successful or not, they do reveal a distinctively practical approach to literature. I can teach anyone to write a successful story, he once advised a literary friend. All that needs to be done is catch the reader's attention with the first sentence and hold it by whatever means are possible to the end. The story flows, he said, as a stream flows, and the storyteller's responsibility is to pilot the reader in safety and comfort through its often meandering channel.

During the twenty years between 1875 and 1894 Samuel Clemens was happiest, and wealthiest, and he wrote his best books. He lived then in luxury among a group of well-to-do litterateurs in Hartford. He lectured, assumed an occasional editorial commitment, and sought attractive books for distribution by his publishing house. His income was breathtaking, probaby mounting more than once to one hundred thousand dollars a year. But money went as fast as it came, especially in speculative enterprises like the typesetting machine into which he poured much of his earnings. He dreamed like Colonel Sellers of making millions, as many of his contemporaries did, but by the mid-1890's he was bankrupt. A world tour then brought him increased fame and respect, produced *Following the Equator* in 1897, paid his debts, and provided new financial security. But at sixty, his effective literary career could be considered finished.

While resident in Europe he completed the writing of *Personal Recollections of Joan of Arc*, an account so seriously intended as the expression of a lifelong admiration that it was published in 1896 without Clemens' familiar pseudonym for fear that readers might expect another comic book from Mark Twain and laugh. The innocent faith of the Maid of Orleans represented a quality pitiably absent from modern life. She seemed "easily and by far the most extraordinary person the human race has ever produced." Untrained and without experience, she had within herself a capacity for goodness so pure and successful that it was condemned as heresy by men whom the world named good. But, hampered perhaps by the necessity of keeping close to what he had learned through years of reading of Joan's history, Clemens did not tell her story well, and few readers have agreed with him that it made his best book.

Grief and increasing bitterness had begun to close in upon him, to darken the rest of his life. His daughter Susie died suddenly while her parents were abroad, Mrs. Clemens was distressingly ill for years and then died, and his youngest daughter died suddenly one Christmas Eve. During the fifteen years which preceded his own death in 1910, Clemens lashed out often in anger at a world which had wounded him or reminisced with increasing compulsion on a world which was gone. He could not bear to return to Hartford where he had been happily successful, but moved restlessly from place to place, from residence in New York, to Florence in Italy, to Bermuda for his health, and finally to Stormfield in rural Connecticut, writing furiously at more projects than he could ever complete.

Readers who found Tom Sawyer silly or Huck Finn finally a profitless model were moved to wry approval of *The Man That Corrupted Hadleyburg* which in 1900 presented Clemens' most trenchant testimony to the fundamental dishonesty of man. Piercing the shell of respectability which traditionally had made each small town seem inhabited by kindly hearts and gentle people, he demonstrated how easily even prominently moral citizens could be led beyond temptation when confronted with opportunity to acquire wealth dishonestly but undetected. None were exempt, for every contest was rigged. No more astringent or cynical condemnation of contemporary mores had been issued by an American; even Stephen Crane's *Maggie* eight years before and Theodore Dreiser's *Sister Carrie* of the same year seem tempered with sentiments which Clemens could no longer feel. A year later, in *A Person Sitting in Darkness*, he struck savagely at the militant morality of missionaries, and in *King Leopold's Soliloquy*, in 1905, scornfully denounced pious exploitation of underdeveloped countries. *Extracts from Adam's Diary* in 1904 and *Eve's Diary* in 1906 were whimsical accounts of the dependence of even the first man on the superior management of women, and spoke feelingly by indirection of the loneliness of life without connubial and familial affection.

In 1906 he began to dictate his autobiography, reviewing, often without any defense of humor, incidents and personalities remembered from his rambling career. Some parts were so forthright that he thought they should not be published for a century after his death, but other parts were sent off for immediate serialization in the *North American Review*. Selected portions have been put together for *Mark Twain's Autobiography* in 1924, *Mark Twain in Eruption* in 1940, and *The Autobiography of Mark Twain* in 1959, each adding its effective extension to the image of a favorite American, who grumbled and growled, who smoked too much and cadged Scotch whiskey from his wealthy friends, but who had been places and who was known and loved all over the world.

In 1906 he also issued privately and anonymously what he called his "wicked book," *What Is Man?* which contains his most astringent diagnosis of man as a mechanism, the plaything of chance, his brain "so constructed that it can originate nothing." Man is a chameleon who "by the law of his nature . . . takes on the color of the place of his resort. The influences about him create his preferences, his aversions, his politics, his taste, his morality, his religion." All that he knows, all that he does, is determined by one inexorable law: "From his cradle to his grave a man never does a single thing which has any first and foremost object but one — to secure peace of mind, spiritual comfort, for himself." He is what he is, and nothing will change him. Self-seeking, self-admiring, he babbles of free will and love and compassion, which are fictions made to ensure his satisfaction with himself. "Whenever you read of a self-sacrificing act or hear of one, or of a duty done for duty's sake, take it to pieces and look for the real motive. It's always there."

The book is not wicked, but it is tired, like the posthumous *Letters from the Earth.* Its words speak forthrightly, despairingly, echoing the words of other men who testified to man's slavery to forces beyond himself. They are palliative as well as condemnatory, as if their writer were explaining to himself as much as to other men why it was necessary for all men to do what he and they perforce had done. Resolution is not lacking, nor is anger. On its level, the book argues well. It presents its case. What is no longer there is the power of the inevitable word which is in so intimate a relation to the thing of which it speaks that meaning spills over to intimations which ordinary words can never reach. Once Clemens' words had clung thus close to things, but now they gestured and had less to say.

Six months before his death Clemens released an *Extract from Captain Stormfield's Visit to Heaven,* a favorite tale over which he had been puttering for many years. In it almost every contrivance of humor, sentiment, or dissection of human frailty that Mark Twain had ever used was expended again on the adventures of a crusty, matter-of-fact mariner who went flashing through the air like a bird toward paradise, racing a comet on the way as steamboat pilots used to race on the Mississippi. He has difficulty in finding wings that fit or a harp that suits him. He seeks long before finding the proper resting place for people from a planet so little valued by angels that they call it the Wart. He has trouble conversing with people who speak ridiculous languages, tumbles terribly in learning to fly, is surprised to find Jews and Moslems in heaven, and pleased that Shakespeare is placed "away down there below shoe-makers and horse-dealers and knife-grinders" to make room for an unknown tailor from Tennessee who "wrote poetry that Homer and Shakespeare couldn't begin to come up to; but nobody would print it, nobody read it but his neighbors, and they laughed at it." Recognition of wisdom masked by such burlesque is usually considered a test of an admirer of Mark Twain.

As a philosophical humorist he spoke on two levels, now one, now the other, seldom blending them to unity of tone or consistency of insight. Henry Nash Smith is correct in describing Mark Twain's popularity as a result of his exploitation of the comic contrast between things as they might be and things as they are. But Louis Budd is also correct in discovering Clemens neither original nor objective as a social philosopher. Convictions he had in plenty, and courage also; but he had a place to preserve and boyhood visions to sustain. His miseries were subtilely compounded and his sense of sin extended as young dreams exploded to recriminatory nightmares at last.

No subtlety of interpretation is required for recognition of the bleak despair of Clemens' posthumous *The Mysterious Stranger*. The scene is Austria in 1590, where in the village of Eseldorf, a paradise for play like that which Tom and Huck had known, three boys are joined by a visiting angel, namesake and nephew of the fallen Satan. He entertains them with miracles, making little creatures of clay, breathing life into them, and then mashing them down as if they were flies. It seems cruel to the boys, but Satan explains that it was not cruel, only capricious and, as far as man could understand, ordained. Crippled by moral sense, in bondage to circumstance, his vision distorted by illusion, man pampers himself with ideals which exist only when he imagines them. What an ass he is! How hysterically mad are his expectations: "No sane man can be happy, for to him life is real, and he sees what a fearful thing it is," for "there is no God, no universe, no human race, no earthly life, no heaven, no hell. It is all a dream — a grotesque and foolish dream. Nothing exists," said the angel, "but you. And you are but a *thought* — a vagrant thought, a useless thought, a homeless thought, wandering forlorn among the empty eternities."

Nothing remains of the Widow Douglas' reliance on the religion of love or Huck's possibility of escape from the world through flight. Again Clemens speaks, as he had in 1885, of ideas which unsettled many people of his time, but now others voiced them better than he, for some magic of language has disappeared from these late sputtering insights of anger and despair. The angel Satan speaks, but the words are Clemens', in reprimand as much to himself as to those who read him: "You have a mongrel sense of humor, nothing more," he charged; "you see the comic side of a thousand low-grade and trivial things — broad incongruities, mainly; grotesqueries, absurdities, evokers of the horse-laugh." But the "ten thousand high-grade comicalities" made by the juvenilities of man are sealed from your dull visions. "Will a day come when the race will detect these juvenilities and laugh at them — and by laughing destroy them?" In a perfect world there is no room for laughter, but this world is not perfect, and man in his poverty "has unquestionably one really effective weapon — laughter. Power, money, persuasion, supplication, persecution — these can lift at a colossal humbug — push it a little — weaken it a little, century by century; but only laughter can blow it to rags and atoms at a blast."

"Humor," Mark Twain once wrote when in another mood, "is only a fragrance, a decoration." If it is really to succeed in survival, it must surreptitiously teach and preach. Perhaps that is why so sober an admirer as James T. Farrell sees in Huck and Tom "two

accusing fingers pointing down the decades of America's history,"
relentlessly questioning why it is in America, or perhaps anywhere
else, that a man so rarely becomes what the boy gave promise of
becoming. Samuel Clemens did see the world as a boy sees it, in its
infinitude of possibilities for freedom and fun and in its darkened
depths of disillusionment. And, like a boy, when embarrassed he
laughed; when tentatively serious he laughed first, so that the re-
sponding laugh could be with, not at, him; even in tantrum, he
seemed somehow comic, an object which in brighter spirits he
might have ridiculed. "From a boyhood idyll of the good life to a
boy's criticism of that life," says Wright Morris in accusation, "is
the natural range and habitat of the American mind." Mark
Twain's charm of innocence did isolate him from maturity. What
he achieved artlessly so well that he invented a theory of storytelling art to explain it was received with riotous applause by his countrymen. With so natural a talent why should he then not attempt
more? Clemens' inability to respond to that question explains much
of Mark Twain and the milieu which made him possible. But it
fails to explain all, or even what is most important.

Samuel Clemens created or became Mark Twain who boundless-
ly created laughter, but he was more than a buffoon. As comic
realist he applies for place beside Laurence Sterne, Dickens, Joyce,
Faulkner, and Camus, for his eyes like theirs have seen beyond locality to qualities which men universally, sometimes shamefully,
share. To remember him only as a creator of boyhood adventure
or as a relic of an American frontier or the voice of native idiosyncrasy is to do him disservice. His accomplishment finally contra-
dicts his thinking, thus certifying his literary achievement. Much
that is excellent in American literature *did* begin with him, and
Lionel Trilling is correct when he says "that almost every contemporary American writer who deals conscientiously with the problems and possibilities of prose must feel, directly or indirectly, the
influence of . . . [his] style which escapes the fixity of the printed page, that sounds in our ears with the immediacy of the heard
voice, the very voice of unpretentious truth."

But he was anticipated also, ten years before his first triumphant entry to public notice, by another native observer who admitted men "victims of illusion" and life "a succession of dreams." Samuel Clemens, Mississippi pilot, had not yet become Mark Twain but Emerson had someone much like him in mind when he described "a humorist who in a good deal of rattle had a grain or two of sense. He shocked the company by maintaining that the attributes of God were two,— power and risibility, and that it was the duty of every pious man to keep up the comedy."

Perhaps it was a basic lack of piety in the sense of dedication to the demands of literature ("and all that bosh") which deprived Samuel Clemens of an ability consistently to keep up the comedy. Laughter is not joy, funny fellows are notoriously prone to tears, and the comic view has never sustained man's highest vision of himself or his possibilities because, as Baudelaire once said, the comic is imitation, not creation. But his countrymen seldom chide Mark Twain for what he is not; what he was is good enough, and plenty. It is probably true that the sense of the comic, the ability to laugh, is in him who laughs, and not in the object which excites his laughter. If the thousand low-grade and trivial things which quickened mirth among his countrymen were more often displayed than Samuel Clemens' occasional genuine and high-grade comicalities, the fault was not his alone, and he is not to be blamed for his anger, except that it came too late, when his words were tired. He shocked his countrymen by explaining what they were, and they laughed. Their continuing laughter measures his genius and their own, and the limitations they have shared together.

William D. Howells

As a journalist, poet, travel writer, critic, and novelist, W. D. Howells wrote professionally for nearly seventy years. In 1852, when *The Blithedale Romance* appeared, Howells at the age of fifteen published his first poem; he was still writing a column for *Harper's* in the year of his death, 1920, when *Main Street* burst upon the literary world. Achieving editorial power and a name before he was thirty, he came to know, or to interpret, justly on the whole, every American writer of four generations, the forgotten Melville excepted. He introduced to American readers a host of Continental novelists, at first noticing their fiction in the French, Italian, and Spanish editions. He was the first advocate and editor and became the warm friend of Henry James and Mark Twain. For forty years he made his literary convictions strongly felt, first as editor-reviewer and then as conductor of critical departments in influential magazines.

From 1875 to 1895 he was at his most imaginative and productive. His work earned the praise of Turgenev, Tolstoi, Taine, Verga, Hardy, Shaw, and Kipling. At the same time, certain English reviewers attacked Howells for maligning Dickens and Thackeray while lesser American critics accused him of vulgarity and lack of idealism. Ambrose Bierce sneered at "Miss Nancy Howells and Miss Nancy James" for their gentility. But the effect of this criticism on the reading public was negligible. Howells' fiction and travel volumes continued throughout these years to sell steadily (if never spectacularly). By the turn of the century, however, the tide had shifted. Thereafter, his creative power waning, he was still often praised but less frequently read. As the "Dean of American Letters," he became in effect a dean without faculty or students. Late in life he noted wryly his loss of popularity, saying his statues were cut down, "the grass growing over them in the pale moonlight."

Then, when Mencken in 1919 charged that Howells "has nothing to say"; when Van Wyck Brooks a year later persuaded many readers, even Sherwood Anderson, that Howells had clipped Mark Twain's wings by censorship — Lewis Mumford renewing the charge; and when Sinclair Lewis on winning the Nobel Prize in 1930 identified Howells with "Victorian" restrictive codes, Howells had reached the limbo of being subject rather than object. Certain readers might take pleasure in D. G. Cooke's and O. W. Firkins' critical studies (1922, 1924), or find the letters edited by his daughter Mildred (1928) full of life and intelligence. But the bright spirits of the second American literary renaissance took Mencken and Lewis and especially Brooks at their word. Beyond the usual American whirligig of taste, one reason for their revulsion seems clear. These leaders in a decade dominated by Freudian doctrine were chiefly familiar with Howells' latest, least vigorous writing. Determined to break through the literary conventions governing sexual morality of earlier decades — conventions which they identified with Howells — they convicted Howells of prudery and optimism and condemned him forthwith.

The depression years of the 1930's saw Howells regain some of his lost stature. As Fitzgerald vanished and Steinbeck appeared, the liberal and radical critics, dismayed and protesting, looked to the American past for present comfort and rediscovered Howells as a Christian socialist. In the succeeding decades a group of scholar-critics have further redressed the balance. His life has been well outlined, his best novels have been distinguished from the worst and partially explicated. But his boldness and subtlety as a critic are scarcely recognized even now, and the full breadth and depth of his work need to be understood. To that end the reader must bring something like Howells' own sensibility — an appreciation of irony, social comedy, and style, and a taste for both James and Twain, Jane Austen and Tolstoi, Emily Dickinson and Thorstein Veblen. Howells' "beautiful time," as James envisioned it, and a just valuation of his work are yet to come.

In the meanwhile a new reading of Howells' life, encompassing yet going beyond Edwin H. Cady's solid, full, pioneer biography, ought to be made, and certain of its emphases may be suggested here. One obvious justification for such a new reading is that sketches of his life before Cady's were rendered impossibly gray by adulation, indifference, or ignorance. Another reason, challenging in nature, is that Howells, though willing enough to write of literary acquaintance and literary passions, spoke of his own life infrequently and guardedly. "Cursed with self-consciousness to the core," he hated, he said, to write of his early life "because it's so damned humiliating." His mood of reserve is curiously like Melville's or Hawthorne's when late in life he told Twain: "I'd like immensely to read your autobiography. You always rather bewildered me by your veracity, and I fancy you may tell the truth about yourself. But *all* of it? The black truth, which we all know of ourselves in our hearts, or only the whity-brown truth of the pericardium, or the nice, whitened truth of the shirtfront? Even you won't tell the black heart's-truth. The man who would do it would be famed to the last day the sun shone on." The inner life, in short, of "William Dean Howells" — he disliked his full name heartily — and its intellectual and emotional crises remain only half explored.

Howells began life with a difference. His boyhood and early manhood in post-frontier Ohio (1837–60), typical in many respects, were still such as to make him both proud and self-conscious about the differences between his family and their neighbors in the villages of Hamilton and Jefferson. Jefferson was no more a cultural waste for a lively printer's apprentice, it is true, than the Hannibal, Missouri, of Sam Clemens, "Mark Twain." But the complex of circumstance and temperament was already marking young Howells with inchoate desires for life in city-centers of culture such as

Columbus, Boston, or New York, for experience of the countries of Heine and Cervantes, and for literary fame. Unable to recall a time when he could not set type, the boy grew up with hard work and poverty in a large and close-knit family whose goal was to own a printing plant, a newspaper, and a home. His earliest neighbors had been largely southerners, yet even after the family moved to northern Ohio, their antislavery, Quaker, and Swedenborgian principles set them and him off from others. The backwoods communal experiment which his father and uncle undertook for a year in the country, near Xenia, at "New Leaf Mills," was unusual, if not unique. Other boys shared many of his childhood fears, but few or none of his young friends suffered until marriage and maturity from a private "demon" created by fears of hydrophobia, the ghosts of contemporary spiritualism, the world's coming to an end, and early death. These fears culminated in a recurrent nightmare of fire and alarmed cries of "Arms, Poe, Arms, Poe," induced by his reading of *Tales of the Grotesque and Arabesque*; eventually, in Howells' mid-teens, they led to hypochondria and nervous breakdown. William C. Howells' reassuring his son that he too had suffered from fears when young afforded some release; the rest came for Howells in constant reading, venturing into the classical languages, studying German, Spanish, and French, and writing poetry.

How much of Howells' later writing is fitfully illuminated by his childhood! His portrayal of ineffectual, warmhearted characters, with a touch of Colonel Sellers, like his father. His profound distrust of the Puritan tradition and Quaker dislike of violence, comparable to Whitman's. His ineradicable memories of hard work and bone-deep fatigue balanced against strong contempt for the scrambling life of self-made men. His lifelong preoccupation with communal experiments and with dream analysis. His devotion to principle in the face of popular disapproval. His taste for the "cleanly respectabilities." And withal, his establishing a pantheon of culture heroes and cultivating from the beginning the humors and ironies of Cervantes and Heine.

When Howells became news and literary editor of the *Ohio*

State Journal at Columbus (1857–61), he began to breathe the air of a larger world, in spite of bouts of homesickness. Dickens, Tennyson, and the New England poets joined the pantheon of Heine, Cervantes, Goldsmith, and Shakespeare. James Russell Lowell accepted five of his poems for the *Atlantic* for 1860. He published *Poems of Two Friends* with J. J. Piatt, presumably thinking of Wordsworth and Coleridge. He wrote a good campaign biography of Lincoln. And he danced and talked literature and made friends and courted a visiting New England girl, Elinor Mead, in the deep-lawned homes of the state capital's simple, open society. The royalties from his campaign biography and a contract for newspaper letters made possible a pilgrimage through Canada to eastern publishing centers. In Boston, Lowell introduced him by letter to Hawthorne, and he met Holmes, Emerson, and Thoreau as well. In New York he encountered the *Saturday Press* Bohemians and Walt Whitman at Pfaff's beer parlor. A year after his return to Ohio, his biography and his family's political devotion won for him a long-hoped-for opportunity, a position as American consul in Venice. A familiar cycle in American letters was once again to repeat itself.

The four years in Venice (1861–65), which included his marriage to Elinor Mead in Paris and the birth of Winifred, their first child, in Venice, completed an education begun at the type case in Hamilton, Ohio. Witty, loquacious, something of a bluestocking, talented in art and letters, this girl from an idiosyncratic Vermont family remains a shadow in Howells' biography. Yet in these first years of marriage, Howells was liberated from the fears and the provinciality of his youth and he acquired professional skills as a writer. Though it remains largely undefined, Elinor Howells' influence upon her husband was subtle and strong, and along with his rich experience of Italian life and letters, it prepared him for the central role he would play for over four decades in American literature. Passing a turning point in his life, he had discovered that his gift was analysis of character, both national and individual, in simple, finely wrought prose. He had read Italian history, Dante, contemporary poetry and drama, and he had immersed himself in the stream of vulgar Italian life. Above all he had read (and witnessed in the Teatro Malibran) the plays of Carlo Goldoni and the *commedia dell'arte* which reflected the same life. Thus, having translated Goldoni's memoirs (published in 1877) and produced fresh travel sketches and criticism, the slender, diffident journalist came home stouter and stronger in his craft, an Italianate American.

But it was not to Ohio that Howells returned, for American publishing centers were in the East. Acutely aware that he might be trailing behind in the post-Civil War procession, Howells fell back on literary journalism in New York City for a temporary "basis" and a livelihood. Writing free-lance reviews and editorials quickly led to his conducting a department, "Minor Topics," for E. L. Godkin's *Nation*, and in his column he turned easily from reviews of Dickens, Whitman, and the Longfellow translation of Dante to murder, scandal, divorce, criminal insanity, New York politics, defense of the liberated Negro, the consular service, and the troubles of the Fenian brotherhood.

Boston was still his goal, nonetheless, and when in 1866 James T. Fields, Lowell's successor, offered him the assistant editorship of the *Atlantic*, Howells fulfilled the dream of his mature life (as he then thought), conceived when he first visited New England before the war. Though not officially editor-in-chief until 1871, Howells was soon actually in charge and responsible for a change in character in this avant-garde monthly. Over a fifteen-year period, he made it a national magazine, accepting contributions from the South and the West, introducing new features (music, political comment), and favoring a fresh, colloquial style. He met deadlines, read proof closely, wrote lead reviews, searched out new talent, and made many friends and certain enemies as he rose in these years from the status of minor poet and skilled journalist to that of new novelist and nationally known editor.

Perhaps the chief effects upon Howells of the editorial burden and of established editorial policies were delay in his development as a writer of fiction and limitation, in a degree, of what he might choose to represent in his fiction. The great success of *Venetian Life* (1866), a book which he had fashioned from his travel letters to the *Boston Advertiser*, and of *Italian Journeys* (1867) persuaded

William D. Howells

him to apply his skill in observing Italian characters and manners to the American scene. But *Atlantic* subscribers demanded reserve in the treatment of love and courtship in the pages of the magazine, and Howells therefore had to fit his treatment of sexual mores, in his first stories and novels, to *Atlantic* conventions. "Scene," for example, which depicts a Boston prostitute's suicide by drowning, is the only one of the *Suburban Sketches* which did not first appear in the magazine. Similarly, Howells could not easily forget that his approving Harriet Beecher Stowe's essay in defense of Lady Byron and Fields's publishing it lost the *Atlantic* some thousands of subscribers. Yet another consequence of Howells' editorship was his tendency to overvalue certain of the founders of the *Atlantic*: he had read them in the West, and now they made him — almost — one of them. He knew Emerson and Thoreau and Hawthorne chiefly in their work, and their work encouraged him in the direction of his own talents. But his adulation of Lowell, Longfellow, and Holmes was for many years restrictive and even stultifying, as his reaction to Mark Twain's speech burlesquing the New England worthies at a birthday dinner for Whittier suggests — clearly he overreacted.

If editing the *Atlantic* cramped Howells' talent in certain respects, however, it freed it in others, for the audience was intelligent and critical; certainly it made possible the flowering of other writers' genius. In the postwar years, Howells met Henry James, Jr., in Cambridge, published his early stories, and talked with him about the art of fiction for hours on end. Subsequently he competed with James for subjects, and with him invented the "American girl" and the international novel; he placed James's late novels; and he elucidated James's fiction discriminatingly for four decades. Howells' friendship with Mark Twain, which was even closer, was of prime consequence. It began with his praise of *Innocents Abroad* (1869) in the *Atlantic* — an act comparably free and bold with Emerson's letter praising Whitman in that Howells was approving in print a "subscription book," that is, vulgar "non-literature." Thereafter Howells guided Clemens, so far as a friend and editor might, away from burlesque and failures in *vraisemblance* and mere buffoonery in the direction of his true capacities: an entire spectrum of satire, humor ranging from black to bright, true pathos touched with the tears of things, speech in the mouth, epic action, and living characterization. Howells was the first and most sensitive of Twain's critics, who never touched his copy when it was right and who was midwife to most of the work by which Twain is now known.

Finally, despite the restraining influence of the "countinghouse" and the limited sensibilities of feminine readers, Howells was able to use his editorial power on the *Atlantic* to extend the horizons of American fiction by selecting what to publish and by the great weight attached to his reviews. He gave short shrift to sentimental-domestic-melodramatic tales, and devoted his attention to stories that were autochthonous in setting and probable in action, whose characters possessed "God-given complexity of motive." Thus, early in his editorial career, he detected realistic traits and qualities in certain novels of Elizabeth Stoddard, Bayard Taylor, and Henry Ward Beecher, but praised with greater enthusiasm the work of Björnson, George Eliot, and J. W. De Forest as he discovered it. Later, he discovered realism full-blown in the dramatic method and the sensibility of Ivan Turgenev, the directness and humor of Mark Twain, and the analytic subtlety and moral discrimination of James. And he drew upon each of these three masters as he wrote his own fiction at the time.

During his last years as editor of the *Atlantic*, Howells grew "miserably tired of editing" and correspondingly eager to write plays and fiction full time. The breaking up of the firm of Houghton and Osgood, which had published the *Atlantic*, a severe illness, and Winifred Howells' nervous prostration led him to resign the editorship in 1881 and take his wife and children abroad again for a year. Howells reached the peak of his power as a novelist in the decade that followed and as a critic took the leading role in a violent intercontinental war over realism. In the decade he wrote his best dramatic and international novels, *A Modern Instance* and *Indian Summer*; the transitional novel *The Rise of Silas Lapham*; and the major novels of social criticism *Annie Kilburn* and *A Hazard*

William D. Howells

of New Fortunes. In it he wrote telling criticism of the comparative and rhetorical kind, much of it in "The Editor's Study" column of *Harper's*, on Tolstoi, Dostoevski, Zola, Verga, Galdós, Hardy, James, and Twain. In it too he suffered a painful revolution in his mode of thinking and feeling, a revulsion from self and self-interest comparable to the "vastation" that Henry James, Sr., had undergone more than forty years earlier.

The change began, probably, in his growing uneasiness over the widening social and economic chasm in America, and in his reading of Tolstoi and the American socialists Gronlund, George, and Bellamy. The change grew at a bound when he chose deliberately to risk his career and livelihood by declaring publicly that the Chicago anarchists, in 1887, had been unfairly tried—this from the writer who sought to be regarded as he himself regarded Cervantes. His altered viewpoint made his success taste of ashes. Then, when his daughter Winifred died, after a long, obscure illness, it deepened to the conviction that personal happiness can bear no part in the legitimate goals of a man's life. James had written of Winifred, "To be young and gentle, and do no harm, and pay for it as if it were a crime"—and Howells added, "That is the whole history of our dear girl's life." Howells' last major move, from Boston to New York and a new publisher, Harper and Brothers, took place in these years and has traditionally marked this profound change in his life. The change was scarcely unique: *The Princess Casamassima, A Connecticut Yankee,* and *Looking Backward* attest to the same deep unease. But Howells' "vastation" has not yet been fully understood in its nature and its consequences.

After 1892 as a novelist Howells entered upon a plateau inclining gradually downward. *A Hazard of New Fortunes* was followed by many novels on a smaller scale, but only two of them, *The Landlord at Lion's Head* and *The Leatherwood God,* are of comparable quality. The social criticism becomes direct and overt in a series of articles, or is imperfectly integrated into the Altrurian romances. More significantly, Howells began his series of literary recollections and reminiscences, and after a time returned to literary journalism. Yet his practical criticism of this period, of plays and fiction, is distinguished, and his lecture on "Novel-Writing and Novel-Reading" represents his critical theory at its comprehensive and penetrating best. The criticism becomes less tendentious than it was in "The Editor's Study," is extraordinarily sensitive to the currents of impressionism and naturalism among new writers, and treats the mature realists' work in a deeper perspective. Between ages fifty-five and sixty-five Howells first revealed the special qualities, lesser and greater, of Emily Dickinson, Crane, Garland, Fuller, Frederic, Norris, and Veblen, and of Herne, Harrigan, Ibsen, and Shaw. At the same time, novelists so different as Dreiser and Kate Chopin were reading and profiting from his fiction. Howells was also working, at the century's turn, to syndicate in newspapers the work of a group of novelists, including James, and to gain for them a wider audience and larger royalties; but he had to give up the scheme when he found that its backer was a former book pirate. He largely failed, as well, opposing national policy in the Philippine phase of the Spanish-American War. Even so, his anti-imperialist rhetoric, like that of Mark Twain and William James, is vigorous and memorable.

Until his death at eighty-three, Howells continued to review books and events in the "Editor's Easy Chair" of *Harper's*. He still wrote well when he was stirred by Ibsen or Brand Whitlock or Wells or Zola or Havelock Ellis, or the Irish executions in 1916, and he was still open to such new works as the poetry of Frost, Masters, and Lindsay and the *Education of Henry Adams*. The autobiographical *Years of My Youth* (1916), and *My Mark Twain* (1910), which Edmund Wilson calls the "best character" of Twain we have, bear comparison with the best earlier writings. Howells took keen pleasure in a variety of activities in his green old age: in serving as the first and continuing president of the American Academy of Arts and Letters and in preventing the Academy from accepting endowments; in cultivating his garden at Kittery Point, Maine; in talking about the movies with his admirer and denigrator, Sinclair Lewis. He was writing about Henry James when he died.

Cooper, Melville, and Mark Twain wrote their first novels on a bet or at the urging of friends, turning from active lives to the writer's study. Hawthorne, Emily Dickinson, and James on the other hand became engaged in the craft of literature at an early age, and Howells is one with them in this matter of conscious literary intention. His first ambition was to become a lyric and narrative poet like Longfellow, sustaining himself by literary journalism until poetry would support him. But the popular failure of *Poems of Two Friends* (1860) and of *No Love Lost, a Romance of Travel* (1869) became the "turning point" of Howells' life, as he later explained, especially in the light of the high critical success of *Venetian Life* (1866). In this new kind of travel book, the first of many, Howells had contrasted the high art and the deep past of Venice with people and incidents in the shabby-picturesque present. The point of view is distinctly American, the tone is ironic in the manner of Heine, the style is finished. His "fatal gift of observation" already apparent, the young ex-consul and *Atlantic* editor turned to fiction.

From "The Independent Candidate, a Story of Today" (1854–55, never collected) to *The Leatherwood God* (1916) Howells wrote thirty-five novels — and more than forty tales and sketches. Apart from the juvenile "Candidate" story, *Suburban Sketches* (1871) is Howells' first tentative venture into fiction. With an eye educated by the Italian experience, Howells drew Irish and Italian and Negro figures in the Cambridge background, and expanded his scenes from the serving girl at home and doorstep acquaintance, through horsecar vignettes, to Boston and Nahant. Two scenes, however, are very largely imagined. The first depicts recovering from the Charles River the body of a drowned prostitute, the second an ex-convict's "romantic" yarns about his past. "If the public will stand this," Howells wrote to James, "I shall consider my fortune made." The public response was favorable, and Howells took a long step toward the novel in his next book.

"I wrote 'Their Wedding Journey,'" Howells remarked to an interviewer long afterward, "without intending to make it a piece of fiction. . . . It was simply a book of American travel, which I hoped to make attractive by a sugar coating of romance." Howells' distrust of his "fitness for a sustained or involved narration," however — he admitted it in the first page of his book — was quickly dissipated. A family friend whom he had asked to mark passages embodying real incidents marked instead "passages which were purely invention," and Howells was elated: he had proved his fictive art. He was also gratified when the first edition of 1500 copies sold out in a day.

The biographical elements in *Their Wedding Journey* (1872) are apparent in Howells' letters of the time and in the manuscript. Howells framed his narrative on his summer's travel with his wife, in 1870, from Boston to New York and Albany, Buffalo, Montreal, and Quebec. He also used descriptive bits and thumbnail character sketches which he had already printed in the travel columns written for Ohio newspapers in 1860, when he had made his literary pilgrimage to New England by way of Canada. Within this framework, nonetheless, *Their Wedding Journey* is fiction. Rapidly limned characters encountered along the route come to life as Basil and Isabel March, delayed honeymooners, talk with them and react to them. The Marches, in fact, provide such action as there is by humorous persiflage and frequent clashes of opinion and occasional quarreling. They also lend depth to the travelogue by recalling Francis Parkman's interpretations of the French-Canadian past, and by comparing Canadian to European sights. Howells provided a rationale for his story thus: "As in literature the true artist will shun the use even of real events if they are of an improbable character, so the sincere observer of man will not desire to look upon his heroic or occasional phases, but will seek him in his habitual moods of vacancy and tiresomeness." More positively, Howells has March tell his wife the story of Sam Patch, who invented the saying "Some things can be done as well as others" and tested it by jumping over Niagara Falls twice. From this tall tale, March then infers that Americans will never have a poetry of their own "till we get over this absurd reluctance from facts . . . till we consent to face the music in our simple common names, and put Smith into a lyric and Jones into a tragedy." *Their Wedding Journey*, which

William D. Howells

Henry Adams called "a pleasing and faithful picture of American existence," thus exemplifies Howells' early, anti-romantic, Emersonian theory of realism, a tradition that led to Eugene O'Neill's *The Emperor Jones*.

The Saguenay-Quebec travel scene again forms the background for *A Chance Acquaintance* (1873) — "There's nothing like having railroads and steamboats transact your plot for you," said Howells to a friend in 1871. But Kitty Ellison, who had appeared briefly in *Their Wedding Journey*, is a real creation. She is a girl from the West, brought up to revere John Brown and the abolitionists of Boston, bright and witty and unconventional, with natural good manners and taste. She finds the Canadian scene and character as rich and strange as Miles Arbuton of Boston thinks them dull, especially by comparison with European counterparts. Howells probably found his idea for the clash of such differing temperaments in Jane Austen, but his characterization is original — and so is his conclusion. Kitty in the end rejects Arbuton's suit, wholly in accord with Howells and James's shared determination, at this time, to avoid the "everlasting young man and young woman" as a subject for serious fiction. Howells' satire, moreover, on one kind of Boston manners — the stiffness, coldness, and extreme self-regard of Arbuton — is pointed and amusing. James considered Kitty too pert, in the early serial chapters, and also wondered whether Arbuton's proposal might not have been dramatically rendered. But, he wrote his friend, he delighted in a figure "so real and complete, so true and charming." It is no wonder, for Kitty is the older sister of James's Daisy Miller, the first fictional portrait of "the American girl" who would make for Howells and James a linked reputation.

Howells' first "true novel," *A Foregone Conclusion* (1875), was also his first international novel. He was now prepared to venture beyond Canadian-American or native East-West contrasts, and by juxtaposing characters of the New World in the Old, to dramatize a tragic *donnée*. "The hero is a Venetian priest in love with an American girl," he wrote James. "There's richness!" The idea for the novel he had presumably been recurring to since 1866, when he thought of beginning "a romance — the scene of it to be laid in Italy, or Venice, rather" and composed an editorial for the *New York Times* on the celibacy of the priesthood as a cause of corruption in Italian society. He argued further that the current advocacy for clerical marriages was "the most natural and consequent growth from present conditions." Howells drew certain touches in the career of his skeptical inventor-priest from the life of Padre Libera, with whom he had read Dante a decade earlier, and introduced his friend Padre Giacomo, of the Armenian convent, very briefly as Padre Girolamo, a character who serves as a foil to Don Ippolito. But these, along with details of setting repeated from *Venetian Life*, are borrowings at the surface. *The Tragedy of Don Ippolito*, as Howells first titled the novel, gains its depth from four fully imagined characters, a tragic action that develops from their relationships, and a highly functional setting.

In the development of his American consul, Ferris, Howells breathes life into the anti-romantic convention that people rarely fall in love at first sight: for all his intelligence, Ferris is inwardly diffident and slow to recognize that he has become jealous of Don Ippolito, a priest. Howells' Mrs. Vervain, the wealthy widow of a choleric American army officer, is as addlepated as she is amiable. She is thus unable to perceive that Don Ippolito is falling in love with her daughter while he tutors her in Italian, and she is even capable of leading the young priest to believe that he might make his way in the then dis-United States. The moody seventeen-year-old "heroine," Florida Vervain, wavers between sharp-tongued outbursts and remorseful self-abasement. After humiliating Don Ippolito, she promises misguidedly to help him leave the church in which he has never truly believed and find a career in America as an inventor. With these three portraits, Howells' grasp of character matured. But the relationship of the Americans, all of them types of innocence, to the dreamy Italian cleric who has turned his oratory into a forge marks an even greater advance of the novelist in his craft, for it is Don Ippolito's character and the breakup of his illusions that count most. Into this figure Howells dissolves faint aromas of Don Quixote, of Arthur Dimmesdale, of Shylock, in order to show him a divided man, inwardly tormented by "a black and deadly lie." Don Ippolito is both unbelieving priest and impractical inventor, "under sentence of death to the natural ties between himself and the human race" and increasingly deluded in the belief that Florida may love him. Howells had thus firmly prepared his actors, his entangling action, and his setting for the climactic chapter. In the moonlit, walled garden of Casa Vervain, the priest declares his love to Florida, who first repels him in unconscious shock and distaste — and then embraces him in pity and understanding before she runs out of his presence. The unobtrusive symbolism and symbolic reference made in earlier chapters now reach their height simultaneously, as the garden fountain that Don Ippolito had repaired to run briefly every day from its limited supply of water, "capering and babbling on," "all at once, now, as a flame flashes up and then expires . . . leaped and dropped extinct at the foot of the statue."

Howells marred the perfect verity of this ending, under pressure from James T. Fields, by adding a foreshortened epilogue in which he shifted his setting, reported the death of Don Ippolito, and concluded with the marriage of Florida to Ferris. "If I had been perfectly my own master . . ." Howells admitted to C. E. Norton, "the story would have ended with Don Ippolito's rejection." As it was, he kept the final action credible and somber enough. Ferris and Florida speculate fleetingly about Don Ippolito's feelings and motives; and in their consciousness finally he "ceased to be even the memory of a man with a passionate love and a mortal sorrow."

Howells' development as a novelist cannot always be neatly periodized. After completing a major work, he frequently lapsed into an earlier accustomed manner before venturing further — or continued to satisfy the taste of his public for psychologized tales of courtship. So, although it comes after *A Modern Instance* (1882) and *The Rise of Silas Lapham* (1885), both works of more scope, *Indian Summer* (1886) may be said to culminate Howells' first period of small-scale novels of manners, and is probably the best of them. Two interim works preceding *Indian Summer* are "Private Theatricals" (*Atlantic*, 1875) and *The Lady of the Aroos-*

took (1879). The first is a brilliant comic account of Belle Farrell's destroying the friendship of two young men who both become her suitors. A master of feminine psychology, Howells surpassed himself in delineating Mrs. Farrell, a New England Hedda Gabler before Ibsen. Like De Forest's Mrs. LaRue, she is beautiful and clever and irresponsible and yet somehow sympathetic, because she is driven by passions she does not fully understand. The second is a once very popular but much slighter work. In Howells' own words, it is the story of a girl, who, by a series of misunderstandings, "finds herself the only woman on board a vessel going to Italy with three young men" who "do everything they can to keep her from embarrassment or even consciousness," one of whom marries her when they get to Venice.

Howells took especial pleasure in writing *Indian Summer*, chiefly because the realistic comedy of manners (one surmises) was the form most congenial to his temperament in his first period. The story grew out of his revisiting Italy in 1882–83 with his family, and duplicates certain pictures and episodes from Florentine history in *Tuscan Cities* (1886), a travel book that overlapped the novel in serial parts. The runaway carriage episode, the artist Inglehart (Duveneck), and the wish of the point-of-view character, Colville, to write a cultural history of Florence stem from Howells' recent direct experience. Understanding of the pervasive tone of the novel, however, its color and flavor, must be sought in his ambivalent attitude toward Italy revisited and in his response to the values of melancholy and nostalgia in Turgenev's fiction. The sense of loss was all the more clearly defined for him by the rapturous encounter of his daughter Winifred, then eighteen, with the country of her birth.

Indian Summer, Howells told Mark Twain, "is all a variation on the one theme" of January and May, of youth and age. The variations are amusing and complex. Effie Bowen, whom De Forest considered "the most perfectly painted child in fiction," appears to be twelve. Her mother, Lina Bowen, is a charming widow of thirty-eight. Imogene Graham, their guest in Italy, twenty, a happier Florida Vervain, is counterpointed against mother and daughter.

And the forty-one-year-old Colville, involving himself with all three, creates discords among them and multiplies the bemuddlement and the humor before final harmony is attained. Two memorable "confidants" help to spin the plot and clarify the theme. Elderly, curious Mrs. Amsden is always one stage behind in tracing the changes within the triangle and thus maintains the comic note. The Reverend Mr. Waters, aged seventy, who has cheerfully left Haddam East Village for Florence, forever, considers Mrs. Bowen and Colville young and provides Howells perspective.

The narrative method of *Indian Summer* is dramatic. The mood is nostalgia for lost youthful love and the Italian past, in the manner of Turgenev, well tempered by irony and wit. The characters, as noted, are Americans in Italy, of all ages. The action is single, culminating in Colville's marriage to Mrs. Bowen, after his engagement to the girl, Imogene, breaks of its own sentimental weight. But Howells' transforming into fictional life his leading ideas — that longing for youth when youth is past results only in the waste of human energy and devotion, and that the notion of self-sacrifice may prove a pure mischief — is achieved only by close attention to motive and characterization. When Imogene strikes youthful attitudes, or confides her delusions to her astonishing diary, or teeters happily at the edge of a mis-marriage, she errs foolishly and openly. Mrs. Bowen's faults are more subtly, though quite as clearly, indicated. The older woman's repressed jealousy and her wish to conform to European codes of behavior lead her to bewilder Colville and to torture Imogene and herself. Colville, though he often acts like a proto-Prufrock, is a paragon of common sense compared to the women of the novel. As for the carriage accident that reveals Colville's love for Mrs. Bowen, or Effie's appeal at the last moment to prevent Colville's leaving, these are acceptable *coups de théâtre*, because Colville now recognizes Imogene's immaturity, and Imogene has weighed Colville's social ineptitudes and found him wanting. The tone is high comedy. Only the dullest reader would expect disaster in *Indian Summer*.

Colville's sentimental dream of recapturing his lost love, re-embodied in Imogene, thus ends happily in the "clear light of common day" and an uncommonly happy marriage. Colville's inner conflict, however, the tug of war within him between American present and European past, remains unresolved, to profounder but equally satisfying effect. Howells' skill as a novelist is well displayed in the natural symbolism by which he represents this wavering equilibrium. At key points in the action, scene, and internal dialogue, he enriches the theme of Indian summer by contrasts in age, in weather, in season, in history, in country. To name only three: When Colville first glances out on the piazza where he is lodging, it seems full of snow, until he discovers that "it was the white Italian moonlight." Further, Howells manages a most delicate and natural allegory of Florentine flowers to illuminate Colville's varying relations with Effie, Imogene, and Mrs. Bowen — the flowers he gives or forgets to give and the flowers they prefer. (The reference is as unforced in *Indian Summer* as it is exotic and artificial, for example, in Melville's *Mardi*.) And again, at Etruscan Fiesole, the mild Italian spring and the ancient landscape with "history written all over it" are set in Colville's consciousness against the raw country around Buffalo, New York, bursting impatient and lavish with "blossoms and flowers and young leaves and birds." In short, *Indian Summer* embodies the international theme in high comedy, and Colville is an earlier, more fortunate Lewis Lambert Strether. On finishing the work, Howells consciously abandoned the international field to James, and turned his full attention to the American scene.

In Howells' first period, therefore, he began by adapting his formula of travel and observation to fiction, with the sanction of the picaresque novel and perhaps of Heine's *Pictures of Travel*. The methods of Hawthorne and Turgenev and maturing concepts of motive and character led to the comedies of manners and courtship — with the Howellsian difference. Toward the end of the period Howells considered himself a "built-in novelist" because he was competent to begin serializing a work before he had finished it. Yet, despite increasing intensity in plot, the early books are alike in their depending on intersectional and international clash and contrast and on dramatic encounter between "two persons only, or three or four at the most." In the second period, 1880–86, Howells turned to the American scene and to certain large problems of contemporary life. His characters increased in number and variety; his novels grew longer, from six to eight or ten magazine installments. He found justification first in Zola and then in Tolstoi for his matter and his motives. Most strikingly, he had come to the decision to excise those humorous or reflective comments on which he had heretofore leaned heavily in order to win approval for a character or an action — asides which formed for many readers a signature of his style and manner. Thus, the manner of Goldsmith or Thackeray or Heine is much diminished in *A Foregone Conclusion*, and by the time of *Indian Summer*, it has either vanished or become an element of the speech of Colville, a created character.

The second period opens with *The Undiscovered Country* (1880), "a serious work" Howells called it, which ventures into an area that he would explore again and again: the channels into which the will to believe was flowing in contemporary America, as religious convictions decayed and religious sanctions weakened. In this novel Howells sets the delusions of spiritualism in New England against Shaker belief and practice. Dr. Boynton's long decline as a spiritualist parallels the growing liberation of his daughter and medium, Egeria, and reaches its climax in his discovery that his spiritualism has been only a grosser kind of materialism. Apart from its intrinsic interest and its treatment of the father-daughter relation, the novel forms an interesting link between Hawthorne's *The Blithedale Romance* and James's *The Bostonians*.

Dr. Breen's Practice (1881) and *A Woman's Reason* (1883) also explore the growing feminist mood of the decade, but the author's stance is at least as masculine and satirical as it is sympathetic. Though Dr. Grace Breen, a homeopathist fresh from medical school, is first humbled by and then humbles the allopathist Dr. Mulbridge, her marriage to the man she loves cannot alter her bottom nature. She is a belated Puritan, a devotee of New England "dutiolatry." *A Woman's Reason* reduces the Boston society girl

Helen Harkness to destitution at her father's death, and depicts her failures as she attempts to paint vases, sell sketches, write book reviews, and make fashionable hats. Her plight is further complicated by proposals from a vulgar American banker and a shy, intense English lord. It is difficult to tell how cynical Howells was when he brought back to life the young naval officer whom he had shipwrecked, early in the story, in the Pacific Ocean — but it is certain that the marriage of Helen Harkness, like Egeria Boynton's and Grace Breen's, ends the story on a decidedly subdued note. Howells failed to make *A Woman's Reason* interesting, either as melodrama or as burlesque.

A Modern Instance (1882) is a very different story. It was born in Howells' mind as "The New Medea" when he conceived an Indiana divorce case as a commonplace example of the dire ancient conflict in Euripides' drama. It grew with Howells' experience of the quarrels between his summer landlord and landlady in 1875 and 1876 — a "tragedy, dreary and squalid beyond conception," he called it. It was written under the stimulus of reading Zola, "everything . . . I can get my hands on," and displayed a powerful motive and a firm grasp of the characters. Ostensibly the novel treats divorce and the failure of belief; less obviously but more truly it probes the mystery of love turned to hatred.

Marcia Gaylord is a most intensely imagined and realized character — pretty, self-centered, full-blooded, bewildered, hotly jealous. She is the child of parents who are as attached to her as they are cold to each other. Her marriage to Bartley Hubbard ends disastrously, partly because her uncontrolled temper and tendency to self-indulgence find counter-traits in her good-humored but amoral husband. Squire Gaylord, the agnostic lawyer of Equity, Maine, and his reproachful self-effacing wife habitually allow Marcia her way but do not give her a sustaining standard of conduct or belief. Hubbard, an orphan who has made his own way through college into small-town journalism, achieves his majority like Marcia with few convictions and grows increasingly sure that only those of his acts that the world sees can be of any account. Given a chance at the bar, enough money, a few friends, Hubbard might have prospered and lived out his life, however stormily, with his wife and child—so Howells seems to imply. But the virus of countinghouse journalism and Marcia's loss of faith in him lead to his cheating Kinney, a devoted friend, for money. This using of a friend brings on, in turn, the break with Ricker, his friend and conscience, the losing of his editorial job, and a final violent quarrel with Marcia over his encounter with a former Equity girl turned prostitute. When Hubbard leaves Boston and loses his pocketbook, return seems impossible. He perjures himself seeking an Indiana divorce, again runs away when confronted in court by the enraged Squire Gaylord, and dies—so it is reported—in Whited Sepulchre, Arizona.

James's well-known charge that the American scene too meagerly nourished the novelist's needs is refuted in this novel. As Howells wrote his publisher, J. R. Osgood, his story was to be on "no mean scale geographically." He was fully aware how the background, East and West, might add life to his characters and clarify his theme. So tight-fisted Equity, where the rats smell in the wainscoting, prefigures Boston as the Hubbards know it, a city of high rents and mean streets and sharp social cleavages, and the raw town of easy divorce, Tecumseh, Indiana, as well.

The Tecumseh courthouse and its tobacco-chewing idlers form the backdrop for Howells' most intense scene. There Squire Gaylord, accipitrine in feature and in his hatred of Bartley, defends his daughter's conduct and proves his son-in-law a liar, only to be brought down in the midst of the trial with a stroke. Howells does not end *A Modern Instance* at this point, however. True to his realistic tenets he returns to half-crippled Ben Halleck's futile struggle between his conscience and his long-indulged love for the widowed Marcia, and to the debate, still further removed from reality, of Clara Kingsbury and her wealthy lawyer-husband, Atherton, as to Ben's proper course. But the issue is no issue. Bartley is dead. Halleck regresses to Calvinist orthodoxy and self-punishment. In Marcia the spring of tenderness is broken, and she will, surely, return to the narrow life of Equity and "stiffen into the old man's aridity." Though the ending of the novel is open, it is not indeterminate.

When *A Modern Instance* appeared, Robert Louis Stevenson (who had married a divorcée) withdrew an invitation to Howells to visit him because he thought Howells was condemning divorce. Much later Edith Wharton accused Howells of "moral timidity" that had checked him from arriving at a logical conclusion, even as she acknowledged his pioneer treatment of "the tragic potentialities of life in the drab American small town." Neither writer had followed the long logic of the tale or understood Howells' view that "the novel ends well that ends faithfully." No second marriage could ever redeem the past for either Halleck or Marcia Hubbard. Despite the weakened dramatic tension in the last chapters, Howells achieved his "strongest" work, as he himself believed, in *A Modern Instance*. It is a moving representation of moral ignorance and moral decay, unmatched until Dreiser imagined Hurstwood and Fitzgerald created Dr. Diver.

The Rise of Silas Lapham (1885) opens dramatically with an interview between Bartley Hubbard, still a struggling reporter, and the newly rich paint-king of Boston, on the perennially fascinating subject of how he had made his million. The novel has always been popular, partly because it presents Lapham's financial and social failure as "consciously and deliberately chosen" when he has to decide whether he shall cheat and stay on top in business, or tell the truth and fail irrecoverably. Lapham's true rise is therefore moral, and all the more dramatic in the context of the elastic business codes of the Gilded Age and his own business failure.

How much the novelist had learned of his art by the age of forty-eight appears in the complexities of the plot. Lapham's physical strength and bulk and country speech indicate that he is still the son of a hard-scrabble Vermont farmer. He is vigorous, raw, naive, uneducated, and socially ambitious for his wife and two daughters — a man who had risen fast as a competent soldier and officer in the Civil War. In sharp contrast, Bromfield Corey is physically slight, well-educated, once fought under Garibaldi and has lived much abroad, lives moderately on family money, and plays at painting.

William D. Howells

In wit and ancestry he represents the Boston Brahmin type par excellence. Howells' device for bringing the two families into contact and conflict is chiefly the confused triangle of Tom Corey, the son, and Irene and Penelope Lapham, the daughters. Tom's polite attention to both girls and Irene's charming but nitwit egotism lead the Laphams to believe that he loves Irene, so that Tom's eventual proposal to witty, reserved Penelope precipitates a period of harsh learning of "the economy of pain," as the Reverend Mr. Sewell calls it, before Tom and Penelope marry — and leave for Mexico.

But the heart motive of the novel, as Howells' original synopsis shows, is Lapham's determination to emulate Boston society and to make his family a part of it. The first clear sign that he will fail occurs in the dinner party scene at the Coreys', midway in the novel, when Lapham becomes boastfully tipsy — the result of his being unused to wine and of Corey's lapse of tact as he fails to note this fact. The vividest symbolic indication of Lapham's determination is Silas' "letting out" his mare and cutter one winter afternoon on the Longwood road. Driving with iron control and unmolested by the mounted policemen, he passes a "hundred rival sledges" with little apparent risk. The effective symbol of Lapham's desire is his building a new house on the Back Bay — a handsome, airy structure, with library and music room, to be decorated in white and gold. It is the product of an architect's taste, chiefly: Lapham contributes only money. The impression of this new house is strengthened by contrast to the ugly farmhouse of Lapham's childhood; the dark, overheated, over-finished house in Nankeen Square; Mrs. Corey's "old-fashioned" house with a classic portico and "bare" interior; and Bromfield Corey's "ancestral halls" in Salem, presumably of the seventeenth century. When the new house burns to the ground, the insurance on it lapsed, Lapham must confess that he had set it on fire himself, carelessly, trying out his new fireplace. In the end, Lapham wrestles, like Jacob, with an angel and achieves an unhappy victory with his conscience; he tells Sewell that if "the thing was to do over again, right in the same way, I guess I should have to do it." Howells presents the larger conflict of Laphams and Coreys more stringently, however, and despite the marriage of the

177

most businesslike Corey and the most cultured Lapham, the couple cannot remain in Boston. Of this conflict, Howells says: "It is certain that our manners and customs go for more in life than our qualities. The price that we pay for civilisation is the fine yet impassable differentiation of these. Perhaps we pay too much; but it will not be possible to persuade those who have the difference in their favour that this is so."

The Rise of Silas Lapham is more finely proportioned at the beginning than in the last third. This may be due to Howells' need to foreshorten Lapham's slow business decline; but it also stems from his inability to make business loss as interesting as social climbing, or even as Irene's error in love and her hardening into maturity. James's comment on his *Roderick Hudson*, that its head was too big for its body, applies equally here. But in terms of style, the novel deserves its reputation. Bromfield Corey's wit and Penelope's tartness gain from contrast with Colonel Lapham's boastful speech, in the idioms and rhythms of his New England vernacular. Howells' narrative prose is equally functional, concrete, and clear. This was the style that both James and Twain, themselves stylists, found so distinctive and took so much pleasure in.

The serious motive and the large impression of occupations and professions that Howells sought in the fiction of his second period gave way to profound concern with social and economic questions in the third period, the decade from 1887 to 1894. In these years he suffered his profound spiritual and psychological crisis. The ground shifted under his feet when he stood, almost alone, in a glare of publicity after he asserted the rights of the Chicago anarchists. His daughter's death brought sharp suffering: perhaps he had sought the wrong treatment. He experienced a sense of alienation, as well as excitement, in moving to New York. In 1886, almost inadvertently he became involved in a sharp, often bad-tempered, running battle concerning the new realism with a host of critics because of his "monthly ministrations of gall and wormwood" in "The Editor's Study" of *Harper's*.

Howells plunged into this storm of change, weathered it, and emerged from it largely by learning the "transcendent vision" of

William D. Howells

Leo Tolstoi and adopting Christian socialism. Most of his novels in the period have been characterized as "economic" novels, and it is true that they share certain characteristics of the *tendenz-romansk* or propaganda novel, a form Howells scorned. Ideologically they culminate in *A Traveler from Altruria* (1894), a Utopian romance that brings together Howells' ideas in defense of liberty, equality, and fraternity in that altruistic "other land" which America only partially shadowed forth. But "novels of complicity" is a more accurate tag than "economic" novels, because complicity is the dominant concept in them; and a "panoramic theory of fiction" — Howells' own phrase as Van Wyck Brooks later reported it — is equally useful since it fits these works concerned with the lives of many rather than few characters. These definitions, however, apply only to the main stream in the third period; they will not account for *April Hopes* (1888) or *The Shadow of a Dream* (1890) — both substantial novels and each different in form and motive.

In *The Minister's Charge; or, The Apprenticeship of Lemuel Barker* (1887) Howells first fully stated his doctrine of complicity, combining it with that major motif of the nineteenth-century novel, the provincial in the city. The minister, Sewell, has unintentionally encouraged Lemuel to come to Boston from his home in the country by politely dishonest praise of the boy's poems. Lemuel becomes his "charge." And in a sermon he is driven to conclude that "no one for good or for evil, for sorrow or joy, for sickness or health, stood apart from his fellows, but each was bound to the highest and the lowest by ties that centred in the hand of God. . . . If a community was corrupt, if an age was immoral, it was not because of the vicious, but the virtuous who fancied themselves indifferent spectators." Sewell's rhetoric is heightened by echoes from the marriage ceremony, and takes on additional ironic force in the context of Barker's fortunate escape later from marriage to a factory worker, "poor, sick, flimsy little Statira" Dudley. The reason for Barker's escape is striking. Just as sexual passion turning to hatred and the persistent tie between father and daughter had spun the plot of *A Modern Instance*, so masculine, "whopper-jawed"

'Manda Grier retains her hold, implicitly sexual, upon Statira, against Barker's sense of obligation to the girl. Thus "The Country Boy in Boston"— this was Howells' first title for the novel — fails and returns to the country; and thus Howells stands the American drama of the self-made man on its head. The work is suffused with other and subtler ironies that delighted Mark Twain, for example, which make up for the blurred double focus on Sewell and Barker. To suggest only two: Sewell preaches complicity but is unable to conceive of Barker's torment when he falls in love with the gentle Jessie Carver while he is still pledged to Statira. (One thinks of Clyde Griffiths.) The society girl Sibyl Vane treats Barker as her inferior with cutting arrogance, even as she finds time to bestow "a jacqueminot rosebud on a Chinaman dying of cancer" in a charity hospital.

The naked issue of charity versus justice becomes, in fact, the central issue of *Annie Kilburn* (1889), though Howells keeps his actors in this Tolstoian novel thoroughly limited and human. For all his social passion, Peck, the egalitarian minister of Hatboro, Massachusetts, cares little for his motherless child. Putney, the lawyer who defends the mill workers in labor disputes, is a periodic drunkard. And Annie Kilburn, Lady Bountiful with a conscience, fails utterly in her efforts to help the working poor of her company town, marries the apolitical doctor, and "waits, and mostly forgets, and is mostly happy."

Between March 1889 and October 1891, Howells published in serial form three extraordinary books: *A Hazard of New Fortunes* (1890), *The Shadow of a Dream* (1890), and *An Imperative Duty* (1892). The third is an intensely imagined study of miscegenation. The second, taking its title from *The Scarlet Letter*, explores the morbid psychology of jealous delusion; it is an experimental novel rendered from three points of view, anticipating rather than following James. The first is very simply Howells' biggest novel. It sets forth panoramically, as *Manhattan Transfer* would later, the struggles of fifteen major characters and a host of minor figures to establish a national magazine in New York City and to enter into its "vast, gay, shapeless life." The execution of the Chicago anar-

William D. Howells

chists and the Brooklyn trolley-car strike of 1889 provided Howells with a "strenuous action" and an "impressive catastrophe." A "moment of great psychological import" both national and private added tensions. And his theme, the American scramble for success with the inner revulsions bred by that struggle, lent the whole fable "dignity," as Howells himself later claimed.

A Hazard of New Fortunes envisions the city as a magnet and a microcosm. In social terms it contrasts Margaret Vance, the sensitive girl of old New York society, with the Dryfoos daughters, Christine and Mela, whose one aim is to break into society under the guidance of the well-paid Mrs. Mandel. The elegant but unsure Beaton wavers in the middle, courting independent Alma Leighton and flirtatious Christine. At the bottom are Lindau and a prostitute pursued by the police, slum-dwellers, the one by choice and the other by necessity. In political-economic terms, the novel presents Dryfoos as the coldest of newly rich entrepreneur-speculators, with Fulkerson as his prophet, in contrast to Conrad Dryfoos, the son, who turns from his father and his father's life to passive resistance and Christian socialism. Similarly, Colonel Woodburn, whose private integrity matches his admiration for the feudal institutions of the prewar South, is set against Lindau, a German revolutionary who has lost his forearm fighting slavery in the Civil War. Still another kind of contrast appears in the characters' attitudes toward art: Beaton's great talent, Alma Leighton's aspirations, the barbarous taste of the Dryfoos family. In moral worth as well, Howells sets his characters in a kind of hierarchy, as George Arms has argued, from lowest to highest: Beaton, Dryfoos, Fulkerson, March, Woodburn, Lindau, and Conrad Dryfoos.

The measure of Howells' skill in representing "God-given complexity of motive" within these characters is that they act out their roles credibly. Beaton fails in a half-comic attempt at suicide. Lindau, a new John Brown, fights with the police in the strike and, his arm again shattered, dies of injuries. Conrad attempts conciliation in the strike and is shot in the heart. Dryfoos suffers, and takes his half-savage daughters off to Europe. Margaret Vance becomes a nun in a charitable sisterhood. March, the witness and chorus-character, is now able to buy the magazine that originally brought the group together. Yet at the moment of his success, March says to his wife, ". . . so we go on, pushing and pulling, climbing and crawling, thrusting aside and trampling underfoot; lying, cheating, stealing . . . to a palace of our own, or the poorhouse," blind to the principle that "if a man will work he shall both rest and eat." "And so we go on," March cries, "trembling before Dryfooses and living in gimcrackeries."

Howells had looked at Boston society from the bottom in *The Minister's Charge*. He had surveyed a Massachusetts mill town from the top in *Annie Kilburn*. Now in *A Hazard* he consciously employed the "historical" form, anatomizing New York City through many eyes. Though James thought the "composition" weak, he found the novel as a whole "simply prodigious," just as Twain considered it "a great book" wrought with "high art." One may not dismiss these appraisals as friendly prejudice: the novel singularly combines the wit of Jane Austen and the elaborate irony of Thorstein Veblen, before Veblen. It is a broad, vital comedy, as provocative in its implications as it is entertaining in its fable, in which Howells artfully and unobtrusively colored the public dream of success with private awareness of complicity.

Following the period of novels of complicity, which ended in the romance *A Traveler from Altruria*, Howells reverted to smaller canvases in his fiction, now persuaded that the great social questions must be represented from within rather than from without. Characteristic and perhaps best of the novels between 1894 and 1908 is *The Landlord at Lion's Head* (1897). Here Howells' idea was to bring a true New England rustic type into conflict with Cambridge and Harvard society, and his bottom motive was to realize "that anti-Puritan quality which was always vexing the heart of Puritanism." The great ambition of his hero, Jeff Durgin, is to build a fashionable summer hotel on the shoulder of his native mountain, Lion's Head. In the course of realizing it, the aggressive Durgin hardens from the contempt he suffers as a "jay" at college, and from his experience with three young women. Genevieve Vostrand refuses Jeff's offer of marriage, preferring a titled Italian, but at the last after separation from her husband and her husband's death, accepts the successful "landlord." Bessie Lynde, a Cambridge society girl, flirts and has a tentative affair with Jeff before her alcoholic brother horsewhips him. Cynthia, the country girl with whom he has grown up, who loves him, is reluctantly forced to give him up. With all three girls, but especially with Bessie, Jeff gets a dark glimpse into "the innate enmity between the sexes" in the game of courtship and passion — "passion lived" and "passion played." As the novel ends, Durgin is thoroughly successful on his own terms, taking for his motto, "You pay, or you don't pay, just as it happens." His career has borne him out. He might have succumbed to drink, except for his will and his constitution. He might have formed a dangerous liaison with Bessie Lynde, but her brother whipped him. He might have murdered Alan Lynde, but circumstance and obscure impulse spared him. He might have committed arson and been caught, but the old hotel burned by accident. Clearly, Howells created this new Bartley Hubbard, the successful failure who suffers from an incapacity for good, with special sympathy and entire aesthetic control. More nearly naturalistic than any other story by Howells, it is as Delmar Cooke judged it "a master novel."

Finally, *The Leatherwood God* (1916) represents a late, fine flowering of Howells' talent and his one punitive tragedy. It recreates the rise of an actual Ohio backwoodsman of the 1840's, who deluded others and even himself momentarily into believing that he was God. Dylks's power arises from his stallion-like sexuality and from the will to believe of spiritually starved women of the frontier. His fall is necessary, but it is moving because it carries so many with him.

Turning from Howells' fiction to his critical theory, one may observe that interpretation of his fiction is further advanced than elucidation of his critical principles or his practical criticism in their full range. Three reasons for this condition may be suggested. First, the mass of Howells' critical writing remains uncollected and it is therefore difficult to view it in sequence or as a whole. Second, Howells' usual critical stance implies that criticism is a secondary form of discourse. Third, the body of critical writing by which he has usually been judged, *Criticism and Fiction* (1891), is argumentative, rhetorical, for the moment, and not wholly representative. It is well to recall that the novel came to be treated seriously, as "literature," only within Howells' lifetime, and that much contemporary criticism was vitiated by irresponsible anonymity or puffery or exhibitionism or ignorance. Howells wrote reviews and critical essays in every year from 1859 to 1920, as a journalist. But he loved literary art, especially the art of fiction. His best criticism is reasoned, reflected, distilled. He was a critic in spite of himself.

Despite his low opinion of the critical office, then, Howells formed a theory of fiction that was subtler and more eclectic than literary history has allowed. Certainly its effect was and has been far-reaching. (It is possible that he is one of those masters "who are more accepted through those they have influenced than in themselves," but this is not the view taken here.) Hackwork and journalism aside, few critics of his day are comparable to him in breadth, in subtlety when he is engaged, and in clairvoyance.

The first element, at once apparent, in Howells' early theory of the realistic novel is his dislike for "*Slop, Silly Slop*," as Nanny Corey characterizes a popular novel. The generic sloppiness of such fiction, Howells believed, derived from sentimental thought, melodramatic action, and poorly motivated character. Of course, James, Twain, De Forest, and many lesser realists shared Howells' revulsion and strengthened him in his view. Very early, Howells and James decided to ignore or play down, so far as they could, simple-minded courtships in favor of other significant relations — of mother and son, father and daughter, husband and wife — and of other passions than love, such as avarice, ambition, hatred, envy, devotion, friendship.

Conversely, Howells early developed a positive concept of form from the example of Turgenev and by reaction against the method of his early idols, Dickens and Thackeray. If readers were to take the novel seriously, then the novelist himself must take his craft seriously, and without intruding or commenting or appealing to the reader, learn to represent, to describe, and to dramatize. That is, if the illusion of life was worth creating, it was worth preserving unbroken. "Everything necessary to the reader's intelligence should be quietly and artfully supplied," Howells maintains, "and nothing else should be added." In these early years Howells distrusted the French writers for the moral vacuity or the obsessive sexuality in their tales, but he accepted as law Flaubert's dictum that the writer must be everywhere present in his work and everywhere invisible. A corollary of this dramatic ideal of Howells was that a strong motive and a firm, long-brooded-over grasp of character were equally necessary for the aspiring realist. It was character that counted, and not the "moving accidents" and thrilling adventures of earlier or popular contemporary tale-telling. In short, Howells' first concept of the novel was that the writer ought to begin by imagining several characters in the round, then bring them together to work out a credible dramatic action. He accepted the ideal of the novel of character the more readily because biography and autobiography fascinated him, both their form and their matter, and he was already writing and translating plays. Howells stated this double principle clearly in his essay on "Henry James, Jr.," in the *Century* (1882).

Plot, then, in the sense of continual gross or overt actions, Howells found less interesting than the slower pace of life as he observed it, "interiorly" and "exteriorly." It followed that a novel might end inconclusively, in the view of readers accustomed to the usual marriages, prosperity, and tying up of loose ends, and yet end faithfully and "well." Howells' youthful passion for Cervantes, his fondness for the episodic "memoirs" of Tom Sawyer and Huckleberry Finn, and his pleasure in the moral logic of Isabel Archer's final decision all confirmed him in his approving the open or ironic ending. To cite only one example, from his fictional practice, he brought *April Hopes*, a sardonic story of courtship, to this conclusion: "If he had been different she would not have asked him to be frank and open; if she had been different, he might have been frank and open. This was the beginning of their married life."

As the vehicle for the "new fiction," Howells advocated, published, and practiced a new, supple, colloquial English, taking as his authority writers so diverse as Dante and Emerson, James Russell Lowell and Artemus Ward, Mark Twain and Henry James. The "language of the street" in many regional varieties functions vitally in his own fiction, and he praised it as it appeared in the "local color" stories of Harte, De Forest, Cable, Frederic, Garland, and even Norris and Crane. He even taught it with some success to his Norwegian protégé, H. H. Boyesen. Mark Twain chiefly created a revolution in the language of fiction; Howells was the architect of the revolution. For many years Howells effectively and persistently advocated the use in fiction of native backgrounds, manners, and speech, often in the light of national difference. Hence it is no wonder that he pioneered, with James, in the international novel, and invented a new kind of city-novel. H. L. Mencken, who cites Howells frequently in *The American Language*, brackets him only a little grudgingly with Twain and Whitman as a chief proponent of American English. Thus, the language line from Emerson through Howells, Twain, and Whitman to Stephen Crane, Robert Frost, Gertrude Stein, Sherwood Anderson, and Ernest Hemingway is a line of direct descent.

These, in sum, are the major propositions of Howells' earlier theory of fiction, and most of them persist in his later theory. He modified his views in several respects during the free-lance years, 1881–86, and the period of novels of complicity and argumentative criticism, 1886–94. Most obviously, he wrote panoramic novels with larger casts of characters under a compulsion to treat the "social question" in an economic chance-world. A less apparent but equally significant change was his creating chorus characters, to serve as centers of consciousness or to focus upon ethical issues implicit in the action. Atherton, Evans, Sewell, the March couple, and others create the illusion of an ongoing society by their reappearance; but their prime reason for being is to debate moral questions more lucidly than less conscious or less dispassionate characters can. But, despite the success of *A Hazard of New Fortunes*, Howells never lost his interest in the psychological "novelette."

William D. Howells

Both *The Shadow of a Dream* (1890) and his liking for Stephen Crane's economical, effective stories suggest this persisting interest. In fact, Howells came in the end to believe that "the phenomena of our enormous enterprise" were not truly the "best material for fiction," except as such wonders of the "outer world" could be related to the "miracles of the inner world."

Defining Howells' key terms, especially as they are used in his later essays on major writers and in his lecture "Novel-Writing and Novel-Reading" (delivered 1899, published 1958), will serve to round out this sketch of his fictional theory, and to suggest his view of the ends of literature. Howells conceived of three ways of representing life in fiction: the novel, the romance, and the romanticistic novel. The novel, which comes from the sincere endeavor "to picture life just as it is," deals with character and incidents that "grow out of character." It is the "supreme form" of fiction, exemplified in *Pride and Prejudice*, *Middlemarch*, *Anna Karenina*, *Fathers and Sons*, *Doña Perfecta*, and *Marta y María*. The romance, Howells says, deals with life "allegorically," in terms of the ideal, of types, and of the passions broadly treated. *The Scarlet Letter* and *The Marble Faun*, Sylvester Judd's *Margaret*, and Stevenson's *Dr. Jekyll and Mr. Hyde* exemplify the form. Romances, he adds, partake of the nature of poems and are not to be judged by "the rules of criticism that apply to the novel." But the romanticistic novel seeks effect rather than truth, according to Howells: its motives are false, it is excessive in coloring and drawing, and it revels in "the extravagant, the unusual, and the bizarre." Two very great men, Dickens and Hugo, wrote books of this kind. Their success is due to readers, prevailing in number, who have childish imaginations and no self-knowledge.

As to the "outward shape of the inward life of the novel," Howells contends, the three principal kinds are the autobiographical, the biographical, and the historical. The first he holds to be the most perfect literary form after the drama, because the tale-teller is master of the situation and can report his first-person narrator's mind with authority. But the "I" narrator cannot go outside his own observations, the range of the form is narrow, and none of the greatest novels have been written in it except *Gil Blas*, though it is the form of *The Luck of Barry Lyndon, The Blithedale Romance*, and *David Copperfield*. (One wonders if Howells exempted, or forgot, *Adventures of Huckleberry Finn*.) The biographical novel, as Howells defines it, is the form in which the author's central figure, who must be of "paramount importance," reflects all the facts and feelings involved. Though he considers it "nearly as cramping as the autobiographical," he asserts that Henry James had used it in *Roderick Hudson* and has lately cast in it "work of really unimpeachable perfection." Here Howells is in effect predicting James's work of "the major phase." But the "great form," however impure and imperfect, he declares with much force and eloquence, is the "historical" form — the novel as if it were history. In it the novelist enters into the minds and hearts of his characters, invents speeches for them, gives their innermost thoughts and desires, and has their confidence in hours of passion or of remorse or even of death itself. He is a "universal intelligence" in this world. In spite of the contradictions, absurdities, improbabilities, and impossibilities inherent in the historical form, Howells prizes it as the "primal form of fiction" and a form of the future. "Think," he says, "of *Don Quixote*, of *Wilhelm Meister*, of *The Bride of Lammermoor*, of *I Promessi Sposi*, of *War and Peace*, of *Fathers and Sons*, of *Middlemarch*, of *Pendennis*, of *Bleak House*, of *Uncle Tom's Cabin*, of *The Scarlet Letter*, of *L'Assommoir*, of the *Grandissimes*, of *Princess Casamassima*, of *Far from the Madding Crowd*," all masterpieces. The historical form may be "sprawling, splay-footed, gangling, proportionless and inchoate," he concludes, "but if it is true to the life which it can give no authority for seeming to know, it is full of beauty and symmetry."

The term "symmetry," drawn from Howells' study of art and architecture, introduces related ideas in his terms "perspective," "relation," and "proportion." All of them stem from his fondness for eighteenth-century English thought: concepts of rationality and control, measure and balance. The novel, he explained to Stephen Crane in an interview (1894), is "a perspective made for the benefit of people who have no true use of their eyes. The novel

William D. Howells

. . . adjusts the proportions. It preserves the balances." And again, it is "the business of the novel to picture the daily life . . . with an absolute and clear sense of proportion." What Howells means by these terms is presumably formal skill in representing norms of experience within the "microcosm" of the novel. Thus a storyteller like Maupassant, in Howells' view, often fails because he is "obsessed" with his own rather than with universal experience. Like Arnold, quoting Sophocles, Howells' goal is to "see life steadily and see it whole."

The effect that a novelist may achieve by representing his characters and their actions in "relation and proportion" is beauty and repose — terms not ordinarily associated with Howells' theory but central to his deepest intent. Repose, he explains (even as he admits he cannot define it), may arise from squalor or grief or agony in a piece of fiction; yet it is the quality that charms readers in every age, it is "the soul of beauty in all its forms." By repose, Howells may mean catharsis, "all passion spent," or he may mean the reader's rational pleasure in the inevitable working out of fictional logic. Perhaps he means both. As for truth, from truth to beauty is scarcely a step in Howells' theory of fiction. Realism is but the "truthful treatment of material," or the "truest possible picture of life." Truth, which is the only beauty, is "truth to human experience, and human experience is so manifold and so recondite, that no scheme can be too remote, too airy for the test."

If Howells seems vague in this definition of truth in the novel, he is far more precise in asserting what the business of the novelist is and what effect the masterwork of fiction has on its audience. The novelist, he asserts, had "better not aim to please," and he "had still better not aim to instruct." His story must be a work of art, outside the realms of polemics and ethics, and if his story does not tell, nothing in it tells. What, then, he asks, is the purpose of the novel, the chief intellectual stimulus and influence of the day, this "supreme literary form, the fine flower of the human story"? His answer is both shrewd and penetrating. Though *The Scarlet Letter* or *Romola* may at once instill the dread of falsehood, he says, the novel can affect readers only so far as it shall "charm their minds

189

and win their hearts." It can do no good directly. "It shall not be the bread," Howells urges, "but the grain of wheat which must sprout and grow in the reader's soul and be harvested in his experience, and in the mills of the gods ground slowly perhaps many years before it shall duly nourish him." In his essay on Ibsen (1906), Howells restated his resolution of the ancient dispute over literature's instructing or pleasing. He said: "The great and dreadful delight of Ibsen is from his power of dispersing the conventional acceptations by which men live on easy terms with themselves, and obliging them to examine the grounds of their social and moral opinions." In the end of ends, Howells made this slow-working indirect power the prime tenet of his critical theory. He sought it in his own fiction. He achieved it in his best novels.

Henry James

HENRY JAMES was the "largest" literary figure to come out of America during the nineteenth and early twentieth centuries. He was not "large" as Melville is large; he did not have Melville's global vision, nor did he dream of epical landscapes. His largeness stemmed rather from the literary territories he annexed to the New World and the career he fashioned in two hemispheres. At a time when American literature was still young and certain of its writers were still sharpening their pens, Henry James crossed from the New World to the Old and was able to take his seat at the table of fiction beside George Eliot and Turgenev, Flaubert and Zola. He found the novel in English still the easy undisciplined and relaxed form it had been from its early days, and he refashioned it into a complex work of literary art. If he was junior to the fellow crafts-men whom he joined in Europe, he achieved, in the fullness of time, a status equal to them, and in some instances he surpassed them. For he was not only a practitioner of fiction; he was one of its finest critics and theorists. It was he who gave us the terminology most useful in our time for the criticism of the novel.

Henry James wrote for fifty years; he was a prolific writer and several times glutted his own market. Never a "best seller," as we know best sellers today, he nevertheless earned an honorable living by his pen. He was fortunate in being born into an affluent family; but from his early twenties he began to earn his own way and wholly by literary work. He was alone among major American writers in never seeking any other employment. He was devoted to his art; and his productivity did not affect his meticulous style — that style by which he believed a writer gains his passport to posterity. At first his prose was clear and fresh; later it became magnificently weighted and complex in its allusiveness and imagery — and its evocative power. His goals remained always aesthetic. He believed from the first that the artist in fiction is a historian of that part of life never found in history books: the private life that goes on behind the walls of dwellings but is also a part of the society in which it is lived. Literature for him was the great repository of life; and he believed that if the novel is a mirror in a roadway, it reflects not only the panorama of existence, but the countenance of the artist in the act of experiencing the world around him.

During his five decades of creation he brought into being twenty novels and one hundred and twelve tales, some of them almost of novel length. He was the first of the great psychological realists in our time, on a much more complicated and more subtly subjective level than his Russian predecessors, Turgenev, Tolstoi, and Dostoevski. In his productivity and the high level of his writing, in his insight into human motivation, and in his possession of the architectonics of fiction, he was a remarkable innovator, constantly fertile, bold, and independent — and a man with a style. R. P. Blackmur has imaged him as a sort of Shakespeare of the novel, in the power with which he brought into being, at the century's turn, with extraordinary rapidity, his three magisterial works — *The Ambassadors*, *The Wings of the Dove*, and *The Golden Bowl* — as Shakespeare set down in fast succession his three great tragedies at the turn of another century. René Wellek has spoken of James as a kind of American Goethe, Olympian in his view of literature and life, certainly in his capacity to hold both at arm's length as he analyzed and reflected upon them — upon poetry and truth, man and reality. Such a continuing reassessment of James's reputation — so recently set aside and disparaged — has brought him to his proper place among the world's large literary figures, and established him among the greatest artists of the novel.

Criticism has perhaps not done sufficient justice to Henry James's uniqueness in fiction. He alone created the cosmopolitan novel in English and made of it a rich study of men, manners, and morals on two continents. More significant still, he was able to treat both as comedy and as tragedy his transatlantic vision of the New World's relations to the Old. In doing this he anticipated the central fact of the twentieth century — America's assumption, among the nations of the world, of those international responsibilities from which it once isolated itself. James early recognized the drama of the confrontation of the New World and the Old — at a time when Americans were too busy on their own expanding continent to be aware of it, and when Europe considered itself sufficiently distant to be able to ignore its transatlantic offspring, or to be interested in it essentially as the land of Fenimore Cooper's Indians — or as a land to be viewed with that "certain condescension" of which Lowell complained.

In James's fiction Americans are often treated as if they still possess the innocence of Eden; and in their unawareness of evil they are shown as highly vulnerable once they venture outside their American paradise. This large drama James projected, during his later phase, as a drama of consciousness, for he had a profound sense of man's inner life. All his virtuosity was addressed, in his fiction, to discovering how to capture in words the subjective, the reflective, and even the phantasmagorial side of man.

It is because Henry James wrote so much and experimented so widely, was so complex a literary "case," that criticism has found it difficult to see him whole. In recent years, however, his authority and his vision have increasingly imposed themselves, and certain of his formulations have entered into the very texture of twentieth-century literary thought. As one of the first modern psychological analysts in the novel his influence has been pervasive. Joseph Conrad, Ford Madox Ford, James Joyce, Virginia Woolf, Dorothy Richardson, Graham Greene are among the many novelists who derived technique or aesthetic ideas from the fount of Henry James. It was no accident that even during his lifetime certain of his fellow novelists abroad addressed this American in their midst as "Master."

The literary career of Henry James extended from the last days of the American Civil War to the middle of the first world war. He was born in New York City and belongs, in America's literary annals, with two other sturdy children of Manhattan, Herman Melville and Walt Whitman. The three can now be seen as distinctly urban artists: their vision was of the sea-girt city and of the ocean attaching America to the world; of ferries and teeming commerce, and a city-community — as distinct from the local vision of the rooted children of the orchards and woods of Concord. Thus, where the New England writers were more abstract and philosophical — their works still linked to the pulpit and the sermon in spite of a disengagement from them — the writings of the New Yorkers dealt with things concrete and palpable. Melville's glimpse of faraway life in the Pacific made him forever a great cosmopolite of the spirit; and Henry James's transatlantic life made him a cosmopolite of fact. Walt Whitman, for all his "cosmos," also dealt in concretions. All three paid their respects to a "flowering" New England, but they represented on their side a great urban flowering — a great urban impulse — in the new American literature.

It is not surprising that James, in later years, was to speak of his Concord predecessors as "exquisite provincials," and indeed, of Thoreau, as being "worse than provincial — he was parochial." He said this not in an altogether derogatory sense: he was simply describing their limited untraveled state, their adherence to homely things and the worldly wisdom that came out of reflection on native ground rather than out of action and life abroad. James spoke of them as would a cosmopolite for whom the Old World and the New had figured from the very first as a kind of double-landscape. For, although he was born just off Broadway, at No. 21 Washington Place, he was taken abroad when he was less than six months old. He opened his eyes of childhood upon European lawns and gardens; and one of his earliest memories was of the Napoleonic column in the Place Vendôme. Nevertheless he was returned to Manhattan when he was just learning to walk. If his eyes had first observed Europe, his feet planted themselves firmly upon American soil — that of Washington Square, within a stone's throw of where he had been born and the Square that would furnish him with the title of one of his most popular short novels. He spent a boyhood in the streets of what was then "uptown" but what is to-day the lower part of Fifth Avenue. With summers on Staten Island, and trips up the Hudson, with the familiar teeming scenes of Broadway, and in a New York of muddy streets with chickens on the sidewalks and pigs rooting in the gutters, James reached the age of twelve a thorough little Manhattanite.

His grandfather had been an Irish immigrant who amassed a large fortune in Albany. His father was a religious visionary who embraced the exalted dreams of Swedenborg and Blake. His elder brother, William James, grew up to found at Harvard the first psychological laboratory in America, to write the *Principles of Psychology*, and to become America's philosopher of pragmatism. The senior Henry James had a comfortable income and was a restless wanderer. Twice during his adolescence Henry was taken to Europe, from twelve until sixteen, and again during his seventeenth year. The father gave his sons tutors and governesses, and Henry attended an assortment of schools, but his education was erratic. Much of it was carried on in European museums, galleries, and parks. From the first, the future novelist had before him the two worlds: the early-forming America, in all of its indigenous rawness and with its European borrowings — and the European scene, as a series of cities, Geneva, Paris, London; there was also the Boulogne-sur-Mer of Thackeray, as well as the suburbs of the British metropolis.

The young Henry was a sensitive and shy boy; he tended to assume a quiet observer's role beside his active elder brother. He was an inveterate reader of novels; indeed it might be said that no novelist before James had had so thorough a saturation in the fiction of both sides of the Atlantic. Having learned French in childhood, he read through shelvesful of French novels as well as the great English novelists from Richardson to the then-serialized Dickens and Thackeray. His father spoke of him as a "devourer of libraries"; for a while the parent worried about this and sent his son to a preparatory school for engineers. Henry resisted this experience as he was to resist the study of law two or three years later. He wanted to be simply "literary" and he realized this goal more rapidly than might have been expected.

On the eve of the Civil War the family returned from the third of their European journeys and settled at Newport in Rhode Island. The seventeen-year-old Henry here formed a friendship with John La Farge, the painter, his senior by several years, who guided him in his reading of French works and encouraged him to begin writing. During the early weeks of the war Henry suffered a strained back while helping to put out a fire and this "obscure hurt," as he called it in his memoirs, kept him from military service. In 1862 he registered at the Harvard Law School but soon withdrew, for he was already writing short stories and book reviews.

The earliest identified piece of fiction is an unsigned tale, "A Tragedy of Error," published in the *Continental Monthly*, a New York magazine, in February 1864. It is a precocious tale, lurid and melodramatic, yet strangely talented. It reveals that James, on the threshold of his manhood, already possessed a vigorous grasp of certain storytelling techniques which were to guide him in all his work and culminate in the remarkable architecture of his final novels. His second tale dealt with life on the civilian front of the Civil War and was accepted by the *Atlantic Monthly* in 1865 when he was twenty-two. From then on the pages of this magazine were open to him. The *North American Review* and the newly founded *Nation* accepted his book reviews and when William Dean Howells began to work for the *Atlantic* he gave James encouragement and editorial support, recognizing at once that he had to do with a young man of extraordinary talent. By the time James had published half a dozen short stories a reviewer in the *Nation* spoke of him as one of the most skillful writers of fiction in America. From the first, however, critics complained that his heroes did not lead a life of action; they tended to be self-absorbed and reflective, and the tales themselves took as their subjects problems in human behavior. The stories of this early period deal entirely with the American scene and show the leisurely existence of the well-to-do in Newport, Boston, and New York. James's models were largely French: Balzac, Mérimée, George Sand. But his writing at this time shows also an attentive reading of Hawthorne.

There is a touch of Hawthorne in "The Romance of Certain Old Clothes" (1868), first of the many ghostly tales James was to write. His most ambitious story of this period was "Poor Richard" (1867), which described a young man's helplessness in courtship when faced with vigorous rivals. James republished a few of these tales, much revised, in England in a series of volumes called *Stories Revived* (1885), among them "A Landscape Painter" and "A Day of Days" of 1866, "A Most Extraordinary Case" (1868), and "A Light Man" (1869). Later he disavowed all his early stories and chose to date his literary debut from the appearance of "A Passionate Pilgrim" in the *Atlantic Monthly* during 1871.

During 1869 and 1870 Henry James went abroad on his first adult journey. He was twenty-six and the experience was unforgettable. For the first time he crossed the Alps into Italy, but before doing this he renewed his old boyhood impressions of London. Here he found Charles Eliot Norton, the Harvard professor of fine arts who had published him in the *North American Review*, and through Norton met William Morris, Rossetti, and Ruskin. He also paid a call on Darwin. As he traveled, he gradually became aware of the theme that was to be central to his writings: he observed his journeying fellow Americans in hotels and pensions and captured their sense of dislocation while trying to imbibe foreign culture; he studied particularly the itinerant American families with passive mothers and undisciplined children, and noted the absence from their lives of any standard of culture and behavior. These were the shortcomings of American innocence. On the other hand James was not blind to certain other aspects of life abroad; it is striking how often the adjective "corrupt" precedes the word "Europe" in his writings. He found in the old countries, nevertheless, a continuing spectacle of life and art. The Italian towns on their hillsides, the spires of the churches gleaming in the landscape, customs and manners bearing witness to time and tradition, served as a constant stimulus to his vision and imagination.

The galleries of Europe provided a feast for his eyes. His complaint on returning home was at one with Hawthorne: in America there was only raw nature, the forest primeval, and a broad, daylight prosperity. Eden would have been a dull place for a novelist. While he was in England the news reached him that his beloved cousin, Minny Temple, to whom he had formed a deep if unvoiced attachment, had died. This was the climax of his "passionate pilgrimage"; and it was to be remembered in *The Portrait of a Lady* and years later in *The Wings of the Dove*. The twelvemonth of wandering in England, France, and Italy — the countries in which he was to travel for the rest of his life — had set the scene for all his future. He was to remain satisfied with this terrain; he traveled neither to Spain nor to the Isles of Greece; he only briefly visited the Low Countries, and on two trips cast a hurried glance at Munich. The capitals in Jamesian geography, extending from the New World to the Old, were Boston and New York, London, Paris, and Rome. Florence and Venice were way stations. And occasionally James explored the rural scenery of these countries. But his particular landscape was that of the prosperous and civilized humans who peopled or visited these places and whose lives he dealt with as a part of a continuing Americano-European *comédie humaine*.

Before Henry James recognized that this was his fundamental theme, he made a serious attempt to discover what he could accomplish as a writer within the United States. Twice between 1870 and 1875 — first in Boston and then in New York — he sought systematically to gain a livelihood by the writing of fugitive journalism and fiction within the American scene. In Boston he wrote a short novel entitled *Watch and Ward*. For a brief moment he entertained the common fantasy of novitiates in fiction that this would be a "Great American Novel": even the supersubtle James allowed himself this cliché-dream of overnight fame and power. Set in Boston and its suburbs, the novel told of a wealthy young man who adopts an orphan and rears her in the hope that she will some day become his wife. The strange thing about this novel was James's failure to paint any background; he became fascinated by the relationships between the orphan, her guardian, her suitors; but the story might have taken place anywhere. In the book may be found an early sketching out of some of the material he would use with finished art in *The Portrait of a Lady*.

More important, at this time, was James's writing of "A Passionate Pilgrim." In it there is the rhapsodic note of his rediscovery of Europe. The tale has all the ingredients of James's later "international" stories: the narrator, discovering Europe, infatuated with the things of the Old World; the contrast of American cultural barrenness with the old traditions and manners of Europe and at the same time an acute sense of the New World's egalitarianism, for if the American protagonist dies in England, there is an Englishman at the end of the story who goes forth with new hope to replace him in America.

During his stay in Boston James continued to write book reviews; and he tried his hand at art criticism. Early in 1875 he went to New York, spending the winter there, but found it artistically — and financially — unremunerative. Between these brief "sieges" of Boston and New York he made another journey to Europe, spending in particular a winter in Rome (1872–73) where he met many American artists and closely observed the life of the long-established American colony on the banks of the Tiber. Out of this experience came his first important novel: *Roderick Hudson*. In substance and setting it seems to take up where Hawthorne left off in *The Marble Faun*. Hawthorne attempted a characteristic "romance," reworking, in terms of the real and the mystical, the Puritan struggle between guilt and goodness in a Roman setting. James, on the other hand, wrote a novel romantic in theme — that of an American artist destroyed by his passion for a beautiful woman — yet realistic in its painting of the American art expatriates in the Holy City. On a deeper level *Roderick Hudson* reflects the conflicts that were experienced by James during his search to discover what it meant to be an American, and an artist, at this moment of history. If the novel did not find the answer, it at any rate stated the problem and weighed the possibilities. Written in a clear and highly readable style, it suffered from the excesses of first novels:

the author was trying to say too much, to cram too many future novels into this one. Yet it is a work of great charm and feeling; compared with the novels being published in America at the time, it is indeed an extraordinary performance.

The novel was completed in New York in 1875 and ran through twelve installments in the *Atlantic Monthly*. With it James established the pattern by which he was to earn his living for the next forty years — that of publishing a serial in a magazine and thereby assuring himself of a steady monthly income, and augmenting this by the writing of articles, reviews, and tales. It was clear to him now that he could expatriate himself without difficulty. He could live more cheaply in Europe, and make money by his travel articles; he would find the material for his fiction and have the leisure in which to write it. By 1875 Henry had devoted a full decade to periodical publication; and now he made a substantial debut between book covers: in that year appeared *A Passionate Pilgrim and Other Tales*; a collection of travel articles, *Transatlantic Sketches*; and the novel *Roderick Hudson*. From this time on he was to publish a book or more every year — drawing upon the great backlog of his periodical writings, which he never exhausted, to make up volumes of tales, criticism, and travel that came out at the same time as his novels.

In the autumn of 1875 he settled in Paris and one of his first acts was to call upon the Russian novelist Ivan Turgenev. James had greatly admired his work and he found in this older writer a congenial mentor. If from Balzac James had learned how to set a scene and launch a drama, and from Hawthorne how to suffuse the drama with charm and fancy, and from George Eliot the value of endowing his story with intellectual illumination, he learned his most important lesson of all from Turgenev. This was to make his novel flow from his personages. The Russian writer provided James with the concept of the "organic" novel; he helped James to see that the novel need not be a haphazard story, but one in which characters live out their natures. This might be called "psychological determinism," and James was to become perhaps the greatest (and often misunderstood) exponent of it in his work. He was one of the rare writers of fiction to grasp the psychological truth that an action properly derives from a character, that a novel creates the greatest illusion of truth when it grows out of a personage's observations and perceptions. This is why, in James, we find an insistence upon the fundamental truths of human behavior, rather than the cheerful coloring of these truths indulged in by so many of his contemporaries. Like Turgenev and the other Russian novelists — but at an opposite emotional pole — James concerned himself with character above all else, and with people in relation to one another. Unlike the characters in Russian novels, James's personages tended to subordinate their emotions and passions to their intellect; but with extraordinary subtlety James could show the force of passion and emotion behind the intellectual façade.

Turgenev took James to meet Flaubert; and in Flaubert's apartment, high in the rue du Faubourg St. Honoré, the American made friends with Zola, Edmond de Goncourt, Daudet, Maupassant. Later he was to know Loti, Coppée, and Bourget, who became a particularly close friend. He had found the men of Concord to be "exquisite provincials"; he felt that these Parisians lived also within parochial horizons. He felt indeed, and understandably, that he was more cosmopolitan and possessed wider experience of the world than they did, if less experience of an immediate physical environment. He amusedly remarked in a letter home that he could talk French to them but they, in their insularity, knew not a word of English.

A year in Paris sufficed. In December of 1876 Henry James crossed the channel and settled in the heart of London, a few blocks from Piccadilly Circus; and little more than a twelvemonth later he was famous both in America and England as the author of "Daisy Miller."

The career of Henry James has been divided, for convenience, by most critics into three "periods" and these were once humorously characterized by a British writer as falling (by dynastic arrangement) into those of "James I, James II, and the Old Pretender." The "Old Pretender" was an allusion to James's elaborate manner in his old age, his involuted sentences and his search for precision of statement at the expense of the patience of his listeners. A closer examination of the sequence of his works gives to his first period a distinctive unity; it is the period of his apprenticeship and his success, his discovery of his great cosmopolitan subject and his exploitation of it. It may be said to end with the triumphant writing of *The Portrait of a Lady*, long planned — and brought to completion according to plan. The second period has often been spoken of as the period of James's "social" novels; but it would be more exact to see this period as falling, in itself, into three stages: the abandoning for the time being of the "international" theme and the writing of three long novels in the naturalist mode; then the abandoning of fiction for five years of play writing; in 1895 there is a return to the novel, followed by half a dozen years of experimental writing in which James assimilates the techniques derived from the theater. Out of these experiments emerged the third period, which — far from being that of an "Old Pretender" — has been more accurately described as a "major phase," certainly "major" in terms of its influence upon the twentieth-century novel. During this final period James wrote, within four years, the three novels by which he makes his greatest claim on posterity.

The first period extended from 1865 to 1882, and it is symbolized by the tale of "Daisy Miller" — the "ultimately most prosperous child of my invention," James called her many years later. During his lifetime his reputation was to rest largely upon his "studies" of young American girls encountering Europe. Daisy was their prototype. His stories of American families touring in the Old World as if it were a painful duty rather than a civilized pleasure were famous and much discussed. Like Hawthorne's young heroes, these Americans have to discover that the world is not as innocent as it seems; behind the smiling façades of castles and picturesque ruins lurk centuries of wrongdoing and the evil things of the human spirit. "Daisy Miller" dramatized this on a level of comedy and pathos: the tale of the young and radiant Daisy, with the dew of her homeland still freshly sprinkled over her, arriving in Rome and never realizing for a moment that European life and

Henry James

European standards may be different from those she has known in Schenectady, N.Y. What she deems to be a pleasant flirtation with a friendly Italian is viewed by Europeans, and even more, by Europeanized Americans, with deadly seriousness. Daisy knows no evil and is unable to think it; she cannot comprehend why her behavior, which seems harmless enough to her, should be the cause of so much social anxiety. As James himself put it: "The whole idea of the story is the little tragedy of a light, thin, natural, unsuspecting creature being sacrificed as it were to a social rumpus that went on quite over her head and to which she stood in no measurable relation. To deepen the effect, I have made it go over her mother's head as well."

The story indeed gained its power from the sketches of the mother who has abdicated all parental authority and Daisy's undisciplined young brother; the picture is that of an upper-middle-class family (whose "permissive" and indulgent parents have been wholly subjugated by their children) transported to a foreign environment where the parents are helpless — and ignorant — and the children run wild. The drama is heightened by the skill with which James shows this family through the sophisticated eyes of an American expatriate who feels he has lost touch with his native land. His failure to understand the "new" American girl, represented by Daisy, in the end only accentuates her sense of isolation; in Europe the transplanted American Daisy can only wither and die.

In *Roderick Hudson* James had portrayed the American artist, going abroad to find the schooling and traditions of art not available to him in his homeland. In *The American* of two years later, his "easiest" and most romantic novel, he had drawn a picture of a businessman possessing great charm of character and the candor of a trusting and innocent nature, seeking to win for himself a wife in the French aristocracy. The novel is a mixture of melodrama and romance, yet it dramatizes most clearly the irony James was seeking to express to his readers. For Christopher Newman, bearing the name of Columbus, represents one type of new man from the New World, who has strayed among the nobles of the Old. They are corrupt. They want to make use of him and his wealth. They also have complete contempt for him. The American has his chance for revenge. But he throws it away with the remark that two wrongs do not make a right; he thereby reveals himself more noble than the nobles, more the Christian gentleman. James has shown him equally, however, in all his crudity, his curious self-assurance, his predilection for strenuous action without thought, and his ignorance of the ways of the civilized world. The novel ends in a splendid passage of muted emotion as Newman walks away from the bleak Paris street in which his love is immured in her convent, and hears the "far-away bells chiming off into space at long intervals, the big bronze syllables of the Word." Revenge, he meditates, is not his "game."

With the success of "Daisy Miller" James promptly recognized that the public liked his Americano-European stories and particularly his tales of international marriages and of bright young American girls discovering Europe. "The Last of the Valerii," "Madame de Mauves," "Four Meetings," and "Daisy Miller" itself had fully attested to this. And now he began to play out his themes in all their variations — stories of the self-made girl, who arranges life for her fiancé so she may make a splendid marriage; stories of English noblewomen who marry Americans but despise them; and of Americans unable to grasp the guile and duplicity of certain kinds of Europeans. His tales were clever, witty, charming; he was in all the magazines and editors asked for more — which he always gave them; it seems now, when one looks over the long list of his "international" productions, as if he wrote at this time with both hands. When London laughed too heartily over Daisy and her young brother, James replied by writing a tale in which Americans could laugh at the smugness and fatuity of Britons visiting America ("An International Episode"). But he was playing upon national sensitivities: the Americans and English enjoyed laughing at each other; they did not care to laugh at themselves.

In his late prefaces James spoke of his "Americano-European legend," and showed how clearly he had envisaged his international dramas. What his stories had represented, he said, was a record of the American "state of innocence," that of the Americans being "almost incredibly *unaware of life* — as the old European order expressed life"; he had studied "their more or less stranded helplessness" abroad. And he went on: "Conscious of so few things in the world, these unprecedented creatures were least of all conscious of deficiencies and dangers; so that, the grace of youth and innocence and freshness aiding, their negatives were converted and became in certain relations lively positives and values." Out of their experience he fashioned the comedy and pathos and beauty of their state. His long observation of traveling Americans, his thorough knowledge of the American character, his saturation in European life, had given him his data. He was artist enough to make of it splendid literary capital. But if he treated it in his shorter tales on a level of wit and comedy — and in a comic spirit which has never been sufficiently recognized — he found in it also larger and more tragic implications. These he embodied in the novel which marked the end of this phase — *The Portrait of a Lady.*

It was planned for almost a decade. To write it, James produced in fast succession three short novels and a nonfictional work — his *Hawthorne* — earning in this way the funds needed to pursue his big novel at leisure. During the next fifteen months his works literally tumbled from the presses in England and America. *The Europeans* came out in October 1878; "Daisy Miller" and two other tales, in a two-volume edition, appeared in February 1879; in October of the same year he issued another collection of tales, and in December there came out, within two days of each other, the short novel *Confidence* and the *Hawthorne.* By this time James had also completed the last of this group, *Washington Square,* which was published during 1880 while he was preparing the first installments of *The Portrait of a Lady.*

The *Hawthorne* was written at the request of John Morley for the English Men of Letters Series. It is a finished piece of work, the tribute of one American genius to another. The argument of the book was that America had been bare of society and history when Hawthorne came upon the scene; having no rich social fabric such as English novelists could draw upon, he tissued his fiction out of the haunted Puritan history of New England. In depicting the America of Hawthorne's time, and in describing certain institutions "absent" from American life, James touched American editorial sensitivities. "In the United States, in those days, there were no great things to look out at (save forests and rivers); life was not in the least spectacular; society was not brilliant; the country was given up to a great material prosperity, a homely bourgeois activity, a diffusion of primary education and the common luxuries." Sentences such as this one, while accurate enough, seemed to certain of his readers depreciatory. Perhaps James used the word "provincial" too many times. Perhaps his easy cosmopolitanism was interpreted as condescension. A formulation such as "in the light, fresh American air, unthickened by customs and institutions" invited challenge. And when James described the materials available to the English novelist of manners — court, church, society, peerage, and so forth — he was held to be making invidious and undemocratic comparisons. His book set off a sharp flurry in the American press, and from this time on there was formed the legend that James was an expatriate who mocked his countrymen and exalted Europe at the expense of America.

Today we can see the *Hawthorne* for what it is: a finely sketched picture of Hawthorne's Salem and Concord, and a profoundly accurate critique of his work. The tone and the style of the book is felicitous at every turn. It contains a large measure of devotion to New England and its traditions, and its picture of Brook Farm and the Transcendentalists is drawn with affection and from intimate sources. But there was no denying that the book served equally to veil James's defense of his own work, and the shortcomings of *his* America — for the kind of novelist he was and sought to be.

The three short novels were thrown off in a happy and spontaneous vein. They represent James at his most gifted "professionalism." The least important was *Confidence*, which is talented hack work, a minor comedy of manners. The most important, *Washington Square*, set in New York, was the story of a plain girl who lived in a big house in the Square with her wealthy father, but who

was prevented by him from having the shoddy lover she wanted
to marry. This novel, written as if it were a piece of naturalism by
the Goncourts or a neo-Balzacian *Eugénie Grandet*, has long been
a favorite with readers of James and won him wide popularity long
after his death when it was dramatized and cinematized as *The
Heiress*. James always regarded it as a trifling work, stale and flat
and without the richer experimental values of his best narratives.
It is nevertheless a vigorous drama of parental misunderstanding
and cruelty. His third potboiler was *The Europeans*, written in response to an appeal from William Dean Howells that he give the
Atlantic Monthly a story less sober and tragic than *Roderick* and
more cheerful than *The American*. To accomplish this James re-
versed his "international" situation; instead of showing Americans
abroad, he brought back to Boston two Americans who had lived
in Europe for so long that they had little knowledge of their own
country. How they fare among a group of rigid New Englanders
was the situation out of which James's comedy of *The Europeans*
grew. Boston readers were not amused. Today, however, the story
reads as one of the brightest and most humorous of the novelist's
inventions.

Now he could finally set to work on *The Portrait of a Lady*. He
took a vacation in Italy and got the book under way, carefully revising each section. He had succeeded in selling it to *Macmillan's*
magazine in London as well as to the *Atlantic* and this brought him
a substantial income during the period of serialization. More important still, it firmly established him before a public on both sides
of the ocean. The novel was his largest and most carefully wrought
canvas to date; and if his career had ended after producing it he
would still rank as a major figure in the history of American fiction.

The Portrait of a Lady was the third in James's group of fictional American expatriations; he had "done" the artist in Rome and
the businessman in Paris. Now he brought Isabel Archer, the
young girl from Albany, to England, and placed her among her
suitors in the Old World. She, too, is an heiress; she is given the
freedom for which she romantically strives. She is an idealistic and

intelligent girl, not the flirtatious hunting-for-a-husband type James had pictured in Daisy Miller or Pandora Day. And the drama in which she becomes involved resides in the choice which she thinks she "freely" makes. Having the opportunity to marry a British lord, she shrinks from being drawn into the life of the nobility, with its rituals and its responsibilities; she shrinks equally from marrying an intense and overinsistent, but upright, American. Neither marriage, she feels, would leave her free. When she makes her choice, it is to marry the one man who in the end limits her freedom most — an American dilettante, fastidious and fussy, who "collects" her — and her money — as he collects his *objets d'art*. But if Isabel has been the victim of her romantic illusions, her self-absorption, and her ingrained egotism, she has also been the victim of a carefully laid plot: the man she marries has a daughter by a former mistress, Madame Merle, who has become Isabel's best friend; and it is through Madame Merle's connivance that the heiress has been steered into the orbit of the dilettante that she may assure, by her fortune, the future of the child.

The melodramatic underpinning of the story is handled with the novelist's characteristic realism. He knew that he could make the reader accept almost any story if his people were truly drawn; and the series of portraits of the characters surrounding Isabel — no less than Isabel herself — give the novel its remarkable force and intensity. Few "psychological" villains have ever been sketched with greater power than Gilbert Osmond, the pretentious and cynical husband, whose egotism surpasses Isabel's; and his scheming yet sympathetic mistress, Madame Merle, is one of James's most completely realized characters. The novel shows step by step how the unconventional and "free" Isabel is "ground in the very mill of the conventional." The "portrait" of the lady — her private history, her illusions and her disillusionment, the clash of ego with ego — is in essence a psychological portrait. Isabel confronts her destiny with courage and determination: but James shows us that behind her egotistical boldness there are fears and uncertainties. What is dramatized in the novel is New World ignorance foundering upon hard realities long known to the Old World. The novel's success lies in its brilliant projection of the American girl, the delineation of her character, and the establishment also of a *tone*: this is achieved in great part by a remarkable narrative movement, an unfailing sense of narrative rhythm.

When the novel was nearing its end in the magazines, Henry returned to America. He was received in Boston, New York, and Washington as the successful if often criticized author who had made a reputation for himself abroad. His mother died during his stay in America; and he had barely returned to England when he was summoned back to Boston, to the deathbed of his father. He was named executor, and after arranging for the division of the family property, he once more crossed the Atlantic. This time he was to remain abroad for twenty years. He inherited a modest income, but he was making his way so successfully that he turned this over to his sister. He continued to live by his pen.

The novelist now entered upon the second period of his writings. It was marked by his decision to attempt new subjects. He was tired of the "international" theme and he felt that he had exhausted it. With extraordinary energy he wrote two long novels during the next three years — *The Bostonians* and *The Princess Casamassima*. The American novel dealt with New England reformers; the *Princess* with another and more dangerous kind of reformer, the European anarchists. These novels are, in a sense, tales of two cities — Boston and London. They are brilliantly "social" in their painting of certain scenes of urban life and they are a calculated attempt by James to write a "naturalistic" novel. A visit to Paris in 1884 and long talks with Zola, Edmond de Goncourt, and Daudet had deeply impressed him. James failed this time, however, to take the measure of his public: it was awaiting more tales from him about helpless and bright Americans in Europe, and wandering foreigners in the United States (such as those described in "A Bundle of Letters"). Instead James offered his readers a realistic and minutely painted picture of Bostonian suffragettes and another of London radicals; this was the kind of novel which was not to gain a firm hold until the Edwardian period, and which in America would have as its foremost exponents Norris and later Dreiser. *The Princess Casamassima* anticipated by five decades the major theme of the twentieth century — the young man who seeks to overthrow the very society in which he in reality also seeks acceptance. It is a valuable study of individuals who seek to rise to power by exploiting working-class causes. James's picture of the British laboring class in its pre-Fabian confusion, while sympathetic, tended to be too generalized and impressionistic; and his plea for the grandeur of art at the expense of human suffering could not convince his readers. In attempting to place the American novel into the stream of the Zolaesque Continental fiction, James alienated his limited but appreciative public. The novels were flat failures.

He made one more attempt. This time he wrote of the world of art and tried to record the problems confronting a young politician-painter and an actress. *The Tragic Muse* ran for many months in the *Atlantic Monthly*, yet it had small success with its readers for all the intellectual brilliancy of its writing: it is, in many ways, a "cold" novel although admirable in its study of the "egotism of art." James, with his experimental attitude toward fiction, had done more than switch from his main theme: he had tried "naturalism" but he was an incomplete "naturalist" — naturalism relying on literalism and the portrayal of primitive passion and violence. What James created was a series of subtle studies of individuals caught in forces and movements beyond their control, undone by conflicts between their temperaments and their environment. James's "determinism" was essentially psychological, where Zola's was physical.

While he was writing these novels he continued to turn out a remarkable series of tales; some of them were of such length that by current measurement they are counted as short novels. During a sojourn in Italy in 1886–87 and immediately after, he created a group of short masterpieces of which the best known is "The Aspern Papers" — with its evocation of a dying Venice and a dying old lady trying to keep from a privacy-invading age the love letters written to her more than half a century before by a great poet.

Henry James

He based the tale on a brief anecdote of a Boston collector who had taken rooms in the Florentine home of Claire Clairmont, Byron's mistress, in the hope of finding Shelley and Byron relics. The story moves with the rhythmic pace and tension of a mystery story; and the double climax — the unmasking of the "publishing scoundrel" and the proposal made to him by the middle-aged niece, that he marry her and receive the Aspern papers as a "dowry" — give this tale the high drama reflected in the success of the play version. Between the lines of "The Aspern Papers" James is saying that an artist's life should be preserved from prying hands, that he should be read in his work alone. Yet James is also, ambivalently, on the side of the biographer who seeks the human elements in the artist's work.

In 1889 Henry James faced the fact that if he had had great success a decade earlier, he was now a distinguished man of letters with several distinct public failures on his hands. He knew that he was more than ever the master of his art; he had, as always, a sense of his destiny; but he had written three big novels which we now know were destined for posterity rather than for his time. He sought accordingly to revive his fortunes by turning to the theater. During the next five years, from 1890 to 1895, he wrote seven plays. Two of them reached the stage: a dramatization of *The American* which had a modest run, and *Guy Domville*, a carefully written costume play, produced in 1895 by the popular London manager George Alexander. This was booed by an ill-tempered audience which vented its anger on James himself, when he came out to take a bow on the first night. Repudiated once again by his public, and this time in an open and violent fashion, James turned his back on the theater and resumed his writing of fiction.

In a sense he turned his back on his public altogether. He withdrew from London after having lived there for more than two decades. At first he rented, and later purchased, a handsome square Georgian house in the picturesque coastal town of Rye, in Sussex, known as Lamb House. It had a walled garden and a detached pavilion which he used as a workroom; and it became his permanent abode, although he later kept a room at his London club and in his last years also had a flat in Chelsea. The once-inveterate traveler made only two trips to the Continent during the rest of his life. But if he seemed thus retired, and pleased with his "rusticity," he worked with greater resource than ever. Between the failure of his play and the writing of the late novels there was an important "transition" period during which James wrote a series of short works using techniques derived from his play writing. The first work of the transition was *The Spoils of Poynton*, a tightly written story of a struggle between a mother and son for possession of a houseful of antiques. The scenic method here used was successively employed by James in *The Other House* (a play scenario converted into a novel), *What Maisie Knew*, the long tales "The Turn of the Screw" and "In the Cage," and *The Awkward Age*, a novel written wholly in dialogue. These works, produced between 1895 and 1900, explore three important themes — that of childhood in a corrupting adult world; the psychology of the supernatural, and, in a semi-autobiographical vein, the paradox of literary "success." In the group of "tales of the literary life," among them "The Death of the Lion," "The Figure in the Carpet," and "The Next Time," James mocked journalistic reviewers and the "newspaperized" image of the artist. The stories are told by little journalistic hacks whose naiveté and philistinism underline James's ironic view of literary celebrity and what would today be called the "public image" of the artist. James sought to show that one could not "make, as it were, a sow's ear out of a silk purse." In "The Next Time," a writer, a distinct public failure but a creator of masterpieces, is approached by a woman who can write only best sellers and who would like, just once, to be a "distinguished failure." She cannot, however, teach her formula for success to the desperate artist who needs money and wants, on his side (as James put it in his notebook) "to do something *vulgar*, to take the measure of the huge, flat foot of the public." Nor can he teach her how to be an artist. In a personal sense these tales were self-consolatory; they helped soften the injury of his public failure. At the same time they are searching parables of the artist-life.

The most celebrated tale in his supernatural group, combining

Henry James

both the theme of tormented childhood and the ghostly element, is
"The Turn of the Screw." James himself dismissed the tale as trivial: he called it a "down-on-all-fours pot-boiler." Nevertheless it
promptly captured the imagination of his readers. No work of
James's has, indeed, stirred up more argument or provoked more
insistent claims by critics, each offering his particular interpretation. The truth is that every reader can supply his own reading.
James revealed on more than one occasion how he deliberately
sought ambiguity so that his reader would imagine his own "horror"
— on the theory that a nightmare is most frightening to the person
who dreams it. In this fashion he established the ground for an unusual collaboration between author and reader. The haunted governess is the narrator, but she supplies few tangible "facts," and the
reader is placed in the difficult position of having to determine,
from the story she tells — and the way she tells it — how reliable a
witness she is. James warned that he had created "a trap for the un-
wary." Most readers, caught up in the movement of the narrative,
understandably take the governess's account in good faith. But if
the reader begins to study her testimony he notices that it does not
always hang together, and that the very language she uses is filled
with imagery which reveals her own terror in the midst of her apparent composure.

By the governess's own account the children never see the ghosts
which are haunting her. The reader, on his side, consciously or un-
consciously, is sensitized to one of two horrors, or indeed to both:
he may participate in the governess's terror that the children are
exposed to damnation, or be terrified himself at the children's being exposed to such an anxiety-ridden governess. Out of such shad-
owings, such "gleams and glooms," the novelist created one of the
most profoundly evocative stories ever written. "The Turn of the
Screw" illustrates James's matured theory of the ghostly tale. Awe
and mystery, he held, do not hinge on the crime and the cadaver,
the dark castle, chains, and frankensteins walking at midnight.
James's ghosts walk mostly in broad daylight. He creates his eerie
atmosphere by having the unusual occur on the margin of the usual.
In this way horror is greatly intensified. What James added to the

ghostly tale, in reality, were a series of acute studies of forms of human anxiety — of the capacity of humans to scare themselves with phantoms of their own creation.

Among his novels of troubled childhood were *What Maisie Knew*, the story of a little girl who lives alternately with each of her divorced parents and is flung from one to the other as if she were a tennis ball, and how she tries, in the process, to fathom the strange moral world in which she sees them living; "In the Cage," the tale of a girl in late adolescence, who works in a branch post office and seeks to construct in her imagination the fashionable world whose telegrams pass through her hands; and *The Awkward Age*, a novel concerned with the female adolescent who reaches the time when she can put up her hair and join her elders in the drawing room. A kind of childish curiosity is at the center of these stories, curiosity about sex and manners and the ways of the adult world. And James conveys in them the bewilderment — and often the terror — of the young plastic consciousness trying to come to terms with a world that it can experience but cannot wholly comprehend. If the theme of these stories reflects a regression by James to his own bewildered early state when *he* had tried to fathom the adult world (and was now trying again, since it had rejected him), they also show the delicate probing by a subtle artist of the sexual mores of Victorian England. These works have greater interest for the student of fiction than the general reader for whom they must be accounted as failures. And the novel which completed the decade, *The Sacred Fount*, is a complex tour de force in which James seems to ask himself whether anything he has seen as artist has validity and reality, or whether he has been living in an unreal fantasy-world.

The technical innovations in these tales are perhaps even more important than their themes: for James was led to explore methods of narration which would accurately render the consciousness of childhood *in terms of its own unawareness*. To do this he resorted increasingly to the lessons he had learned in the theater: revelation of action through scene, use of dialogue as narration, removal of the omniscient author from his role as informer and commentator.

This meant also imposing upon the reader the burden of ferreting out for himself what is happening in the story. In a sense it converts the reader into an author, it places him at the author's window in the "house of fiction." Few readers were willing during James's lifetime to accept the responsibility he asked them to assume, or yield that "attention of perusal" which he demanded. His discovery of the possibilities of merging stagecraft with fictional method is one of the great moments of revelation in his notebooks, in which he recorded "*the singular value for a narrative plan* of the . . . divine principle of the Scenario."

That James fully discovered this "singular value" may be discerned in the final period of his career, the years from 1900 to the first world war. The three large novels which Henry James wrote between 1900 and 1904 — in which he returned to his "international" subjects and this time on a grandiose scale — can be understood only in the light of the techniques of James's maturity. At the end, form and substance coalesced to give us the psychological drama of James's highest comedy, *The Ambassadors*, the brooding pathos of *The Wings of the Dove*, and what might be called James's supreme novel of manners, *The Golden Bowl*. He had sought to be a naturalist: he became in the end a symbolist.

The Ambassadors, published in 1903 but written between 1899 and 1901, exemplified both James's use of "point of view" (that is, the telling of the story through various angles of vision) and his method of "alternation of scene." By the "point of view" method James was able to make the reader feel himself at one with the given character, and impart to him only as much of the story as that character perceives at any given moment; by alternating scenic action with his narrative of the reflective and analytic side of his personages, James created a novel unique in the history of fiction. His "ambassador" is a middle-aged New Englander who discovers how little he has been emotionally awake, because of the inhibitions of his youth and those of his environment; he finds himself balancing the rigidity of New England against the flexibility of Paris, without altogether being able to shake off his New England conscience. But he at least has been opened up to experience and has gained insight into himself. The "envoys" of *The Ambassadors* are sent out at various times to bring home the American lingerers in Paris, including the original "ambassador" himself. At the core of the novel is James's mature belief that life is a process of *seeing*, and through awareness the attaining of understanding; that if man is a creature with a predetermined heredity and a molding environment, he still can cherish the "illusion of freedom." He should, therefore, James holds, make the most of this illusion.

Written in the high style of James's late years, *The Ambassadors* represents the novel form carried to a level of extraordinary "art": mere storytelling has given way to intricate effects, as on a stage. There is no scene in James more brilliantly realized than that in which Lambert Strether, thinking of an old painting of the French countryside he had once seen in Boston, wanders into the Parisian suburbs and finds himself, as it were, inside the frame of that painting, walking about in its landscape.

Technique is also a key to *The Wings of the Dove*, published a year before *The Ambassadors* although written immediately after that novel. It clearly exemplifies the way in which James insisted that his subject dictate its structure and why he believed he could thus achieve an "organic" novel. Wishing to write the story of a doomed girl (the disease is not specified), he told himself that fiction cannot concern itself with dying, but is concerned wholly with the act of living; and so he arranged the scenic structure of the book to keep the picture of Milly Theale's dying state from the reader save at certain moments when she affirms her will to live. The novel focuses rather on the personages around her, and on the cruel plot of her friends to supply her with a "lover" who will inherit her money and thus be free, after her death, to make the marriage he wishes. This is one of the strangest variants ever introduced into the old love triangle and James rigorously adhered to his plan: the "big" scenes, those in which the dying heroine is involved, are never written. They would have turned the novel into mere pathos. The characters hear about the events afterwards; they have occurred offstage, as in classical tragedies. And James realizes the artistic unity of his work not only in his study of a passive young man in the hands of a fascinating and power-driven woman, but in the way in which, in the end, the dead Milly, "the dove," has changed the course of the lives of all the characters in the novel. In a remarkable way *The Ambassadors* and *The Wings of the Dove* were an elaborate rewriting, in terms of his late maturity, of *The American* and *The Portrait of a Lady*, a weaving of a new and complex fabric out of old materials within the large vision the novelist had finally achieved of the Western world — its greatness and its glory, its corruption and its decay. James wrote from a charged consciousness and, as he said of Shakespeare, "out of the history of his soul and the direct exposure of his sensibility." In doing this he bethought himself of "our towering idol" — the man who had tried to write the history of the world into the France of his day, Balzac, saluted by James as "the master of us all."

Balzac had tried to create certain novels which would serve also as "philosophical studies" within the frame of his "human comedy." They had been rather poor novels, but James had looked at them attentively. And there is an implied homage to them, or to their intention, in these late works. Thus James named the hero of *The Ambassadors* Lewis Lambert Strether, after Balzac's *Louis Lambert*. To be sure, Strether himself remarks that Balzac's novel "is an awfully bad one" — but James nevertheless makes his, like Balzac's, the story of an education. There is perhaps a more profound relationship between *The Wings of the Dove* and another of the *études philosophiques*, Balzac's Swedenborgian novel *Séraphita* (which, in our time, fascinated Yeats). A great Christian awareness pervades both the *Wings* and *Séraphita*: and both tell of a young woman who enacts the sacrifice of Christ. Séraphita says "there are two ways of dying — to some death means victory, to some it is defeat" — and Milly's great moral triumph is in making of her death a victory and a sacrifice. Balzac's work is, however, mystical whereas James's is grounded in the human stuff of nobility and betrayal, grandeur and defeat. To Balzac James may be said to be indebted for the symbolism of his novel — in both works we seem to hear a beating of great angelic wings, and the heroines are found perched on the edge of great abysses, surveying the precipices and terrors of the life they are to leave. Séraphita wishes she had "wings to cover you withal" and "the wings of the dove" in James's book in the end enfold those who sought to betray her. In these novels James created dramas of man, within the large social organisms he has shaped for himself, and within the ideas by which he reared his churches and his civilization. Perhaps for this reason, certain critics have tried to read allegories into them, overlooking the fact that James rejected this form of writing and held himself a realist concerned with things visible and palpable. His tradition was not that of the Divine Comedy, but of the *comédie humaine*.

If these two major works of the final phase reached back to earlier fictions, James's ultimate novel, *The Golden Bowl*, reveals him breaking new ground and finding a resolution to questions left unresolved in his other novels. He chooses a triangle — husband, wife, mistress — but the twist this time is that he marries off the mistress to the father of the wife, makes her the stepmother of the betrayed heroine. A subject as "adulterine" as this James had wanted to treat for many years, complaining that the American "family" magazines made him write at the level of adolescents. But *The Golden Bowl* was not serialized; moreover, the Victorian era was at an end and he was free to handle his subject with less indirection. The novel is, for once, the record of an innocent American girl who really does grow up: in the end she not only has won back her husband, but has emerged from her all-but-fatal attachment to her father. She sends the father back to America with his young wife and remains in Europe to work out her own future; her marriage is restored, her relationship with her husband "reconstructed" on the firm foundation of adult life: the immaturities had been her own. This time in James, the marriages are not failures: the alliances between Europeans and Americans are consummated and made strong and durable, and possessed of a future. To say this is but to give the bald elements of a remarkable work, rich in James's most elaborate metaphors. His exploration of the consciousness of the Italian Prince and his American Princess is subtle — she at first as innocent and as ignorant as Isabel Archer; he an aristocrat, taking life as it comes, and ready to ignore his wife if she fails to live up to his high sophistication. She learns actively to *see*; and through awareness triumphs.

These three novels would seem to be accomplishment enough for any writer; but James, asserting always that he was a slow and poor "producer," also put forth during this time the series of brilliant stories contained in volumes titled *The Soft Side*, *The Better Sort*, and *The Finer Grain*. Perhaps the most famous of these tales, certainly the most widely read in recent years, is "The Beast in the Jungle," whose forty-odd pages encompass the entire life of an individual — an individual so wrapped in his own egotism that his eyes are sealed to the essential experiences of life. He knows only the jungle of his own existence. The beast that waits to spring is the emptiness of his life, his failure to understand and to love.

If, at the end of the *The Golden Bowl*, Henry James sent Adam Verver and Charlotte, his wife, back to America, it was perhaps because he was about to return himself. He had been away during all his middle years — from his fortieth to his sixtieth year. He was curious, he wanted to take a look at his past. America received him with enthusiasm; he was invited to lecture and to write his impressions; he traveled to the South for the first time and he realized a long-cherished dream when he crossed the continent and saw California. Although he returned to England with a sigh of relief, after a strenuous year, it was with the sense that he had captured the whole new aspect of the United States. His book *The American Scene* is one of his great prose works: with the brush of an impressionist painter he restlessly analyzes things as they were, and as they had become; he had known old New York and now confronted the skyscrapers; he had known a tight parochial Boston; he now saw a sprawling city. Only Concord seemed much the same, and he wondered whether it had not been in its time a sort of "American Weimar." He revisited it with warm memories of Emerson. He revisited also the family plot in the Cambridge cemetery and wrote into his notebook a lyrical passage that expressed all the felt intensity of that experience. What bothered him about America was that so booming a civilization, capable of the greatest things, was addressed so markedly to material ends. This is the repeated refrain of *The American Scene*, one of James's most poetic works of travel.

While in the United States he reached an agreement with his publisher to assemble his novels and tales into a definitive edition. For three years after his return to Lamb House he labored on this task, thinking of Balzac and the way in which the French novelist had harmonized his stories and novels and created categories for them in his *comédie humaine*. The "New York Edition," as James titled it, was rigorously selective. It emphasized the cosmopolitan character of his work, and he selected for inclusion his "international" and psychological stories. He left out those novels and tales which had America for a setting, apparently planning to add these, as a separate group, at some later time. All his early works were carefully revised. The changes he made in his text were not, however, substantive; he sought rather to "point up" the prose, to create a richer verbal texture, to give the edition a uniform polish and maturity. At times old simplicities were sacrificed to the over-ornate; nevertheless the revisions invariably result in more explicit statement.

To each novel, and each collection of tales, James affixed a long and tightly written preface. These are of a piece with the novelist's critical writings — the reviews, portraits, and essays he had written for periodicals and newspapers during his entire career. His criticism had reflected from the first the clearly formulated canons of his novelist's art. The collections he put forth himself during his lifetime testify to this — *French Poets and Novelists, Partial Portraits, Essays in London*, and *Notes on Novelists*. As a critic, James is eclectic and classical in his mode of thought: he insists upon form, on style, on integration of form and substance. He unerringly selects the very writers we today consider to have been "major" in his time; and he reads them for what they may teach him of his own process, and for the "quality of mind" he may find in their work. He believes that the artist is to be discovered in his work; but that the work must be created as an "invulnerable granite" to the seeker.

The late prefaces, since collected in a single volume, are composed of three elements: there is the author's interest in his creative process, the "story of the story," how he came to write it and the personal memories and associations aroused by the rereading of his own work; there is the discussion of the technical problems involved in each case; and, with all this, there are James's generalizations on the art of novel writing which form the heart of these essays and give them remarkable force as critical documents. The pages are crowded with critical ideas; they show the creative and analytical vision of an artist who meditates on his career and on old artistic problems long since resolved in his workshop. He felt, as he wrote the prefaces, that they would someday be a manifesto on the art of the novel and would serve as a guide for writers of fiction. His belief was well founded; the prefaces gave to criticism for the first time a valuable terminology for the discussion of the novel. To be sure, the craft of novel writing had been discussed on many occasions during the nineteenth century, but James, in some measure, codified this discussion in these last and most personal of his critical essays, gave it system and authority in the light of his half century of practice.

Although he wrote no more novels, James's productivity during his final years was remarkable. Following the pattern of the New York Edition, he revised his travel writings and consolidated them; thus *English Hours* appeared, and then *Italian Hours* which, with his *Little Tour in France*, commemorated the pathways James had taken during his lifetime on the Continent. He issued a final collection of essays on the eve of the war, *Notes on Novelists*, containing magisterial studies of Flaubert, Zola, and Balzac and his protest against the forms naturalism had taken in the new English novel, particularly as exemplified in the realistic fiction of H. G. Wells and Arnold Bennett. In addition he wrote two remarkable volumes of reminiscence — *A Small Boy and Others* and *Notes of a Son and Brother*, looking back at his own past with the same search for the truths of the emotions which Proust was to show in *A la recherche du temps perdu*. James's *Notes* embodied also his memories of his brother William, who had recently died, and those of his father. A third volume of reminiscence, destined to deal with his years in

London and Paris, was left a mere fragment, and was published as *The Middle Years* after James's death.

The English-speaking world honored him on his seventieth birthday; and while efforts to obtain the Nobel Prize for him failed, James was given a golden bowl by 250 friends and admirers who also asked him to sit for his portrait to John Singer Sargent. That portrait is now in the National Portrait Gallery in London.

With the outbreak of the war James threw himself into various activities: he visited hospitals, aided refugees, and wrote on behalf of the American volunteer motor ambulance corps in France. Ill and suffering, he decided in 1915 to yield the American citizenship he had retained during his forty years' residence in England, and throw in his lot with the British cause. A stroke three or four months later was followed by pneumonia, and although he survived into 1916, and was given the Order of Merit by King George V, it was clear that there would be no recovery. He died on February 28. His ashes were brought to America and interred in the family plot in Cambridge. An inscription on his grave describes him as the interpreter of his generation on both sides of the sea.

At first, after James's death, there was a period during which his works were dismissed as thin and lifeless by a generation that had read only a few of his books and had lost sight of the total structure of his literary edifice. For a decade or more the view put forth by Van Wyck Brooks, that James, in uprooting himself from his native land, had produced a rootless art, prevailed. Moreover the publication of James's letters in 1920 tended to establish for posterity the "Old Pretender" James, the heavy long-winded figure of Rye and Chelsea, rather than the robust bearded creative James of the turn of the century. This was due to the fact that much of the earlier correspondence was not available to Percy Lubbock, the editor of the letters, who in particular did not have James's "working" letters, his correspondence with editors and publishers; he assembled two volumes which show James the social being and "theorist" of fiction, but not the Balzacian "professional."

The only posthumous works published were the two unfinished novels, *The Sense of the Past* and *The Ivory Tower*, and the frag-

ment of autobiography, *The Middle Years.* James's other papers
were allowed to remain in the trunk in which they had been
packed and sent back to America. They ultimately passed into the
possession of Harvard University, at the time of the James centenary in 1943, when it became clear that there was still much of
James to be given to the world. Most important of all were certain
of his working notebooks, which when published in 1947 showed
the source material out of which the prefaces had been written.
These notebooks constitute one of the most remarkable records of
an artist-life ever preserved. Written often in the full blaze of creation, they demonstrate James's way of reimagining his materials
and the strange, often calculating intellectual force he brought to
bear upon his work.

James had been a constant letter-writer from the first. His letters
are the surplus production of a writer who, having done his day's
work, is unable to stop, and writes on with a free flow and an easy
play of imagination. More than ten thousand letters survive, the
majority unpublished, and his professional letters, no less than
those written in friendship, are filled with remarkable observation
of the people and places of his time.

His friendships were numerous. He moved everywhere in the
literary and art world and crossed the path of nearly all the leading
writers of his day. He knew more intimately among writers, critics, painters, Robert Browning, Robert Louis Stevenson, George
Meredith, Edmund Gosse, Alphonse Daudet, Ivan Turgenev, Paul
Bourget, George du Maurier, John Singer Sargent, John La Farge,
Émile Zola, Jules Jusserand, Mrs. Humphry Ward and later Joseph Conrad, H. G. Wells, Rudyard Kipling, Edith Wharton. He
had met Matthew Arnold in Rome and in London, had chatted in
London drawing rooms with Pater, and had encountered Tennyson and George Eliot, William Morris and John Ruskin. If we add
the earlier friendship with Emerson, and his close ties with Norton
and Howells, it can be seen that James was far from being the recluse of Rye, as he has sometimes been pictured. He touched his age
largely during his half century in the creative world. He tends increasingly to dominate the literature of America because the rami-

fications of his career are considerable — and complex — beside the simpler lives and simpler works of other American novelists. His achievement resides in his fertility and inventiveness, his grasp of the New World myth in its relation to the Old; and the skill with which he exploits his often delicate materials. His shortcomings reside in the narrowness of his actual world and sometimes in the triviality of his social comedies, as well as in the more tortured effects of certain pages of his late style. Some readers find him, in this phase, subtle to the point of exasperation. Yet in all that he wrote he represented the old civilized world at its most searching and questioning.

He was content to be the historian of his society. If there is any "social message" in his work it might be that he would have the human animal less animal and more human. He would teach men and women to open themselves to experience and to feeling — endow them with greater awareness of the world's beauty and of the potential of their imagination. As the poet of civilization, his quest was wholly aesthetic and his religion is a religion of art. He was so secure in his tradition and in his roots that he could shape his art at his will, remake the world in the light of his imagination, believing, as he said, that "art makes life," and that what remains from generation to generation is the sum of man's visions, the transfigured realities of creation.

From the American point of view, his cosmopolitanism, of which so much has been made, was nothing more than a desire to read his land and his people into the culture of the West, even as Jefferson and Franklin before him had sought to read America into the community of nations after the Revolution. To this extent James worked in the tradition of his country's founders and discovered himself alienated from the new generation which concerned itself with the nationalistic and material opening up of the continent. As for the stuff of his fiction, it is that of the human nerves and the mind; his concern is with intellectual and emotional relations rather than with physical being. His own life, compared with that of other American artists, was one of great depth and richness; he drew upon his inner resources to create a work exquisite in feeling, in humor, in irony. Of his own craft — the craft of fiction — he was a master. The so-called "revival" of Henry James has in reality been the discovery of the writer and the man as a world literary figure, a remarkable New World bridge from the Enlightenment to all that is "modern" in the literary art of the twentieth century.

SELECTED BIBLIOGRAPHIES

Selected Bibliographies

JAMES FENIMORE COOPER
Principal Works

NOVELS

Precaution. New York: Goodrich, 1820.
The Spy. New York: Wiley and Halstead, 1821.
The Pioneers. New York: Charles Wiley, 1823.
The Pilot. New York: Charles Wiley, 1824.
Lionel Lincoln. New York: Charles Wiley, 1825.
The Last of the Mohicans. Philadelphia: Carey and Lea, 1826.
The Prairie. London: Henry Colburn; Philadelphia: Carey, Lea, and Carey, 1827.
The Red Rover. Paris: Hector Bossange, 1827; Philadelphia: Carey, Lea, and Carey, 1828.
The Wept of Wish-ton-Wish. London: Henry Colburn; Philadelphia: Carey, Lea, and Carey, 1829.
The Water-Witch. Dresden: Walther; Philadelphia: Carey and Lea, 1830.
The Bravo. London: Colburn and Bentley; Philadelphia: Carey and Lea, 1831.
The Heidenmauer. London: Colburn and Bentley; Philadelphia: Carey and Lea, 1832.
The Headsman. London: Bentley; Philadelphia: Carey, Lea, and Blanchard, 1833.
The Monikins. London: Bentley; Philadelphia: Carey, Lea, and Blanchard, 1835.
Homeward Bound. London: Bentley; Philadelphia: Carey, Lea, and Blanchard, 1838.
Home as Found. Philadelphia: Lea and Blanchard, 1838.
The Pathfinder. London: Bentley; Philadelphia: Lea and Blanchard, 1840.
Mercedes of Castile. Philadelphia: Lea and Blanchard, 1840.
The Deerslayer. Philadelphia: Lea and Blanchard, 1841.
The Two Admirals. London: Bentley, 1842; Philadelphia: Lea and Blanchard, 1842.

The Wing-and-Wing. London: Bentley; Philadelphia: Lea and Blanchard, 1842.
Wyandotté. London: Bentley; Philadelphia: Lea and Blanchard, 1843.
Afloat and Ashore. London: Bentley; Philadelphia: The author, 1844.
Afloat and Ashore, second series (later retitled *Miles Wallingford*). London: Bentley; New York: Burgess, Stringer, 1844.
Satanstoe. London: Bentley; New York: Burgess, Stringer, 1845.
The Chainbearer. London: Bentley; New York: Burgess, Stringer, 1845.
The Redskins. London: Bentley; New York: Burgess, Stringer, 1846.
The Crater. London: Bentley; New York: Burgess, Stringer, 1847.
Jack Tier. London: Bentley; New York: Burgess, Stringer, 1848.
The Oak Openings. London: Bentley; New York: Burgess, Stringer, 1848.
The Sea Lions. London: Bentley; New York: Stringer and Townsend, 1849.
The Ways of the Hour. London: Bentley; New York: G. P. Putnam, 1850.

CRITICAL PROSE AND HISTORY

Notions of the Americans: Picked up by a Travelling Bachelor. London: Henry Colburn; Philadelphia: Carey, Lea, and Carey, 1828.
A Letter to His Countrymen. New York: John Wiley, 1834.
Sketches of Switzerland, Parts I and II. London: Bentley; Philadelphia: Carey, Lea, and Blanchard, 1836.
Gleanings in Europe. London: Bentley; Philadelphia: Carey, Lea, and Blanchard, 1837 (*France*), 1837 (*England*), 1838 (*Italy*).
The American Democrat. Cooperstown, N.Y.: H. and E. Phinney, 1838.
The Chronicles of Cooperstown. Cooperstown, N.Y.: H. and E. Phinney, 1838.
History of the Navy of the United States of America. Philadelphia: Lea and Blanchard, 1839.
Ned Myers. London: Bentley; Philadelphia: Lea and Blanchard, 1843.
Lives of Distinguished American Naval Officers. Philadelphia: Carey and Hart, 1846.

COLLECTED EDITIONS

Cooper's Novels. Illustrated from drawings by F. O. C. Darley. 32 vols. New York: W. A. Townsend, 1859–61.
J. Fenimore Cooper's Works. Household Edition, with Introductions by Susan Fenimore Cooper. 32 vols. New York and Cambridge, Mass.: Hurd and Houghton, 1876–84.
The Works of James Fenimore Cooper. Mohawk Edition. 33 vols. New York: G. P. Putnam's Sons, 1895–96.

LETTERS AND JOURNALS

Correspondence of James Fenimore Cooper, edited by James Fenimore Cooper. 2 vols. New Haven, Conn.: Yale University Press, 1922.

Selected Bibliographies

The Letters and Journals of James Fenimore Cooper, edited by James F. Beard. 6 vols. Cambridge, Mass.: Harvard University Press, 1960–67.

Bibliographies

Spiller, Robert E., and Philip C. Blackburn. *A Descriptive Bibliography of the Writings of James Fenimore Cooper*. New York: Bowker, 1934.

Spiller, Robert E., and others, editors. *Literary History of the United States*, Vol. II: *Bibliography*. 3rd edition. New York: Macmillan, 1963.

Biographies

Boynton, Henry W. *James Fenimore Cooper*. New York: Appleton-Century, 1931.

Grossman, James. *James Fenimore Cooper*. New York: Sloane, 1949.

Lounsbury, Thomas R. *James Fenimore Cooper*. Boston: Houghton, Mifflin, 1882.

Spiller, Robert E. *Fenimore Cooper: Critic of His Times*. New York: Minton, Balch, 1931.

Critical Studies

Bewley, Marius. *The Eccentric Design*. New York: Columbia University Press, 1959.

Clavel, Marcel. *Fenimore Cooper: Sa vie et son oeuvre: La jeunesse (1789–1826)*. Aix-en-Provence, France: E. Fourcine, 1938.

Cunningham, Mary E., editor. *James Fenimore Cooper: A Reappraisal*. With an Introduction by Howard Mumford Jones. Cooperstown, N.Y.: New York State Historical Association, 1954. (Cooper centenary papers.)

Lawrence, D. H. *Studies in Classic American Literature*. New York: Thomas Seltzer, 1923. Pp. 50–92.

Parrington, V. L. *Main Currents in American Thought*. New York: Harcourt, Brace, 1927. Vol. II, pp. 222–37.

Pearce, Roy H. "The Leatherstocking Tales Re-examined," *South Atlantic Quarterly*, 46:524–36 (October 1947).

Philbrick, Thomas. *James Fenimore Cooper and the Development of American Sea Fiction*. Cambridge, Mass.: Harvard University Press, 1961.

Ringe, Donald A. *James Fenimore Cooper*. New York: Twayne, 1961.

Smith, Henry Nash. *Virgin Land*. New York: Knopf, 1957.

Walker, Warren S. *James Fenimore Cooper*. New York: Barnes and Noble, 1962.

Waples, Dorothy. *The Whig Myth of James Fenimore Cooper*. New Haven, Conn.: Yale University Press, 1938.

NATHANIEL HAWTHORNE

An edition of the complete works intended to be definitive is in preparation by the Ohio State University Press, edited by William Charvat, Roy H.

Pearce, and others. Until it becomes available the standard complete editions are the Riverside Edition, 12 vols. (Boston: Houghton, Mifflin, 1883), and the Old Manse Edition, 22 vols. (1904).

Principal Works

Fanshawe. Boston: Marsh and Capen, 1828.
Twice-Told Tales. Boston: American Stationers Co., 1837. Second series, Boston: James Monroe, 1842.
Mosses from an Old Manse. New York: Wiley and Putnam, 1846.
The Scarlet Letter. Boston: Ticknor, Reed, and Fields, 1850.
The House of the Seven Gables. Boston: Ticknor, Reed, and Fields, 1851.
The Snow-Image and Other Twice-Told Tales. Boston: Ticknor, Reed, and Fields, 1851.
The Blithedale Romance. Boston: Ticknor, Reed, and Fields, 1852.
The Life of Franklin Pierce. Boston: Ticknor, Reed, and Fields, 1852.
A Wonder Book for Girls and Boys. Boston: Ticknor, Reed, and Fields, 1852.
Tanglewood Tales for Girls and Boys. Boston: Ticknor, Reed, and Fields, 1853.
The Marble Faun. Boston: Ticknor and Fields, 1860.
Our Old Home. Boston: Ticknor and Fields, 1863.
Passages from the American Note-Books, edited by Sophia Hawthorne. Boston: Ticknor and Fields, 1868. (*The American Notebooks*, edited by Randall Stewart. New Haven, Conn.: Yale University Press, 1932.)
Passages from the English Note-Books, edited by Sophia Hawthorne. Boston: Fields, Osgood, 1870. (*The English Notebooks*, edited by Randall Stewart. New York: Modern Language Association, 1941.)
Dr. Grimshawe's Secret, edited by Julian Hawthorne. Boston: Osgood, 1883. (*Hawthorne's Dr. Grimshawe's Secret*, edited by Edward H. Davidson. Cambridge, Mass.: Harvard University Press, 1954.)
Hawthorne as Editor: Selections from His Writings in the American Magazine of Useful and Entertaining Knowledge, edited by Arlin Turner. Baton Rouge: Louisiana State University Press, 1941.

Bibliographical Aids

Browne, Nina E. *A Bibliography of Nathaniel Hawthorne.* Boston: Houghton, Mifflin, 1905.
Cathcart, Wallace H. *Bibliography of the Works of Nathaniel Hawthorne.* Cleveland: Rowfant Club, 1905.
Fogle, R. H. Bibliography in *Hawthorne's Fiction: The Light and the Dark.* Norman: University of Oklahoma Press, 1952. (The bibliography at the back of this book is the best available for literary critical purposes.)
Gross, Seymour L. *A "Scarlet Letter" Handbook.* San Francisco: Wadsworth, 1960. (A full and well-selected bibliography on this novel.)
Spiller, Robert E., and others, eds. *Literary History of the United States*, Vol.

Selected Bibliographies

III. New York: Macmillan, 1948. *Supplement*, edited by Richard M. Ludwig, 1959.

Critical and Biographical Studies

Arvin, Newton. *Hawthorne*. Boston: Little, Brown, 1929.

Bridge, Horatio. *Personal Recollections of Nathaniel Hawthorne*. New York: Harper, 1893.

Crews, Frederick C. *The Sins of the Fathers: Hawthorne's Psychological Themes*. New York: Oxford University Press, 1966.

Fogle, Richard H. *Hawthorne's Fiction: The Light and the Dark*. Norman: University of Oklahoma Press, 1952.

Hawthorne, Julian. *Nathaniel Hawthorne and His Wife*. Boston: Osgood, 1885.

————. *Hawthorne and His Circle*. New York: Harper, 1903.

Hoeltje, Hubert H. *Inward Sky: The Mind and Heart of Nathaniel Hawthorne*. Durham, N.C.: Duke University Press, 1962.

James, Henry. *Hawthorne*. London: Macmillan, 1879.

Lathrop, G. P. *A Study of Hawthorne*. Boston: Osgood, 1876.

Lathrop, Rose Hawthorne. *Memories of Hawthorne*. Boston: Houghton, Mifflin, 1897.

Loggins, Vernon. *The Hawthornes: The Story of Seven Generations of an American Family*. New York: Columbia University Press, 1951.

Male, Roy R. *Hawthorne's Tragic Vision*. Austin: University of Texas Press, 1957.

Pearce, R. H., ed. *Hawthorne Centenary Essays*. Columbus: Ohio State University Press, 1964.

Stewart, Randall. *Nathaniel Hawthorne: A Biography*. New Haven, Conn.: Yale University Press, 1948.

Turner, Arlin. *Nathaniel Hawthorne: An Introduction and Interpretation*. New York: Barnes and Noble, 1961.

Van Doren, Mark. *Nathaniel Hawthorne: A Critical Biography*. New York: Sloane, 1949.

Wagenknecht, Edward. *Nathaniel Hawthorne: Man and Writer*. New York: Oxford University Press, 1961.

Waggoner, Hyatt H. *Hawthorne: A Critical Study*. Cambridge, Mass.: Harvard University Press, 1955; revised edition, 1963.

Books Containing Chapters on Hawthorne

Bewley, Marius. *The Complex Fate*. London: Chatto and Windus, 1952.

————. *The Eccentric Design: Form in the Classic American Novel*. New York: Columbia University Press, 1959.

Feidelson, Charles, Jr. *Symbolism and American Literature*. Chicago: University of Chicago Press, 1953.

Hoffman, Daniel G. *Form and Fable in American Fiction*. New York: Oxford University Press, 1961.

Levin, Harry. *The Power of Blackness: Hawthorne, Poe, Melville*. New York: Knopf, 1958.
Lewis, R. W. B. *The American Adam: Innocence, Tragedy, and Tradition in the Nineteenth Century*. Chicago: University of Chicago Press, 1955.
Matthiessen, F. O. *American Renaissance*. New York: Oxford University Press, 1941.
Stewart, Randall. *American Literature and Christian Doctrine*. Baton Rouge: Louisiana State University Press, 1958.
Warren, Austin. *Rage for Order*. Chicago: University of Chicago Press, 1948.
Winters, Yvor. *In Defense of Reason*. New York: Swallow Press and Morrow, 1947.

HERMAN MELVILLE
Works

COLLECTED EDITIONS

The Works of Herman Melville, 12 volumes (London: Constable, 1922–23), with 4 supplementary volumes of poetry and posthumous prose (1924), is the most complete edition of Melville yet issued.
Complete Works (Chicago and New York: Hendricks House) is in two editions, a trade edition with editorial notes and a subscribers' edition with additional textual notes. It includes *Collected Poems*, edited by H. P. Vincent (1947); *Piazza Tales*, edited by E. S. Oliver (1948); *Pierre*, edited by H. A. Murray (1949); *Moby Dick*, edited by L. S. Mansfield and H. P. Vincent (1952); *The Confidence Man*, edited by Elizabeth Foster (1954); *Clarel*, edited by W. E. Bezanson (1960).
The Northwestern-Newberry Edition of *The Writings of Herman Melville*, edited by Harrison Hayford, Hershel Parker, and G. Thomas Tanselle, 15 volumes (Evanston, Ill.: Northwestern University Press, 1967–   ), will provide a critical text for Melville's complete works together with a complete textual history and a historical note on the composition and publication of each volume.

ORIGINAL AMERICAN EDITIONS

Typee: A Peep at Polynesian Life. New York: Wiley and Putnam, 1846.
Omoo. New York: Harper, 1847.
Mardi and a Voyage Thither. New York: Harper, 1849.
Redburn: His First Voyage. New York: Harper, 1849.
White Jacket; or, The World in a Man-of-War. New York: Harper, 1850.
Moby Dick; or, The Whale. New York: Harper, 1851.
Pierre; or, The Ambiguities. New York: Harper, 1852.
Israel Potter, His Forty Years of Exile. New York: Putnam, 1855.
Piazza Tales. New York: Putnam, 1856.
The Confidence Man, His Masquerade. New York: Dix, Edwards, 1857.

Selected Bibliographies

Battle-Pieces and Aspects of the War. New York: Harper, 1866.
Clarel: A Poem and Pilgrimage in the Holy Land. New York: Putnam, 1876.
John Marr and Other Sailors. New York: De Vinne, 1888.
Timoleon. New York: Caxton, 1891.
The Apple Tree Table and Other Sketches. Princeton, N.J.: Princeton University Press, 1922.
Shorter Novels of Herman Melville. New York: Liveright, 1928. (Includes *Billy Budd*, first published in London by Constable in 1924.)

CURRENT EDITIONS OF SPECIAL INTEREST

All of Melville's prose works with the exception of his newspaper pieces and certain sketches unpublished during his lifetime are currently available in inexpensive reprints. Several have notable characteristics:

Billy Budd, Sailor. The Phoenix Edition (Chicago: University of Chicago Press, 1962) is the Hayford-Sealts text. Most others are reprints of either the Weaver or the Freeman texts.
Moby Dick. The Modern Library Giant Edition (New York: Random House, 1944) contains the Rockwell Kent illustrations; the Bobbs-Merrill Edition (Indianapolis, 1964) contains technical illustrations and also explanatory notes; the Oxford Edition (New York, 1967) includes excellent photographs and drawings; the Norton Edition (New York, 1967) includes critical essays, explanatory notes, and textual additions derived from Melville's revision of American proofsheets for the first English edition.
Typee. The Signet Classics edition (New York: New American Library, 1965) records the substantive differences between the first English and the first American editions and the bowdlerizations made in the American Revised Edition.

There are several collections available. *Great Short Works of Herman Melville* (New York: Harper and Row, 1966) includes *Billy Budd* and the complete short stories; various collections under the titles *Four Short Novels* or *Shorter Novels* consist of *Billy Budd*, "Bartleby," "Benito Cereno," and "The Encantadas"; and *The Viking Portable Melville* reprints *Typee*, "Hawthorne and His Mosses," "Bartleby," and *Billy Budd, Foretopman* in their entirety. Melville's poetry is fully available only in the collected editions of his works, but it may be extensively sampled in the Anchor Edition of his *Selected Poems* (New York: Doubleday, 1964).

JOURNALS, CORRESPONDENCE, AND MANUSCRIPTS

"Journal of Melville's Voyage in a Clipper Ship," *New England Quarterly*, 2:120–39 (January 1929).
Journal of a Visit to London and the Continent by Herman Melville, edited by Eleanor M. Metcalf. Cambridge, Mass.: Harvard University Press, 1948.
Melville's Journal of a Visit to Europe and the Levant, October 11, 1856–May 6, 1857, edited by Howard C. Horsford. Princeton, N.J.: Princeton University Press, 1955.

Family Correspondence of Herman Melville, 1830–1904, edited by V. H. Palsits. New York: New York Public Library, 1929.
The Letters of Herman Melville, edited by Merrell R. Davis and William H. Gilman. New Haven: Yale University Press, 1960.
Billy Budd, Sailor (An Inside Narrative), edited by Harrison Hayford and Merton M. Sealts, Jr. Chicago: University of Chicago Press, 1962. (A careful edition of Melville's working manuscript which provides both a reading text and a genetic text with introduction and notes.)

Biographical and Critical Studies

Anderson, C. R. *Melville in the South Seas.* New York: Columbia University Press, 1939.
Arvin, Newton. *Herman Melville.* New York: Sloane, 1950.
Berthoff, Warner. *The Example of Melville.* Princeton, N.J.: Princeton University Press, 1962.
Bowen, Merlin. *The Long Encounter: Self and Experience in the Writings of Herman Melville.* Chicago: University of Chicago Press, 1960.
Brodtkorb, Paul, Jr. *Ishmael's White World: A Phenomenological Reading of Moby Dick.* New Haven, Conn.: Yale University Press, 1965.
Chase, Richard. *Herman Melville.* New York: Macmillan, 1949.
Davis, M. R. *Melville's Mardi: A Chartless Voyage.* New Haven, Conn.: Yale University Press, 1952.
Gilman, W. H. *Melville's Early Life and Redburn.* New York: New York University Press, 1951.
Howard, Leon. *Herman Melville: A Biography.* Berkeley and Los Angeles: University of California Press, 1951.
James, C. L. R. *Mariners, Renegades, and Castaways.* New York: James, 1953.
Leyda, Jay. *The Melville Log: A Documentary Life of Herman Melville, 1819–1891.* 2 volumes. New York: Harcourt, Brace, 1951.
Mason, Ronald. *The Spirit above the Dust: A Study of Herman Melville.* London: John Lehmann, 1951.
Metcalf, Eleanor M. *Herman Melville: Cycle and Epicycle.* Cambridge, Mass.: Harvard University Press, 1953.
Mumford, Lewis. *Herman Melville.* New York: Harcourt, Brace, 1929.
Olson, Charles. *Call Me Ishmael.* New York: Reynal and Hitchcock, 1947.
Sedgwick, W. E. *Herman Melville: The Tragedy of Mind.* Cambridge, Mass.: Harvard University Press, 1944.
Simon, Jean. *Herman Melville, marin, métaphysicien et poète.* Paris: Boivin, 1939.
Stern, M. R. *The Fine Hammered Steel of Herman Melville.* Urbana: University of Illinois Press, 1957.
Stone, Geoffrey. *Melville.* New York: Sheed and Ward, 1949.
Thorp, Willard. *Herman Melville.* New York: American Book, 1938.
Weaver, R. M. *Herman Melville, Mariner and Mystic.* New York: Doran, 1921.

Selected Bibliographies

Special Topics

Braswell, William. *Melville's Religious Thought*. Durham, N.C.: Duke University Press, 1943.

Finkelstein, Dorothee. *Melville's Orienda*. New Haven, Conn.: Yale University Press, 1961.

Franklin, H. Bruce. *The Wake of the Gods: Melville's Mythology*. Stanford, Calif.: Stanford University Press, 1963.

Hetherington, H. W. *Melville's Reviewers, British and American, 1846-1891*. Chapel Hill: University of North Carolina Press, 1961.

Hillway, Tyrus, ed. *Moby Dick Centennial Essays*. Dallas, Texas: Southern Methodist University Press, 1953.

Lanzinger, Klaus. *Primitivismus und Naturalismus im Prosaschaffen Herman Melvilles*. Innsbruck: Universitätsverlag Wagner, 1959.

Parker, Hershel, ed. *The Recognition of Herman Melville*. Ann Arbor: University of Michigan Press, 1967.

Percival, M. O. *A Reading of Moby Dick*. Chicago: University of Chicago Press, 1950.

Pommer, H. E. *Milton and Melville*. Pittsburgh: University of Pittsburgh Press, 1955.

Rosenberry, E. H. *Melville and the Comic Spirit*. Cambridge, Mass.: Harvard University Press, 1955.

Sealts, M. M., Jr. *Melville's Reading: A Check-List of Books Owned and Borrowed*. Madison: University of Wisconsin Press, 1966.

———. *Melville as Lecturer*. Cambridge, Mass.: Harvard University Press, 1957.

Stafford, W. T., ed. *Melville's Billy Budd and the Critics*. San Francisco: Wadsworth, 1961.

Stern, M. R., ed. *Discussions of Moby Dick*. Boston: Heath, 1960.

Sundermann, K. H. *Herman Melvilles Gedankengut*. Berlin, 1937.

Thompson, Lawrance. *Melville's Quarrel with God*. Princeton, N.J.: Princeton University Press, 1952.

Vincent, H. P. *The Trying Out of Moby Dick*. Boston: Houghton, Mifflin, 1949.

———, ed. *Bartleby the Scrivener* (Melville Annual, 1965: A Symposium). Kent, Ohio: Kent State University Press, 1966.

Wright, Nathalia. *Melville's Use of the Bible*. Durham, N.C.: Duke University Press, 1949.

NOTE: The essay on Melville is especially indebted to an important but unpublished study of Melville's imagery by Harrison Hayford.

MARK TWAIN

The most complete edition is *Mark Twain's Works*, 37 volumes (New York: Harper, 1929). See also Merle Johnson, *A Bibliography of Mark Twain* (New York: Harper, 1935), and E. H. Long, *Mark Twain Handbook* (New York: Hendricks House, 1957), which list important critical articles.

Principal Works

The Innocents Abroad; or, The New Pilgrim's Progress. Hartford, Conn.: American Publishing Co., 1869.

Roughing It. Hartford, Conn.: American Publishing Co., 1872.

The Gilded Age (with C. D. Warner). Hartford, Conn.: American Publishing Co., 1874.

The Adventures of Tom Sawyer. Hartford, Conn.: American Publishing Co., 1876.

A Tramp Abroad. Hartford, Conn.: American Publishing Co., 1880.

The Prince and the Pauper. Boston: Osgood, 1882.

Life on the Mississippi. Boston: Osgood, 1883.

The Adventures of Huckleberry Finn. New York: Webster, 1885.

A Connecticut Yankee in King Arthur's Court. New York: Webster, 1889.

The Tragedy of Pudd'nhead Wilson. Hartford, Conn.: American Publishing Co., 1894.

Personal Recollections of Joan of Arc. New York: Harper, 1896.

Following the Equator. Hartford, Conn.: American Publishing Co., 1897.

The Man That Corrupted Hadleyburg and Other Stories and Essays. New York: Harper, 1900.

Extract from Captain Stormfield's Visit to Heaven. New York: Harper, 1909.

The Mysterious Stranger. New York: Harper, 1916.

Mark Twain's Autobiography, edited by A. B. Paine. New York: Harper, 1924.

Mark Twain's Letters from the Sandwich Islands, edited by G. Ezra Dane. Palo Alto, Calif.: Stanford University Press, 1938.

Mark Twain's Travels with Mr. Brown, edited by G. Ezra Dane. New York: Knopf, 1940.

Mark Twain in Eruption, edited by Bernard De Voto. New York: Harper, 1940.

The Autobiography of Mark Twain, edited by Charles Neider. New York: Harper, 1959.

Mark Twain–Howells Letters, edited by H. N. Smith and W. M. Gibson. Cambridge, Mass.: Belknap Press, 1960.

Mark Twain's Letters to Mary, edited with commentary by Lewis Leary. New York: Columbia University Press, 1961.

Mark Twain: Letters from Earth, edited by Bernard De Voto, with a Preface by Henry Nash Smith. New York and Evanston: Harper and Row, 1962.

Critical and Biographical Studies

Andrews, Kenneth R. *Nook Farm: Mark Twain's Hartford Circle.* Cambridge, Mass.: Harvard University Press, 1950.

Asselineau, Roger. *The Literary Reputation of Mark Twain.* Paris: Libraire Marcel Didier, 1954.

Bellamy, Gladys C. *Mark Twain as a Literary Artist.* Norman: University of Oklahoma Press, 1950.

Selected Bibliographies

Benson, Ivan. *Mark Twain's Western Years*. Palo Alto, Calif.: Stanford University Press, 1938.

Blair, Walter. *Mark Twain and Huck Finn*. Berkeley: University of California Press, 1960.

Branch, Edgar M. *The Literary Apprenticeship of Mark Twain*. Urbana: University of Illinois Press, 1950.

Brashear, M. M. *Mark Twain, Son of Missouri*. Chapel Hill: University of North Carolina Press, 1934.

Brooks, Van Wyck. *The Ordeal of Mark Twain*. Revised edition. New York: Dutton, 1933.

Budd, Louis J. *Mark Twain: Social Philosopher*. Bloomington: University of Indiana Press, 1962.

Clemens, Clara. *My Father, Mark Twain*. New York: Harper, 1931.

Cox, James M. *Mark Twain: The Fate of Humor*. Princeton, N.J.: Princeton University Press, 1966.

De Voto, Bernard. *Mark Twain at Work*. Cambridge, Mass.: Harvard University Press, 1942.

———. *Mark Twain's America*. Boston: Little, Brown, 1935.

Eliot, T. S. Introduction to *The Adventures of Huckleberry Finn*. New York: Chanticleer Press, 1950.

Ferguson, J. DeLancey. *Mark Twain: Man and Legend*. Indianapolis: Bobbs-Merrill, 1943.

Hill, Hamlin. *Mark Twain and Elisha Bliss*. Columbia: University of Missouri Press, 1964.

Howells, William Dean. *My Mark Twain*. New York: Harper, 1910.

Kaplan, Justin. *Mr. Clemens and Mark Twain*. New York: Simon and Schuster, 1966.

Leary, Lewis. *Mark Twain's Wound*. New York: Crowell, 1962.

Liljegren, S. B. *The Revolt against Romanticism in American Literature as Evidenced in the Works of S. L. Clemens*. Upsala: Lundequistska Bokhandeln, 1945.

Lynn, Kenneth S. *Mark Twain and Southwestern Humor*. Boston: Atlantic-Little Brown, 1960.

Paine, Albert Bigelow. *Mark Twain: A Biography*. Revised edition in 2 volumes. New York: Harper, 1935.

Schönemann, Friedrich. *Mark Twain als literarische Persönlichkeit*. Berlin: Verlag der Frommanschen Buchhandlung, Walter Biedermann, 1925.

Scott, Arthur L., ed. *Mark Twain: Selected Criticism*. Dallas: Southern Methodist University Press, 1955.

Smith, Henry Nash. *Mark Twain: The Development of a Writer*. Cambridge, Mass.: Belknap Press of Harvard University Press, 1962.

Trilling, Lionel. Introduction to *The Adventures of Huckleberry Finn*. New York: Rinehart, 1948.

Wagenknecht, Edward. *Mark Twain: The Man and His Work*. New Haven, Conn.: Yale University Press, 1935.

Wecter, Dixon. *Sam Clemens of Hannibal*. Boston: Houghton, Mifflin, 1952.

WILLIAM D. HOWELLS

A Bibliography of William Dean Howells by William M. Gibson and George Arms (New York: New York Public Library, 1948) lists Howells' primary writings. Jacob Blanck's *Bibliography of American Literature* (Vol. IV) adds certain contributions to books and pamphlets and refines upon issues. Titles given below are first editions; revised texts are not noted nor are translations. Much of Howells' writing is out of print, but *A Selected Edition of William Dean Howells* in 36 volumes, of which Edwin H. Cady is general editor, is forthcoming from Indiana University Press. The fullest list of criticism of Howells is the "Selected Bibliography" in Clara and Rudolf Kirk, eds., *William Dean Howells, Representative Selections* (New York: Hill and Wang, 1961).

Works

TRAVEL AND PLACE

Venetian Life. London: Trubner, 1866.
Italian Journeys. New York: Hurd and Houghton, 1867.
Three Villages. Boston: Osgood, 1884.
Tuscan Cities. Boston: Ticknor, 1886.
A Little Swiss Sojourn. New York: Harper, 1892.
London Films. New York: Harper, 1906.
Certain Delightful English Towns. New York: Harper, 1906.
Roman Holidays and Others. New York: Harper, 1908.
Seven English Cities. New York: Harper, 1909.
Familiar Spanish Travels. New York: Harper, 1913.

NOVELS

Their Wedding Journey. Boston: Osgood, 1872.
A Chance Acquaintance. Boston: Osgood, 1873.
A Foregone Conclusion. Boston: Osgood, 1875.
The Lady of the Aroostook. Boston: Houghton, Osgood, 1879.
The Undiscovered Country. Boston: Houghton, Mifflin, 1880.
Dr. Breen's Practice, a Novel. Boston: Osgood, 1881.
A Modern Instance, a Novel. Boston: Osgood, 1882.
A Woman's Reason, a Novel. Boston: Osgood, 1883.
The Rise of Silas Lapham. Boston: Ticknor, 1885.
Indian Summer. Boston: Ticknor, 1886.
The Minister's Charge, or The Apprenticeship of Lemuel Barker. Boston: Ticknor, 1887.
April Hopes. New York: Harper, 1888.
Annie Kilburn, a Novel. New York: Harper, 1889.
A Hazard of New Fortunes, a Novel. New York: Harper, 1890.
The Shadow of a Dream, a Story. New York: Harper, 1890.
An Imperative Duty, a Novel. New York: Harper, 1892.

Selected Bibliographies

The Quality of Mercy, a Novel. New York: Harper, 1892.
The World of Chance, a Novel. New York: Harper, 1893.
The Coast of Bohemia, a Novel. New York: Harper, 1893.
A Traveler from Altruria, Romance. New York: Harper, 1894.
The Day of Their Wedding, a Novel. New York: Harper, 1896.
The Landlord at Lion's Head, a Novel. New York: Harper, 1897.
An Open-Eyed Conspiracy, an Idyl of Saratoga. New York: Harper, 1897.
The Story of a Play, a Novel. New York: Harper, 1898.
Ragged Lady, a Novel. New York: Harper, 1899.
Their Silver Wedding Journey. New York: Harper, 1899.
The Kentons, a Novel. New York: Harper, 1902.
Letters Home. New York: Harper, 1903.
The Son of Royal Langbrith, a Novel. New York: Harper, 1904.
Miss Bellard's Inspiration, a Novel. New York: Harper, 1905.
Through the Eye of the Needle, a Romance. New York: Harper, 1907.
Fennel and Rue, a Novel. New York: Harper, 1908.
The Leatherwood God. New York: Century, 1916.
The Vacation of the Kelwyns, an Idyl of the Middle Eighteen-Seventies. New York: Harper, [1920].
Mrs. Farrell, a Novel. New York: Harper, [1921]. First serialized as "Private Theatricals" in the *Atlantic*, November 1875 to May 1876.

STORIES

Suburban Sketches. New York: Hurd and Houghton, 1871.
A Fearful Responsibility and Other Stories. Boston: Osgood, 1881.
A Day's Pleasure and Other Sketches. Boston: Houghton, Mifflin, 1881.
A Parting and a Meeting. New York: Harper, 1896.
A Pair of Patient Lovers. New York: Harper, 1901.
Questionable Shapes. New York: Harper, 1903.
Between the Dark and the Daylight, Romances. New York: Harper, 1907.
The Daughter of the Storage and Other Things in Prose and Verse. New York: Harper, [1916].

POEMS AND PLAYS

Poems of Two Friends, with John J. Piatt. Columbus, Ohio: Follett, 1860.
No Love Lost, a Romance of Travel. New York: Putnam, 1869.
Poems. Boston: Osgood, 1873. Enlarged editions, Boston: Ticknor, 1886.
Stops of Various Quills. New York: Harper, 1895.
The Complete Plays of W. D. Howells, edited by Walter J. Meserve. New York: New York University Press, 1960. (Brings together all 36 plays.)

CRITICISM

Modern Italian Poets, Essays and Versions. New York: Harper, 1887.
Criticism and Fiction. New York: Harper, 1891.

WILLIAM D. HOWELLS

My Literary Passions. New York: Harper, 1895.
Impressions and Experiences. New York: Harper, 1896.
"Novel-Writing and Novel-Reading, an Impersonal Explanation," in *Howells and James: A Double Billing*, edited by William M. Gibson and Leon Edel. New York: New York Public Library, 1958. (A lecture delivered in 1899.)
Heroines of Fiction. New York: Harper, 1901.
Literature and Life, Studies. New York: Harper, 1902.
Imaginary Interviews. New York: Harper, 1910.
The Seen and Unseen at Stratford-on-Avon, a Fantasy. New York: Harper, 1914.

CRITICAL INTRODUCTIONS

Between 1882 and 1920 Howells wrote introductions to works by Kingsley, Tolstoi, Verga, Stoddard, Pellew, Garland, William C. Howells, Galdós, Crane, Dunbar, Du Maurier, Bellamy, Mark Twain, Cawein, James, Artemus Ward, Swift, Maupassant, Howe, Jane Austen, Ibáñez, Merrick, and Zola, as well as to several volumes of American and French stories. *Prefaces to Contemporaries*, edited by George Arms, William M. Gibson, and Frederic C. Marston, Jr. (Gainesville, Fla.: Scholars' Facsimiles and Reprints, 1957), collects 34 of these introductions.

BIOGRAPHY

Lives and Speeches of Abraham Lincoln. Columbus, Ohio: Follett, Foster, 1860.
The Life and Character of Rutherford B. Hayes. Boston: Houghton, 1876.
"Sketch of George Fuller's Life," in *George Fuller: His Life and Works.* Boston: Houghton, Mifflin, 1886.
"Meetings with King," in *Clarence King Memoirs.* New York: Putnam's, 1904.
My Mark Twain, Reminiscences and Criticisms. New York: Harper, 1910.

AUTOBIOGRAPHY AND REMINISCENCE

A Boy's Town. New York: Harper, 1890.
My Year in a Log Cabin. New York: Harper, 1893.
Literary Friends and Acquaintance, a Personal Retrospect of American Authorship. New York: Harper, 1900.
New Leaf Mills, a Chronicle. New York: Harper, 1913.
Years of My Youth. New York: Harper, [1916].

LETTERS

Life in Letters of William Dean Howells, edited by Mildred Howells. New York: Doubleday, Doran, 1928.
Mark Twain–Howells Letters . . . 1872–1910, edited by Henry Nash Smith

and William M. Gibson. Cambridge, Mass.: Harvard University Press, 1960.

Biographical and Critical Studies

Bennett, George N. *William Dean Howells, the Development of a Novelist.* Norman: University of Oklahoma Press, 1959.

Brooks, Van Wyck. *Howells, His Life and World.* New York: Dutton, 1959.

Cady, Edwin H. *The Road to Realism, the Early Years, 1837–1885, of William Dean Howells* and *The Realist at War, the Mature Years, 1885–1920, of William Dean Howells.* Syracuse, N.Y.: Syracuse University Press, 1956, 1958.

———— and David L. Frazier, editors. *The War of the Critics over William Dean Howells.* Evanston, Ill.: Row, Peterson, 1962. (Sixty pieces, from excerpts to full articles, from 1860 to 1960.)

Carrington, George C., Jr. *The Immense Complex Drama: The World and Art of the Howells Novel.* Columbus: Ohio State University Press, [1966].

Carter, Everett. *Howells and the Age of Realism.* Philadelphia: Lippincott, [1954].

Cooke, Delmar G. *William Dean Howells.* New York: Dutton, 1922.

Eble, Kenneth E., editor. *Howells, a Century of Criticism.* Dallas, Texas: Southern Methodist University Press, 1962. (Twenty-eight essays.)

Firkins, Oscar W. *William Dean Howells.* Cambridge, Mass.: Harvard University Press, 1924.

Fryckstedt, Olov W. *In Quest of America, a Study of Howells' Early Development as a Novelist.* Cambridge, Mass.: Harvard University Press, 1958.

Hough, Robert L. *The Quiet Rebel, William Dean Howells as Social Commentator.* Lincoln: University of Nebraska Press, 1959.

Kirk, Clara M. *W. D. Howells, Traveler from Altruria, 1889–1894.* New Brunswick, N.J.: Rutgers University Press, 1962.

————. *W. D. Howells and Art in His Time.* New Brunswick, N.J.: Rutgers University Press, 1965.

———— and Rudolf Kirk. *William Dean Howells.* New York: Twayne, 1962.

McMurray, William. *The Literary Realism of William Dean Howells.* Carbondale: Southern Illinois University Press, 1967.

Woodress, James L., Jr. *Howells and Italy.* Durham, N.C.: Duke University Press, 1952.

HENRY JAMES

For a complete listing of Henry James's writings see *A Bibliography of Henry James* by Leon Edel and Dan H. Laurence (London: Hart-Davis, 1957) which establishes the priority of editions as between America and England, and also lists foreign translations of James's writings. The present selection gives his books under the titles they bore on original appearance and first place of publication.

Works

COLLECTED EDITIONS

Collected Novels and Tales. 14 volumes. London: Macmillan, 1883.

The Novels and Tales of Henry James (New York Edition). 24 volumes. New York: Scribner's, 1907–9. (Two volumes were added posthumously.) Reprinted 1961–65.

Uniform Edition of the Tales. 14 volumes. London: Secker, 1915–19. (There was one tale in each volume – that is, 14 tales in all were published, of the 112 written by James.)

The Novels and Stories of Henry James. 36 volumes. London: Macmillan, 1921–23.

The Complete Tales of Henry James. 12 volumes. Philadelphia: Lippincott, 1962–65.

NOVELS

Roderick Hudson. Boston: Osgood, 1875.

The American. Boston: Osgood, 1877.

Watch and Ward. Boston: Houghton, Osgood, 1878.

The Europeans. London: Macmillan, 1878.

Confidence. London: Chatto and Windus, 1879.

Washington Square. New York: Harper, 1881 [1880].

The Portrait of a Lady. London: Macmillan, 1881.

The Bostonians. London: Macmillan, 1886.

The Princess Casamassima. London: Macmillan, 1886.

The Reverberator. London: Macmillan, 1888.

The Tragic Muse. Boston: Houghton, Mifflin, 1889.

The Other House. London: Heinemann, 1896.

The Spoils of Poynton. London: Heinemann, 1897.

What Maisie Knew. London: Heinemann, 1897.

The Awkward Age. London: Heinemann, 1899.

The Sacred Fount. New York: Scribner's, 1901.

The Wings of the Dove. New York: Scribner's, 1902.

The Ambassadors. London: Methuen, 1903.

The Golden Bowl. New York: Scribner's, 1904.

The Outcry. London: Methuen, 1911.

POSTHUMOUS NOVELS

The Ivory Tower. London: Collins, 1917. (Uncompleted.)

The Sense of the Past. London: Collins, 1917. (Uncompleted.)

TALES

Titles marked with an asterisk are special titles assigned by James to books containing his tales. Otherwise the title is that of one of the tales in the volume. Where the title is not italicized, the tale was published alone.

Selected Bibliographies

A Passionate Pilgrim and Other Tales. Boston: Osgood, 1875.
"Daisy Miller." New York: Harper, 1879 [1878].
"An International Episode." New York: Harper, 1879.
The Madonna of the Future and Other Tales. London: Macmillan, 1879.
"The Diary of a Man of Fifty." New York: Harper, 1880.
The Siege of London and Other Tales. Boston: Osgood, 1883.
* *Tales of Three Cities.* Boston: Osgood, 1884.
The Author of Beltraffio and Other Tales. Boston: Osgood, 1885.
* *Stories Revived.* 3 volumes. London: Macmillan, 1885.
The Aspern Papers. London: Macmillan, 1888.
A London Life. London: Macmillan, 1889.
The Lesson of the Master. New York: Macmillan, 1892.
The Real Thing and Other Tales. New York: Macmillan, 1893.
The Private Life. London: Osgood, McIlvaine, 1893.
The Wheel of Time. New York: Harper, 1893.
* *Terminations.* London: Heinemann, 1895.
* *Embarrassments.* London: Heinemann, 1896.
In the Cage. London: Duckworth, 1898.
* *The Two Magics.* London: Heinemann, 1898.
* *The Soft Side.* London: Methuen, 1900.
* *The Better Sort.* London: Methuen, 1903.
"Julia Bride." New York: Harper, 1909.
* *The Finer Grain.* New York: Scribner's, 1910.

POSTHUMOUS COLLECTIONS OF TALES

"Gabrielle de Bergerac." New York: Boni and Liveright, 1918.
Travelling Companions, edited by Albert Mordell. New York: Boni and Liveright, 1919.
A Landscape Painter, edited by Albert Mordell. New York: Scott and Seltzer, 1919 [1920].
Master Eustace, edited by Albert Mordell. New York: Seltzer, 1920.
The American Novels and Stories, edited by F. O. Matthiessen. New York: Knopf, 1948.
The Ghostly Tales of Henry James, edited by Leon Edel. New Brunswick, N.J.: Rutgers University Press, 1948 [1949].
Eight Uncollected Tales, edited by Edna Kenton. New Brunswick, N.J.: Rutgers University Press, 1950.

AUTOBIOGRAPHIES

William Wetmore Story and His Friends. Edinburgh: Blackwood, 1903. (Biographical memoir.)
A Small Boy and Others. New York: Scribner's, 1913.
Notes of a Son and Brother. New York: Scribner's, 1914.
The Middle Years. London: Collins, 1917. (Uncompleted.)

LETTERS

The Letters of Henry James, edited by Percy Lubbock. 2 volumes. London: Macmillan, 1920.
Letters of Henry James to A. C. Benson. New York: Scribner's, 1930.
Theatre and Friendship. London: Cape, 1932. (Letters of James to Elizabeth Robins.)
Henry James and Robert Louis Stevenson, edited by Janet A. Smith. London: Hart-Davis, 1948.
Selected Letters of Henry James, edited by Leon Edel. New York: Farrar, Straus, 1955.
Henry James and H. G. Wells, edited by Leon Edel and Gordon N. Ray. London: Hart-Davis, 1958.

PLAYS

Daisy Miller, a Comedy. Boston: Osgood, 1883.
Theatricals. London: Osgood, McIlvaine, 1894.
Theatricals; Second Series. London: Osgood, McIlvaine, 1894.
The Complete Plays of Henry James, edited by Leon Edel. Philadelphia: Lippincott, 1949.

ESSAYS, CRITICISM, AND MISCELLANEOUS WRITINGS

French Poets and Novelists. London: Macmillan, 1878.
Hawthorne. London: Macmillan, 1879.
Partial Portraits. London: Macmillan, 1888.
Essays in London and Elsewhere. London: Osgood, McIlvaine, 1893.
Picture and Text. New York: Harper, 1893.
The Question of Our Speech. Boston: Houghton, Mifflin, 1905.
Views and Reviews, collected by Le Roy Phillips. Boston: Ball, 1908.
Notes on Novelists. London: Dent, 1914.

POSTHUMOUS COLLECTIONS OF ESSAYS, CRITICISM, AND MISCELLANEOUS WRITINGS

Within the Rim. London: Collins, 1919.
Notes and Reviews, edited by Pierre la Rose. Cambridge, Mass.: Dunster House, 1921.
The Art of the Novel, edited by R. P. Blackmur. New York: Scribner's, 1934.
The Notebooks of Henry James, edited by F. O. Matthiessen and Kenneth B. Murdock. New York: Oxford University Press, 1947.
The Scenic Art, edited by Allan Wade. New Brunswick, N.J.: Rutgers University Press, 1948.
The American Essays of Henry James, edited by Leon Edel. New York: Knopf (Vintage), 1956.
The Future of the Novel, edited by Leon Edel. New York: Knopf (Vintage), 1956.
The Painter's Eye, edited by John L. Sweeney. London: Hart-Davis, 1956.

Selected Bibliographies

The House of Fiction, edited by Leon Edel. London: Hart-Davis, 1957.
Literary Reviews and Essays, edited by Albert Mordell. New York: Grove, 1957.

TRAVEL

Transatlantic Sketches. Boston: Osgood, 1875. (Titled *Foreign Parts* in Tauchnitz Edition, 1884.)
Portraits of Places. London: Macmillan, 1883.
A Little Tour in France. Boston: Osgood, 1885 [1884].
English Hours. London: Heinemann, 1905.
The American Scene. London: Chapman and Hall, 1907.
Italian Hours. London: Heinemann, 1909.

POSTHUMOUS TRAVEL COLLECTIONS

Parisian Sketches, edited by Leon Edel and Ilse Lind. New York: New York University Press, 1957.
The Art of Travel, edited by Morton D. Zabel. New York: Doubleday, 1958.

Biographical and Critical Studies

Beach, Joseph Warren. *The Method of Henry James.* New Haven, Conn.: Yale University Press, 1918.
Brooks, Van Wyck. *The Pilgrimage of Henry James.* New York: Dutton, 1925.
Dupee, F. W. *Henry James.* New York: Sloane, 1951.
———, ed. *The Question of Henry James.* New York: Holt, 1945.
Edel, Leon. *Henry James: The Untried Years.* Philadelphia: Lippincott, 1953.
———. *The Conquest of London.* Philadelphia: Lippincott, 1962.
———. *The Middle Years.* Philadelphia: Lippincott, 1962.
Grattan, C. H. *The Three Jameses.* New York: Longmans, Green, 1932.
Lubbock, Percy. *The Craft of Fiction.* New York: Scribner's, 1921.
Matthiessen, F. O. *Henry James: The Major Phase.* New York: Oxford University Press, 1944.
———. *The James Family.* New York: Knopf, 1947.
Nowell-Smith, Simon, ed. *The Legend of the Master.* London: Constable, 1948 [1947].
Putt, S. Gorley. *A Reader's Guide to Henry James.* Ithaca, N.Y.: Cornell University Press, 1967.
Wilson, Edmund. *The Triple Thinkers.* New York: Harcourt, Brace, 1938.

ABOUT THE AUTHORS

About the Authors

HYATT H. WAGGONER is a professor of American literature at Brown University and chairman of the American Civilization Program there. He is the author of *Hawthorne: A Critical Study* as well as other books of literary criticism.

ROBERT E. SPILLER is Felix E. Schelling Emeritus Professor of English at the University of Pennsylvania. He is the author or editor of a number of books, including *Literary History of the United States*, *The Cycle of American Literature*, and *The Third Dimension*.

LEON HOWARD is a professor of English at the University of California at Los Angeles. Among his books are *Herman Melville: A Biography*, *Literature and the American Tradition*, and *The Mind of Jonathan Edwards*.

LEWIS LEARY, a professor of English at Columbia University, is the author or editor of a number of books on American literature, including *That Rascal Freneau*, *The Literary Career of Nathaniel Tucker*, and *Contemporary Literary Scholarship*.

WILLIAM M. GIBSON has compiled a Howells bibliography with George Arms and has edited the Mark Twain–Howells letters with Henry Nash Smith. He is a professor of English at New York University and director of the Modern Language Association Center for Editions of American Authors.

LEON EDEL, biographer and editor of James, occupies the Henry James chair of English and American Letters at New York University. He has written or edited more than thirty books, the most important being his *Life of Henry James*, *The Modern Psychological Novel*, and *Literary Biography*.

INDEX

Index

Index

Index

39–40; *Satanstoe*, 37, 38–39, 44; *The Sea Lions*, 41, 43; *Sketches of Switzerland*, 29; *The Spy*, 10, 12, 13, 17, 18–19; *The Two Admirals*, 34; *The Water-Witch*, 23; *The Ways of the Hour*, 41; *The Wept of Wish-ton-Wish*, 17, 22, 35; *The Wing-and-Wing*, 34, 35, 43; *Wyandotté*, 35, 43
Cooper, Mrs. James Fenimore (Susan Augusta De Lancey), 15, 16
Cooper, Susan (daughter of James F. Cooper), 14
Cooper, William (father of James F. Cooper), 14, 16, 36
Cooperstown, N.Y., 14, 31, 33, 36, 40; burial place for Cooper family, 41
Coppée, François, James meets, 201
"Country Boy in Boston, The," 180
Crane, Stephen, 4, 6, 149, 164, 186: quoted, 147; influences Howells, 187; Howells defines novel to, 188–89
Crater, The, 41–42, 43
Criticism and Fiction, 184
"Custom House, The" (Introduction to *Scarlet Letter*), 45

Daily Crescent, 126
"Daisy Miller," 201, 202–3, 204
Dana, Richard Henry, Jr., 36, 94: influence on Cooper, 17
"Dandy Frightening the Squatter, The," 124
Dante Alighieri, 88, 160: Howells reads, 154, 168; influence of on Howells, 186
Darwin, Charles, James meets, 197
Daudet, Alphonse, 223: James meets, 201, 209
David Copperfield, 188
"Day of Days, A," 197
"Death of the Lion, The," 212
Deerslayer, The, 20, 33, 34, 43
De Forest, John William, 184: Howells supports work of, 162; quoted, 170
De Lancey, James, 15
De Lancey, Susan Augusta (Mrs. James F. Cooper), 15, 16
De Lancey, William Heathcote, Bishop (brother-in-law of James F. Cooper), 16: confirms Cooper, 40
Delano, Amasa, 109

Denver, Colo., bans *Huckleberry Finn*, 137
"Devil in Manuscript, The," 50, 51
Dewey, John, 56
Dickens, Charles, 5, 122, 124, 153, 159, 160, 187: Howells criticizes, 155; Howells' reaction against, 184; James reads, 195
Dickinson, Emily, 157, 164, 165
Dimmesdale, Arthur (fictional character), 47, 64, 72, 76, 168
Dix and Edwards, publishing firm, 111
Dr. Breen's Practice, 173–74
Dr. Jekyll and Mr. Hyde, 187
Don Quixote (fictional character), 168
Don Quixote, 188
Dostoevski, Feodor, 163, 192
Dreiser, Theodore, 44, 149, 164, 176, 210
"Dutch Nick Massacre, The," 127
Duyckinck, Evert, 97, 101: Melville meets, 87; quoted, 94

"Earth's Holocaust," 50, 51, 59, 60, 61, 96
"Editor's Easy Chair" (Howells' column in *Harper's*), 164
"Editor's Study, The" (Howells' column in *Harper's*), 164, 178
Education of Henry Adams, The, 164
Edward VI (king of England), 135
"Egotism, or The Bosom Serpent," 52, 73
Eimeo Island (Moorea Island), Melville escapes to, 84
Eliot, George, 191, 223: Howells praises work of, 162; James influenced by, 200
Eliot, T. S., 119: on *Huckleberry Finn*, 137
Elizabeth Islands, Mass., 105
Ellis, Havelock, 164
Embargo of *1807* (shipping law), 46
Emerson, Ralph Waldo, 7, 8, 62, 94, 96, 122, 137, 161, 219, 223: Hawthorne's neighbor, 47, 50; Hawthorne's view of work of, 69; theme of individual vs. society in work of, 139; quoted, 154; Howells meets, 159; influence of on Howells, 186
Emperor Jones, The, 167

Index

Index

Jack Tier, 41, 43

Jackson, Andrew, 122

James, Henry, 3, 4, 6, 7, 8, 11, 139, 157, 163, 164, 165, 167, 172, 173, 178, 180, 184, 188: Hawthorne's writing foreshadows, 54; compared with Samuel Clemens, 131; Howells friend and editor of, 155, 161, 163, 164, 165, 186; on Hazard of New Fortunes, 182; compared with European authors, 191; evaluation of work of, 191–92, 223–24, 224–25; opinion of artist in fiction, 192; style of, 192; develops psychological novel, 192, 193, 201, 208; influence on other authors, 193; early years and family history, 194–95; travels – to Europe as boy, 195, to Europe 1869–70, 197, to Rome 1872–73, 199, to Paris 1875, 200, to Paris 1884, 209, to Italy, 207, 210, to America, 209, 219; withdraws from Harvard Law School, 196; early stories of, 196–97; influences on work of, 197–98; death of cousin, 198; settles in England, 201; compared with Turgenev, 200–1; three periods of, 201–2, 205, 209, 212, 215; use of theme of Americans abroad, 202, 204, 209; writes plays, 202, 211; use of irony, 203–4, 212; death of parents, 209; repudiated by public, 211; writes semiautobiographical stories, 212; technical innovations of, 214–15; use of symbolism, 217; compared with Balzac, 217–18; during World War I, 222; as letter-writer, 222, 223; prefaces to work, 220–21; illness and death of, 221, 222; gives up American citizenship, 222; working notebooks published, 223

Works: The Ambassadors, 192, 215–17; The American, 203–4, 207, 211, 217; The American Scene, 219; "The Aspern Papers," 210; The Awkward Age, 212, 214; The Better Sort, 219; The Bostonians, 139, 173, 209–10; Confidence, 205, 206; English Hours, 221; Essays in London, 220; The Europeans, 205, 207; The Finer Grain, 219; French Poets and Novelists, 220; The Golden Bowl, 192, 215, 218, 219;

Guy Domville, 211; Hawthorne, 205–6; Italian Hours, 221; The Ivory Tower, 222; A Little Tour in France, 221; The Middle Years, 222, 223; Notes of a Son and Brother, 221; Notes on Novelists, 220, 221; The Other House, 212; Partial Portraits, 220; A Passionate Pilgrim and Other Tales, 200; The Portrait of a Lady, 6, 198, 199, 202, 205, 207, 208–9, 212; Princess Casamassima, 139, 163, 188, 209, 210; Roderick Hudson, 178, 188, 199–200, 203, 207; The Sacred Fount, 214; The Sense of the Past, 222; A Small Boy and Others, 221; The Soft Side, 219; The Spoils of Poynton, 212; Stories Revived, 197; The Tragic Muse, 210; Transatlantic Sketches, 200; "The Turn of the Screw," 212, 213–14; Washington Square, 205, 206–7; Watch and Ward, 198–99; What Maisie Knew, 212, 214; The Wings of the Dove, 192, 198, 215, 216–17

James, Henry, Sr., 163, 195

James, William (elder brother of Henry James), 164, 195

Jay, William, Judge, 16

J. B., 54

Jefferson, Ohio, Howells' childhood in, 157

Jefferson, Thomas, 224

Jewett, Sarah Orne, 3, 7

John Bull in America; or The New Munchausen, 24

"John Marr," 115

John Marr and Other Sailors, 114

Jones, Howard Mumford, 40

"Journal of a Solitary Man, The," 50, 51

Joyce, James, 153, 193

Judd, Sylvester, 187

Jusserand, Jules, 223

Kafka, Franz, 81

Keokuk, Iowa, 125

Kierkegaard, Soren, Hawthorne's use of, 56

King Leopold's Soliloquy, 149

Kipling, Rudyard, 155, 223

Kittery Point, Me., 164

Index

Index

Pfaff's (beer parlor), 159
Philadelphia, Pa., 124
Philbrick, Thomas, 23
Piatt, John James, 159
Piazza Tales, 111
Piccadilly Circus, 201
Pierce, Franklin, 48, 106: and Hawthorne, 50, 53
Pierre; or, The Ambiguities, 102-3, 104, 105, 114, 124
Pilot, The, 10, 13, 17, 23, 34
Pioneers, The, 12, 13, 15, 17, 19, 20, 22, 31
Pirate, The, 17
Pittsfield, Mass., 94
Plato, 62
Plymouth, N.H., Hawthorne dies in, 50
Poe, Edgar Allan, 4, 6, 8, 18
Poems of Two Friends, 159, 165
"Poor Man's Pudding and Rich Man's Crumbs," 108
"Poor Richard," 197
Portrait of a Lady, The, 6, 198, 199, 202, 205, 217: plot of, 207-8; success of, 208-9
Prairie, The, 6, 17, 22
Precaution, 13, 16-17
Pride and Prejudice, 187
Prince and the Pauper, The, 135, 136, 145
Princess Casamassima, The, 139, 163, 188, 209, 210
Princeton University, 15
Principles of Psychology, 195
"Private History of a Campaign That Failed," 126
"Private Theatricals," 170
"Prophetic Pictures, The," 52
Proust, Marcel, 137, 221
Pry, Paul, 52
Prynne, Hester (fictional character), 5, 47, 72-73, 79
Punch, Brothers, Punch and Other Sketches, 135
Putnam's Monthly Magazine, 106, 108, 109, 110
Pyncheon, Phoebe (fictional character), 74, 79, 80
Pyncheon family (fictional), 48, 74-75

Quaker City (steamship), 130

Quebec, Canada, 166, 167

Rabelais, François, 4, 88
"Rappaccini's Daughter," 55
Red Rover, The, 23, 43
Redburn: His First Voyage, 90, 92, 100
Redskins, The, 37, 39-40
Revolution (American), 15, 224
Revolution of *1830* (French), 27
Richardson, Dorothy, 193
Richardson, Samuel, 195
Ringe, Donald A., 11, 17-18, 23
Rio de Janeiro, Brazil, 84
Rise of Silas Lapham, The, 139, 162, 169, 176-78
Robertson, Agatha, 106, 107, 108
Roderick Hudson, 178, 188, 199-200, 203, 207
"Roger Malvin's Burial," 79
"Romance of Certain Old Clothes, The," 197
Rome, Italy, 198, 199, 202, 207, 223
Romola, 189
Rossetti, Dante Gabriel, James meets, 197
Roughing It, 127, 129, 131
Ruskin, John, 223: James meets, 197
Rye, N.Y., 40
Rye, England, 222, 223: James moves to, 211

Sacramento Union, Clemens writes for, 128
Sacred Fount, The, 214
St. Louis, Mo., 124, 125
Salem, Mass., 45, 46, 49, 206
Salinger, J. D., 119
Sand, George, 197
San Francisco, Calif., 112, 128
San Francisco Call, Clemens works for, 127
Sargent, John Singer, 222, 223
Sargent's New Monthly Magazine, 61
Sartor Resartus, Melville reads, 96
Sartre, Jean-Paul, 80
Satanstoe, 37, 38-39, 44
Saturday Press, 159
Sawyer, Tom (fictional character), 120, 123, 134, 135, 136, 140, 151, 152, 185: relation to Huck Finn, 139; Clemens' favorite character, 142

267

Index

Tobacco Road, 132

Tolstoi, Leo, 157, 163, 192: praises work of Howells, 155; influence of on Howells, 173, 179, 180

Tom Sawyer Abroad, 125, 142

Tom Sawyer Detective, 142

"Tortoises or Tortoise-Hunting," 108

"Tragedy of Error, A," 196

Tragedy of Pudd'nhead Wilson, The, 145, 146–47

Tragic Muse, The, 210

Tramp Abroad, A, 135

Transatlantic Sketches, 200

Transcendentalism, 100: German, 93–94; Melville's interest in, 95–96, 97

Transcendentalists, 206

Traveler from Altruria, A, 179, 182

Trilling, Lionel, 137

Trollope, Anthony, Hawthorne admires, 69

Turgenev, Ivan, 191, 192, 223: praises Howells, 155; Howells supports work of, 162; influence of on Howells, 170, 184; compared with Howells, 171, 172; James with in Paris, 200, 201

"Turn of the Screw, The," 212, 213–14

Tuscan Cities, 170

Twain, Mark, see Clemens, Samuel Langhorne

Twice-Told Tales, 42, 46

Two Admirals, The, 34

"Two Temples, The," 108

Two Years before the Mast, 36

Tyler, Royall, 24

Typee: A Peep at Polynesian Life, 84–88 passim, 91, 100

Typees (cannibal tribe), Melville captive of, 84

Uncle Tom's Cabin, 188

Undine, 88

Undiscovered Country, The, 173

United States (frigate), Melville signs on, 84

Vanity Fair, 42

Van Rensselaer, Stephen, 37

Veblen, Thornstein, 157, 164, 182

Venetian Life, 160, 165, 168

Venice, Italy, 131, 170: Howells in, 159; used as background in Howells' work, 168; used as background in James's work, 210

Verga, Giovanni, 155, 163

Virginia City, Nev., 127, 128

Waples, Dorothy, 32

War and Peace, 188

War of 1812, 46

Ward, Artemus, 127, 128, 186

Ward, Mrs. Humphry, 223

Warner, Charles Dudley, 132

Warren, Robert Penn, compared with Hawthorne, 54

Washington, D.C., 87, 124, 132, 209

Washington Square, 205, 206–7

Watch and Ward, 198–99

Water-Witch, The, allegory in, 23

Ways of the Hour, The, 41

Wayside (home of Nathaniel Hawthorne), 48, 49, 50

Wellek, René, 192

Wells, H. G., 164, 221, 223

Wept of Wish-ton-Wish, The, 17, 22, 35

Westchester County, N.Y., 40

Wharton, Edith, 223: reaction of to A Modern Instance, 176

What Is Man? 150

What Maisie Knew, 212, 214

White Jacket, 92, 93, 100, 115

"Whiteness of the Whale, The," 99, 103

Whitlock, Brand, 164

Whitman, Walt, 7, 120, 122, 139, 160, 161, 186: Howells compared with, 158; Howells meets, 159; James compared with, 194

Whittier, John Greenleaf, 7, 161

Wiley and Putnam (publishers), 86

Wilhelm Meister, 188

Wilson, Edmund, 164

Wing-and-Wing, The, 34, 35, 43

Wings of the Dove, The, 192, 198, 215, 216–17

Woman's Reason, A, 174

Woolf, Virginia, 193

Wordsworth, William, 159

Wyandotté, 35, 43

Xenia, Ohio, 158